LATIN AMERICAN LITERATURE AT THE MILLENNIUM

BUCKNELL STUDIES IN LATIN AMERICAN LITERATURE AND THEORY

Series editor: Aníbal González, Yale University

Dealing with far-reaching questions of history and modernity, language and selfhood, and power and ethics, Latin American literature sheds light on the many-faceted nature of Latin American life, as well as on the human condition as a whole. This highly successful series has published some of the best recent criticism on Latin American literature. Acknowledging the historical links and cultural affinities between Latin American and Iberian literatures, the series productively combines scholarship with theory and welcomes consideration of Spanish and Portuguese texts and topics, while also providing a space of convergence for scholars working in Romance studies, comparative literature, cultural studies, and literary theory.

Selected Titles in the Series

Rebecca E. Biron, *Elena Garro and Mexico's Modern Dreams*

Persephone Brahman, *From Amazons to Zombies: Monsters in Latin America*

Jason Cortés, *Macho Ethics: Masculinity and Self-Representation in Latino-Caribbean Narrative*

Tara Daly, *Beyond Human: Vital Materialisms in the Andean Avant-Gardes*

Earl E. Fitz, *Machado de Assis and Female Characterization: The Novels*

Earl E. Fitz, *Machado de Assis and Narrative Theory: Language, Imitation, Art, and Verisimilitude in the Last Six Novels*

Naida García-Crespo, *Early Puerto Rican Cinema and Nation Building: National Sentiments, Transnational Realities, 1897–1940*

Thomas S. Harrington, *Public Intellectuals and Nation Building in the Iberian Peninsula, 1900–1925: The Alchemy of Identity*

David Kelman, *Counterfeit Politics: Secret Plots and Conspiracy Narratives in the Americas*

Brendan Lanctot, *Beyond Civilization and Barbarism: Culture and Politics in Postrevolutionary Argentina*

Marília Librandi, Jamille Pinheiro Dias, and Tom Winterbottom, eds., *Transpoetic Exchange: Haroldo de Campos, Octavio Paz, and Other Multiversal Dialogues*

Adriana Méndez Rodenas, *Transatlantic Travels in Nineteenth-Century Latin America: European Women Pilgrims*

Cecily Raynor, *Latin American Literature at the Millennium: Local Lives, Global Spaces*

Andrew R. Reynolds, *The Spanish American Crónica Modernista, Temporality, and Material Culture*

Elisa Sampson Vera Tudela, *Ricardo Palma's Tradiciones: Illuminating Gender and Nation*

Mary Beth Tierney-Tello, *Mining Memory: Reimagining Self and Nation through Narratives of Childhood in Peru*

Alberto Villate-Isaza, *Exemplary Violence: Rewriting History in Colonial Colombia*

LATIN AMERICAN LITERATURE AT THE MILLENNIUM

Local Lives, Global Spaces

CECILY RAYNOR

Bucknell University | University Press
Lewisburg, Pennsylvania

Library of Congress Cataloging-in-Publication Data

Names: Raynor, Cecily, author.
Title: Latin American literature at the millennium : local lives, global spaces / Cecily Raynor.
Description: Lewisburg, Pennsylvania : Bucknell University Press, [2021] | Includes bibliographical references.
Identifiers: LCCN 2020027649 | ISBN 9781684482566 (paperback ; alk. paper) | ISBN 9781684482573 (hardcover ; alk. paper) | ISBN 9781684482580 (epub) | ISBN 9781684482597 (mobi) | ISBN 9781684482603 (pdf)
Subjects: LCSH: Latin American fiction—20th century—History and criticism. | Latin American fiction—21st century—History and criticism. | Local color in literature. | Regionalism in literature. | Globalization in literature. | Literature and globalization—Latin America—History—20th century. | Literature and globalization—Latin America—History—21st century.
Classification: LCC PN849.L29 R39 2021 | DDC 863/.60998—dc23
LC record available at https://lccn.loc.gov/2020027649

A British Cataloging-in-Publication record for this book is available from the British Library.

∞ The paper used in this publication meets the requirements of the American National Standard for Information Sciences—Permanence of Paper for Printed Library Materials, ANSI Z39.48-1992.

www.bucknelluniversitypress.org

Distributed worldwide by Rutgers University Press

Manufactured in the United States of America

For Xavier and Rhian, the future

CONTENTS

LATIN AMERICAN LITERATURE AT THE MILLENNIUM

INTRODUCTION
Patterning the Local within the Global

> We do not live in a kind of void, inside of which we could place individuals and things. We do not live inside a void that could be colored with diverse shades of light, we live inside a set of relations that delineates sites which are irreducible to one another and absolutely not superimposable on one another.
>
> —Michel Foucault, "Of Other Spaces: Utopias and Heterotopias"

As we begin the third decade of the twenty-first century, we have enhanced our understanding of spatial heterogeneity and fluidity. We are no longer contemplating the arrival of globalization, transnational phenomena, or the digital age, but are rather recognizing that these are upon us. The question remains as to how our experiences of these changes are discussed and codified within narrative, particularly in the literature of regions like Latin America, whose experience of globalization is characterized by rapid yet uneven economic development, social stratification, political upheaval, and the collision of existing traditions with new, modernizing regimes. Like the heterotopias described in the epigraph, the local narratives of recent Latin American literature speak to heterogeneous encounters with world processes, illuminating how a range of subjects gain voice and presence as they mediate their local lives in global spaces. These representations of the local often contradict the notion of globalization as an all-encompassing monolith that erases local identities, experiences, and historical frameworks. Contemporary Latin American literature underscores issues of belonging, creating homes within global life through diverse localizing practices that respond to the dissolution of links between geographical place and human experience. As such, this book examines transformations in the narrative construction of the local that respond dynamically to Latin America's position in a time of heightened global integration.

In order to expose these relationships, I examine literary production from the turn of the century as a textual lens through which to consider the changing face of the local. Globalization is a historical phenomenon involving the economic, cultural, and social integration of individuals and nation-states across the world. As a set of interrelated and accelerating processes that bring distant localities into contact and interdependence with one another, globalization reveals points of contact that lend themselves to the idea of a multiplicity of experiences of the world. This approach, as I will discuss later on in this introduction, draws from the work of prominent theorists on globalization and studies of the impact of the former on cultural production. The history of globalization in Latin America is far-reaching and can be traced back to encounters during the colonial period that brought Latin America into collision with ideological and economic systems with globalizing consequences. Thus, the arrival of Christopher Columbus in 1492 can be seen as one such moment whose rippling effects still manifest in Latin America's political, social, and cultural systems. The rise of European colonial empires during the early modern period and the later Industrial Revolution of the nineteenth century are but two additional moments on the timeline of global integration affecting the region, as commodities and bodies formed long-term systems of global exchange. The envelopment of Latin America in global capitalist trade networks is a long-running historical process—to this effect, literary scholars, including Ericka Beckman,[1] have studied the escalation of Latin America's entanglement in global capitalist trade systems during the late nineteenth and early twentieth centuries. Although a historical precedent is clear, this book operates on the understanding that the recent confluence of mass media, technological advancement, and the opening up of the world's economy has intensified globalization to an unprecedented extent.[2] While economists often focus on the financial consequences of globalization, rather than its social or cultural ramifications, Latin American cultural production repeatedly highlights the artistic and thematic role of globalization, as the McOndo and Crack movements in Latin American literature illustrate.[3] From a sociocultural perspective, it is undeniable that an accelerated engagement with the world characterizes the decades examined in this book, spanning from 1990 to 2011. Fundamental advances in information and communication technologies have only furthered Latin Americans' integration within global processes. Indeed, the world has a habit of showing up on our doorstep in an era of globalization, via transnational migration, neoliberal economic policies, or the construction of socioeconomic platforms that destabilize borders or turn capital cities into ruins.

Although numerous studies have noted the new time-space configurations that accompany globalization in late twentieth- and early twenty-first-century Latin American literature,[4] it is only recently that scholars have engaged the localizing practices present in these texts that force us to understand the ways that narrative protagonists mediate their experiences of global and local as interwoven concepts. This book situates itself among a new set of studies by authors who seek to explore the temporal and spatial life of literary texts at the turn of the twentieth and the beginning of the twenty-first centuries, including Gustavo

Guerrero, who examines the spatial fragmentation of globalization; Erica Durante, who studies its temporal multiplicity; and Héctor Hoyos, who argues that contemporary Latin American authors, including Roberto Bolaño, are shaping the notion of world literature and literature as a global phenomenon.[5] In differentiation from these studies, however, the contribution of this work lies in its commitment to exploring how practices of locality mark the cultural production of this era. This interest calls on the widespread assertion among globalization theorists regarding the necessity of studying the local manifestations of global processes. To that effect, Santiago Castro-Gómez and Eduardo Mendieta contend that "la globalización no es un proceso nebuloso y abstracto sino que se haya siempre localizado" (globalization is not a nebulous and abstract process: rather, it has always been localized);[6] similarly, Renato Ortiz finds that for globalization to exist, "debe localizar, enraizarse en las prácticas cotidianas de los pueblos y los hombres" (it must be localized, rooted in the daily practices of people and towns).[7] In this context, should we consider the local a remnant of some secure, bounded, "traditional" space? The notion of locality might equally be read through the totalizing gaze of global capital as marketable, profitable resources to be produced and hawked to foreign tourists: hence *local* flavor, *rich* culture, and other descriptors that portray the local as a consumable object of cultural difference. As Latin American authors question and reimagine the region's role within the phenomenological systems of globalization, they reveal the conflicts and imbalances that underlie a heightened global integration of cultural and economic flows.

In the present work, I endeavor to expand on an understanding of the local as belonging or relating to a particular area, in favor of an interpretation of *area* as an intersection of time and space, so that the understanding of local entails understanding a mode of inhabiting the world: a position from which to speak. In that vein, Néstor García Canclini acknowledges that the statistics of human and capital mobility ring slightly hollow until they are suitably forested with "narratives of heterogeneity," at which point "subjects reappear within structures."[8] This, in turn, raises the question of how to consider the shape of the *local* in Latin American literary subjects' negotiation of global processes. As Carlos Mario Yory points out in his writing on the present role of inhabited territory, "Ser de un lugar será, entonces, desde la perspectiva global, 'ser de un momento,' pertenecer a un intervalo" (Being from a place means, from a global perspective, "being from a moment," belonging to an interval).[9] To dialogue Yory's approach with García Canclini's consideration of the "collection of narratives"[10] that form our knowledge of global processes, it is clear that new representations of the local must themselves be intervals from which to narrate the interplay of near and distant forces.

From a historical perspective, the study of contemporary literature provides a means for investigating the ways that failed economic reform, incomplete development, and displacement of entire generations during the dictatorial regimes have altered the economic, social, and cultural landscapes of Latin America. Citing the immense heterogeneity of Latin American cultural formations, George Yúdice points to the uneven development and modernization processes, the persistence of imperial power relations, and the strategies for survival that emerge in the shadows of the former.[11] Contemporary subjects thus occupy inequitable positions from which to negotiate individual and collective identities. Indeed, as Castro-Gómez and Mendieta write, "La des(re)territorialización de la economía, los imaginarios y las identidades . . . se trata, en el fondo, de una nueva repartición de privilegios y exclusiones, de posibilidades y desesperanzas, de libertades y esclavitudes" (The de(re)territorialization of the economy, of imaginaries and identities . . . is at its core a matter of a new distribution of privileges and exclusions, of possibilities and despairs, liberties and slaveries).[12] The study of the construction of the local in contemporary narrative raises crucial questions: What do these changes mean for contemporary actors and, by extension, perhaps contemporary literary protagonists? In my study of recent Latin American novels, I find that the region's contemporary narrative is faced with reconstructing not only local meanings (to echo Jesús Martín-Barbero) but also the very meaning of *local* itself. Rather than a fixed concept rooted in place—a neighborhood or a town—local becomes a plastic concept, a site for mediating conflicts in identities and imaginaries, for evaluating the tension between past and present modes of inhabiting the world. I use the term *local* to describe the territories of belonging, identity, and memory transited by the many characters engaged in this book—whether they be spatial, temporal, phenomenological, or otherwise.[13] These narrative constructions portray the local as a way of being in a place, a means of inhabiting the world and navigating the ambivalence between familiarity and estrangement, the mediation of immediate and distant influences, and the overwhelming simultaneity and disjuncture of contemporary life.

The many translocalizations of globalization pose challenges to the selection of a literary corpus from which to interpret Latin American authors' representation of contemporary life. Even the question of defining what constitutes Latin American literature may be a futile and reductive exercise, as Jesús Montoya Juárez and Ángel Esteban have noted. These scholars, and many of their peers, have called for a more open, plural approach to the study of the region's literature, one "en la que emerge con fuerza lo local" (in which the local emerges forcefully).[14] With this in mind, I focus this book primarily on the question of technique, selecting my corpus based on the strategies that authors use to illustrate their protagonists' spatial and temporal worlds. Although the integration of Brazilian and Spanish American authors may seem unorthodox, the central goal of this book lies not in contemplating the differences between national literary traditions but in assessing how the impacts of globalization—a powerful force of change in both Lusophone and Hispanophone Latin American literatures—

play out in textual representations of locality. To begin, in chapter 1, I examine Luiz Ruffato's *Estive em Lisboa e lembrei de você* (2009), a novel centered on a working-class Brazilian who moves from Minas Gerais to Lisbon. Next, I turn to the use of language as a mobile spatiality in Wilson Bueno's *Mar paraguayo* (1992), an understudied novella written in Spanish, Portuguese, and Guaraní, along with invented words. To garner a more panoramic view of authors' narrative constructions of universality in multisited narratives, in chapter 2 I examine the breakneck speed and fragmented imagery of Roberto Bolaño's *2666* and its theatrical adaptation by Àlex Rigola (2007). In chapter 3, I study two Brazilian novels distinguished by their ambiguous settings, Bernardo Carvalho's *Teatro* (1998) and João Gilberto Noll's *Harmada* (1993), to further investigate the tension between familiarity and estrangement that characterizes the experience of contemporary subjects. Finally, to close this discussion of the new modalities of the local, in chapter 4 I turn to an analysis of writing and translation as practices that configure space and time in Valeria Luiselli's *Los ingrávidos* (2011). Throughout the novel, Luiselli's characters translate themselves into new locales: their practices of writing and inhabiting spaces highlight the ways in which contemporary subjects reconstruct modes of belonging as they travel and partake in the world around them. Questions of time and space come to the fore in close readings of these texts, whose pages are dappled with lengthy forays into memory, rapid jumps from one locale to another, and malleable territories of language and affective bonds. In this reading, I focus on understanding how contemporary Latin American authors from across the region represent the local amid increasingly destabilized and globalized planes of existence.

UNDERSTANDING LATIN AMERICAN LITERATURE AT THE TURN OF THE MILLENNIUM

The novels I examine in this book—published between 1992 and 2011—span a critical timeframe in Latin American history following the end of the Cold War and through the first decade of the new millennium. Several innovative examinations of space in contemporary Latin American narrative emerged from Última narrativa latinoamericana, a conference hosted at the University of Salamanca in 2009 to examine the new territories that have arisen in the decline of national parameters of narration.[15] In *Narrativas latinoamericanas para el siglo XXI: Nuevos enfoques y territorios*, the editors find that these new narrative settings are marked by the spatial aesthetics of de(re)territorialization: extraterritorial and nomadic narratives, hybridity, and virtual and cyberspaces.[16] In their subsequent volume from 2011, *Literatura más allá de la nación*, editors Francisca Noguerol Jiménez, María Ángeles Pérez López, Ángel Esteban, and Jesús Montoya Juárez argue that globalization has led to a disintegration of national borders, redefining the territories of contemporary literature.[17] Among the works that proceeded from this congress, it is perhaps Montoya Juárez and Esteban's *Entre lo local y lo global* that provides the most pivotal grounds for this continued discussion of how Latin American literature mediates locality in a globalized world.[18] In their introduction to the work, the editors trace several contradictory currents of influence that enveloped the field of literary production in Latin America from the 1990s onward: the decline of Boom and post-Boom styles of narration; the accelerated movement of people, capital, and ideas; the displacement of entire workforces through neoliberal economic policy and globalized trade networks; the expansion of wealth disparities; the decline of the state as sovereign power; and new communication technologies, all of which have notable consequences in the realm of personal experience. It is these changes that lead writers to a new project, one that, in the words of Montoya Juárez and Esteban, "busca escribir . . . esas historias otras, locales, que dialogan con el contexto global e interrogan a una Latinoamérica siempre cambiante" (seeks to write . . . these other stories, local stories, that dialogue with the context of the global and interrogate an ever-changing Latin America).[19] A few crucial features of Latin America's experience of increasing integration within global markets and imaginaries merit further exploration here. During the two-decade period covered by the works studied in this book, the region became increasingly democratic and further embedded in the global economy. The production of narrative reflects both the cultural and economic impacts of globalization: greater movement of people and goods, increased cultural diversity, the expansion of foreign influence and capitalism on a global scale, and a resultant widening of wealth disparities. The cultural shifts that underlie these changes—in particular, the steady decline of formerly resonant frames for understanding the self in relation to place through the medium of nation, and an unprecedented interconnectivity sustained by new communication technologies—present contemporary Latin American authors and their protagonists with the task of mediating multitudes of other times and spaces beyond their immediate surroundings.

While Latin America's economy opened up to greater external influence, widespread migration—sparked by political exile and dramatic economic changes from the 1970s to the 1990s—altered the relationship between place, identity, and belonging in the region, which I investigate at length in this book.[20] Between 1978 and the end of the 1980s, dictatorships fell or elected governments in thirteen Latin American countries. The impact of these authoritarian regimes can be understood first in the context of political imaginaries: the period that followed the dictatorships destabilized the very idea of the nation-state as an integrative concept. Indeed, Latin America's fictional writing reflects dramatic changes in the relationship between the populace and the state, particularly a diminished faith in national institutions and the intermingling of the public and private spheres through state-led reconciliation processes.[21] The question of how to represent the past emerges as a central concern of postdictatorship literature, a topic

Idelber Avelar pursues in *The Untimely Present*, whose ruminations on ruin and allegory I engage in chapter 3 of this book.[22] In addition to the political repression and traumatic legacy of the dictatorships, the decade was marked by decreased spending, the privatization of industry, and the removal of trade and price barriers. In *Literature and Interregnum*, Patrick Dove focuses his analysis on a period of postmodernity between the decline of state sovereignty and before a new order has arisen in its place.[23] And in 2014, Timothy Robbins and José González published a coedited collection of essays arguing that contemporary writers distance themselves from political and social issues at the national level and are uniquely embedded in digital spaces that provide transnational tools for communication and distribution.[24] Robbins and González stress the notion that the nation-state no longer serves as an effective model for defining authorial origin. These considerations for the representation of the nation-state offer an opportunity to reflect on how contemporary Latin American literature is charged with ruminating on the decline of national models of identity. To that effect, Dove writes that neoliberal globalization entails a shift in the dynamics of Latin America's engagement with the world, as economic processes increasingly mediate the relationship between local and global planes of human interaction, a framework formerly administered by the state.[25]

From an economic perspective, the two-decade period explored in this book began with a shift toward economic and cultural globalization coupled with widespread democratization followed by a period of neoliberal disillusionment and recession during the 1990s. In particular, Brazil, Mexico, and Argentina have felt the lingering effects of the Latin American debt crisis of 1982, when their governments' inability to repay the large sums borrowed from international creditors became an unavoidable fact.[26] In chapter 1, I examine Luiz Ruffato's narrative of a lower-class Brazilian's migration to Portugal during the 1980s: the so-called lost decade in which a recession drove Brazilians to seek work abroad.[27] In response to the debt crisis, many Latin American countries shed the formerly dominant import substitution industrialization model and adopted a free market–oriented approach in order to comply with the conditions set out by the International Monetary Fund for financing their debt repayments.[28] These changes, along with a denunciation of state intervention in economic affairs, would become the hallmarks of a neoliberal economic platform that took hold across the region, popularly known as the Washington Consensus.[29] Advocates of market-oriented economic reforms expected that the shift toward a more competitive environment and accompanying change in the role of the state would allow markets to become the main determinant of relative prices and of resource allocation, reducing inefficiencies, increasing productivity, and spurring growth.[30]

Notably, one of the common themes during this period is the economic mediation of relationships between members of different nations. The passage of the North American Free Trade Agreement in 1992 established one of the world's most prominent free-trade zones and laid the groundwork for strengthened economic ties between Canada, the United States, and Mexico. As the borderland setting of Bolaño's *2666* illustrates, although Mexico's new access to the broader North American economy spurred economic expansion, it also placed the country's working class in a precarious position in a system that favored fiscal growth over social development. Latin America faced widespread recessions as early as 1997 and 1998 in which employment growth faltered and the utopic aura surrounding neoliberalism attracted increased scrutiny. This, in turn, facilitated a political transition to the left: by the end of the decade, a so-called pink tide swept through Latin America in response to the shortcomings of the neoliberal platform, leaving Venezuela, Bolivia, Brazil, and Argentina in the hands of left-wing governments by the mid-2000s.[31] This populist turn to the left did not always translate into economic isolationism, as many governments opted to continue free market economics, while regional trade organizations grew during this period. In Brazil, for example, Luiz Inácio Lula da Silva chose to focus on social and structural inequality during his presidency, while also advocating for economic liberalization and private enterprise to sustain the global capital needed to fuel Brazil's massive twenty-first-century economy.

Globalization must be considered as a phenomenon of both simultaneity *and* disjuncture, characterized by the concurrent and interdependent functioning of multiple planes and processes of economic exchange and political influence, without losing sight of inequalities and imbalances in trade—the persistence and concretization of social disparities despite rampant economic growth. *Latin American Literature at the Millennium* destabilizes the tropes of unilaterally accelerated mobility and unification that dominate the popular imaginary of globalization in Latin America. The narrative of global unification through cultural intermingling and economic interdependency—which García Canclini refers to as "the most repeated story about globalization"[32]—is often heralded as the chief impact of neoliberal economic growth, and the mobility of people its prerequisite. However, this perspective is limited by its emphasis on movement and homogenization, and on the dissolution of cultural links to place without a reterritorialization of symbolic processes. To that effect, García Canclini takes a skeptical posture toward the aesthetic of deterritorialization in which "the world came to be regarded as a transit lounge"[33]—a scene that recalls Gilda Simon's refutation of the "nomadic planet" narrative of boundless movement and accompanying dissolution of the frictions of cultural difference.[34] The "nomadic planet" view echoes some of the flattening descriptions of globalization offered by Thomas Friedman and Sheila Croucher, among others.[35] David Harvey furthers the notion of temporal leveling, arguing that the geographical expansion of global capitalism attempts to annihilate space through time, diminishing local difference while situating all of the places of the global market on the same clock.[36] However, the element missing from this consideration of the orientation of Latin America on a global market clock is a study of time and space as they are experienced by contemporary subjects.

These new mobilities of capital and people pose, above all, pressing questions about the way that we understand protagonists' local contacts with *elsewhere*—whether through movement, entanglement in global systems of trade, or psychological awareness of the staggering multiplicity of experiences of the world. The novels I discuss in this book reveal both the grand and the minute, sweeping gestures such as moving across countries or feeling the impact of global processes, while giving equal attention and narrative space to the journey of the human psyche. In that vein, Anthony Giddens proposes *distanciation* as a term that names the conjoining of proximal and distant influences on human sensory experience.[37] The impact of modernity on human perception is that distant events can be equally as familiar as or even more familiar than that which is close at hand, easily integrated into personal experience.[38] Although they may inhabit local physical worlds, the citizens of Latin America and the protagonists of the region's literature often make journeys through intangible and decidedly *global* planes of consciousness as they think and feel in response to distant events that take place outside their immediate niche in time and space.[39]

In an era of increased worldwide integration, contemporary Latin American literature habitually upsets chronological linearity, straddling the local time of multiple geographies or deepening and extending time on a global plane. To this effect, contemporary Latin American literary theorist Erica Durante argues that globalization is a temporal process capable of encompassing distinct notions of time and multiple histories in a continuous flow.[40] This splicing of near and distant happenings produces uncertainties in the relationship between inhabited place and lived experience, which might be understood more conceptually as turbulence in the relationship between lived space and time. To use a ground-level example, the government of the Mexican state of Quintana Roo decided to adopt a time zone that matches that of Eastern Standard Time[41] in order to boost revenues in the resort cities of Cancún, Playa del Carmen, and Tulum by providing an extra hour of daylight in the evening. This change temporally articulated the physical setting of Quintana Roo in relation to a global economic force by aligning the state's clocks with those of its dominant tourist market: the East Coast of the United States. Beyond its impact on tourism, this reformatting complicates the individual-level experience of local time: the resort workers who commute from the neighboring state of Yucatán also travel "back" in time as they cross into another time zone after work. Contemporary historical novels, such as Andrés Neuman's *El viajero del siglo*,[42] reveal the multilayered, narrative quality of history itself. In other instances, the passage of time is made ambiguous, as in César Aira's *Una novela china* and *Váramo*,[43] novels that provide few chronological cues beyond taking place in the twentieth century and in China and Panama, respectively. Numerous contemporary authors—among them Patricio Pron (Argentina) and Tatiana Salem Levy (Brazil)—tend toward the fragmentation and extension of time in multinational micronarratives. Literature thus offers a means of ruminating on the many global contacts embedded in seemingly mundane activities, which become visible through subjects' musings on the disjuncture between space and time. In *2666*, the novel that provides an anchor for chapter 2 of this book, Bolaño describes the experience of jet lag for Oscar Amalfitano:

> Creía (o le gustaba creer que creía) que cuando uno está en Barcelona aquellos que están y que son en Buenos Aires o el DF no existen. La diferencia horaria era sólo una máscara de la desaparición. Así, si uno viajaba de improviso a ciudades que en teoría no deberían existir o aún no poseían el tiempo apropiado para ponerse en pie y ensamblarse correctamente, se producía el fenómeno conocido como jet-lag. No por tu cansancio sino por el cansancio de aquellos que en aquel momento, si tú no hubieras viajado, deberían de estar dormidos.[44]

> [He believed (or liked to think he believed) that when a person was in Barcelona, the people living and present in Buenos Aires and Mexico City didn't exist. The time difference only masked their nonexistence. And so if you suddenly traveled to cities that, according to this theory, didn't exist or hadn't yet had time to put themselves together, the result was the phenomenon known as jetlag, which arose not from your exhaustion but from the exhaustion of the people who would still have been asleep if you hadn't traveled.][45]

Here, the incongruences in time that are made visible by transnational travel are linked with conflictive imaginings of space and the fracturing of human experience over many settings. Thus, at the local level, deeper studies of everyday actors' negotiation of translocal processes reveal heterogeneities that defy simplistic assessments of Latin America's assimilation to a global clock and compass. The staggering growth of multinational trade networks and rapid oscillations between inflationary booms and stark recessions shape the topography of globalized landscapes of people—who lives where, in what way, and at what time—and in the landscapes of development and decline left in the wake of foreign and domestic investment. At the level of the individual protagonist, these disparities play out in terms of inequitable control over lived time and space, highlighting the intimate link between a protagonist's local experience and his or her position of power within global systems of exchange (see, for example, the work of Martin Albrow and Doreen Massey), an inevitable consequence of a world structured by gender, race, and class.

Indeed, a study of the local in contemporary Latin American literature must attend to the narrative illumination of multiple experiences of being in the world:

the conflictive imaginings of borderlands, the cyclical migrations of seasonal work, the returns to a homeland after the displacement of exile, the contrast between the fluid transnational leaps of privileged jetsetters and the perilous journeys of those without documents. The local representations studied in this book often entail sites of tension for the remediation of identity and reckoning with the ground-level impacts of uneven economic development and state and interpersonal violence. Across the chapters of this book, I show that textual engagement with the simultaneity and disjuncture of globalization offers a vision of contemporary life woven from the heterogeneities in these processes of movement and communication. To make the abstract, disorienting phenomenological engagements of globalization visible, contemporary Latin American authors engage new narrative techniques of locale: fragments that speak from multiple voices and settings, lengthy forays into memory, and hybrid geographies that mingle the words and syntaxes of different languages. As local actors embedded in global processes, the protagonists of contemporary Latin American literature must inaugurate new territories of belonging, whether in response to the disorientation of living in foreign locales or the alienating experience of confronting world events and phenomena in local spaces. The region's most recent literature often shows that the opposition between global and local is not a stark contrast at the level of protagonists, who mediate their lives across many contexts. Latin American literature provides local context and nuance to global processes, highlighting individual narratives that punctuate and complicate the broad strokes of historical or economic discourse prevalent at the turn of the millennium. These themes provide insights into the task of contemporary narrative: to reconcile unprecedented contact with other places and perspectives—a staggering multiplicity of experiences of the world.

CHAPTER OVERVIEWS

Rather than present a historiography of the period in question, I have organized the chapters of this book thematically to illustrate varied techniques of capturing the dialogue between local terrains and global processes. I focus first on the role of language as a mobile spatiality, then move to the use of visual snapshots that convey movement between multiple spaces and places. From there, I ruminate on spatial nonspecificity as a vehicle for generalizing local settings into an allegorical contact zone where ruin and memory take precedence. Finally, I examine metanarrative (de)constructions of space through the meticulous staging of interconnected localities and character arcs. This book is divided equally between contemporary Lusophone and Hispanophone Latin American texts, a choice that is deliberate. Indeed, as the region's authors question and reimagine their role within the phenomenological systems of globalization, they reveal common conflicts and imbalances that underlie a heightened global integration of cultural and economic flows. What bridges the linguistic and geographical divides of this book is an evolving thematic focus on expressions and practices of locality within contemporary Latin American narrative. To inaugurate *Latin American Literature at the Millennium,* I focus first on localizing practices in two Brazilian migration-related novels, examining how memory and language help to ground migrant protagonists in the face of estrangement and marginalization abroad. The centrality of movement in these narratives is always accompanied by a weighty dependence on remembered locales to contextualize the present: indeed, as Sara Ahmed writes in her discussion of estrangement and belonging in migration, "The experience of leaving home in migration is hence always about the failure of memory to fully make sense of the place one comes to inhabit, a failure which is experienced in the discomfort of inhabiting a migrant body, a body which feels out of place, which feels uncomfortable in this place. The process of returning home is likewise about the failures of memory, of not being inhabited in the same way by that which appears as familiar."[46] I look first at Luiz Ruffato's *Estive em Lisboa e lembrei de você,*[47] a story centered on a working-class migrant from Minas Gerais who moves to Lisbon in the hope of better economic opportunities. As the young man becomes increasingly embedded in Lisbon's underworld, I study how Ruffato uses typographic techniques and dialect-specific terms to convey linguistic residues of the protagonist's local identity and experience. I examine how Otherness[48] becomes a type of shared identity for the main protagonist and his Brazilian migrant friend. In conversation with Ahmed's work on homemaking and Otherness as grounds for community formation within the process of migration, I examine how the protagonists of *Estive em Lisboa* engage memory as a local terrain and refuge, often enacted in the text through Ruffato's painstaking mimicry of orality. From there, I turn to a lesser-known novella by Wilson Bueno, *Mar paraguayo,*[49] a work known for its rhythmic narrative style and linguistic border-crossing. The *marafona* protagonist of Bueno's *Mar paraguayo* conjures and banishes hybrid geographies of Portuguese, Spanish, and Guaraní as she guides the reader across the precarious linguistic terrains on which her seething story rests. Throughout this section of the book, language serves a trifold function: as a mobile spatiality, as a temporal practice revealing personal history and memory, and finally, as a means of asserting the self through fluid linguistic geographies. I examine language as a grounding practice that aids in preserving identity, thereby operating as a space to inhabit, a local practice that inaugurates geographies through the lyrical *portunhol* (amalgamation of Spanish and Portuguese) of the protagonist of Bueno's *Mar paraguayo* and the boldly *mineiro* Portuguese (a dialect spoken in the state of Minas Gerais) of Ruffato's working-class migrant in Lisbon. The preservation of language as a localizing practice also reminds us of the alienation and marginalization that migrants may experience with respect to their tongues, as the very language that localizes and connects these subjects to their country of origin or heritage can estrange them when placed in a sea of speakers of a different origin or dialect.[50] In my study of *Mar paraguayo*, I examine how the protagonist deploys both Spanish and Portuguese in her polyphonic universe, developing a strong narrative voice that reveals her trajectory in space and time and gives her the ability to articulate herself. This is especially pertinent given the rich linguistic territories of Brazil, long marked by the shifting terrains of immigrant populations. Language serves as a type of anchor in the novella, providing a tool for resistance, as well as an arena for evaluating the intermingling of the local, as understood through her connection to Paraguay and her indigenous language of Guaraní, with the global, in relationship to her time in Brazil and her othered experience of Portuguese and Spanish. I refer to Antonio Cornejo Polar's work on the prominence of orality in Latin American literature,[51] as well as Alastair Pennycook's assessments of language as a local practice.[52] Here, language helps to establish a type of presence in the face of estrangement and lack of community.

In chapter 2, I study multiterritoriality, or the representation and transition between multiple geographies, in Roberto Bolaño's sprawling novel *2666* and its theatrical adaptation by Àlex Rigola.[53] Bolaño creates a vast narrative universe compiled in vignettes, a technique that aids the novel in both complicating time and moving the central plotline between multiple planes. This layering of narratives makes visible the many faces and facets of the global, highlighting readers' inability to see globalization in its panoramic expression. Literature often handles spatial distances in incongruent ways, making jumps in space that rely on the constant and renewed expression of the local. In this way, *2666*'s micronarratives counteract the very speed they create, as Bolaño habitually focuses in on a narrative moment with a level of meticulousness that borders on excess, addressing the local in its minutiae. Observing these incongruences, I argue that it is in fact the contrast between speed and stasis, between the external plot development and the internal drawing out of time, that defines the novel, capturing the fragmentation of our collective global experience. I look then at how these translate into a temporal disjuncture that Bolaño expresses through breakneck speed punctuated by moments of stillness. To illuminate many uneven experiences of globalization—or, to recall Yory, many intervals—*2666* hurtles across desert landscapes, literary conferences, and manufacturing plants, skidding to a halt in the backyard of a distressed Mexican academic, the desolate crime scene of a femicide, and a lunch counter in Arizona.

In its response to the novel, Rigola's play interweaves music, film, and projected texts and images to complicate the notion of speed and mobility in the text, at times running in frenzy, on other occasions zeroing in on the slow passage of time through shadows, inner dialogue, and scenes enacted in slow motion. With every scene change, audiences observe how Rigola re-creates the multiplicities of local time with an intimacy that plays out in contrast to broader questions of global movement, to which the work is also attentive in its use of film and moving platforms on the stage. Ultimately, Bolaño (and Rigola) reminds readers and audiences of the incongruences of contemporary life, a testimony to the fact that globalization is never experienced homogeneously. From an elusive transnational writer, to a black American journalist covering a boxing match on the borderlands with Mexico, to a German expatriate prisoner in a border-town jail, to the hundreds upon hundreds of poor female workers whose corpses blend into the landscape of the factory-laden desert created by the North American Free Trade Agreement, the novel reflects on inequitable mobility in an era of globalization in which certain ethnicities, nationalities, and genders dominate over others. In dialogue with the work of Doreen Massey and Martin Albrow, I assess how inequitable access to temporal and spatial resources in our current era are illuminated in the novel and play, highlighting absences and inconsistencies in the textures of globalized local life. In both contemporary literature and theater, the treatment of time and space reminds us of the ways in which we collide in the twenty-first century, but also how greatly our experiences differ in terms of mobility and power. Many of the female protagonists of *Latin American Literature at the Millennium*—such as the *marafona* (a sex worker) in Bueno's *Mar paraguayo* and the numerous victims of femicide in Bolaño's *2666*—provide narrative examples of how women (especially poor women and women of color) are muted into the background of globalization discourses and struggle to articulate their presence verbally and physically. This coercive silencing is only exacerbated by these women's entanglement within the processes of neoliberal capitalism or transnational migration, making them particularly vulnerable to oppression and exploitation. The ability of literary representations of such marginalization to subvert or perpetuate these inequalities remains a significant question, as I discuss at length in chapters 1 and 2: What might these representations tell us about literature as a site of cultural negotiation in the face of global phenomena?

In chapter 3, I transition from multiterritoriality to spatial ambiguity in my analysis of two Brazilian novels from the 1990s: Bernardo Carvalho's *Teatro* and João Gilberto Noll's *Harmada*.[54] The novels' shared focus on ruin guides readers through an exploration of spatial and temporal ambivalence. Both works operate in nationally undefined contexts, while exploring spatial tropes central to the region: the borderland and a return to the capital city, respectively. The novels present settings that are general enough to belong anywhere and to anyone, yet the nonspecificity of these settings also renders them a kind of no-man's-land. For example, in the case of *Teatro*, the borderland is undefined but clearly articulates a power dynamic that evokes the relationship between the United States and Mexico. Within this ambivalent zone, *Teatro* reflects on borderlands broadly and on Latin America as a region in which borders—ideological, political, social, linguistic, ethnic, and economic—abound. In order to approximate questions of the particular within the universal, I dialogue my textual analysis with Andreas

Huyssen's and Henri Lefebvre's work on the abandonment and repurposing of space. Both Noll and Carvalho depict conditions of decadence and decay, achieved in explorations of physical sites and in the portrayal of antiheroic protagonists on the brink of downfall. In their rendering of ruin, both works provide vivid images of a failed modernity; in the case of Noll, readers experience the ills of a shambolic city in which unemployment and material and bodily decay abound; in Carvalho's text, the borderland becomes a place of abandoned lives and objects, a desert of wreckage not dissimilar to that of *2666*'s Santa Teresa (Ciudad Juárez). Ruin illuminates important issues pertinent to the landscape of the 1990s in Latin America, including poverty, underdevelopment, and the systematic violence of life on the margins. The narrative subjects of *Harmada* and *Teatro* must mediate conflicting selves and settings in a liminal zone between belonging and estrangement: a task that manifests in one character's return to a once-decadent city that has fallen into social and economic decline since his departure and in another protagonist's struggle to speak his parents' mother tongue.

Finally, I close the book with a study of *Los ingrávidos* by Valeria Luiselli,[55] a young Mexican writer with a multinational footprint. Concluding our extended examination of locality with *Los ingrávidos* is appropriate in a number of ways, as the text is the most contemporary work of the collection and brings in a critical young female voice to the analysis of spatial representations in current Latin American literature. Luiselli's work is distinct in its overt ruminations on time and space: her polyvocal narrative centers on a young translator's hunt for traces of a deceased Mexican poet, Gilberto Owen, ensconced within her older self's struggle to write amid her domestic obligations in Mexico City. As the story progresses, Luiselli constructs and then compresses places and narrative worlds, arriving at a denouement in which boundaries across space and time collapse. In engaging Luiselli's novel, I refer to the work of Doreen Massey on the openness and interconnectedness of place and further dialogue with Yi-Fu Tuan's differentiation of space and place in my study of the settings of *Los ingrávidos*.[56] Given the centrality of polyvocality and multiple perspectives in this discussion, it is worth noting the prominence of affective patterning of public spaces transited by many people, as Luiselli's protagonists pattern their own readings of space over the liminal canvas of subway stations and park benches.[57] The work's actors move through ruptures and overlaps in different times and spaces, colliding with each other as they mediate their stories and selves across other cities and other lives. This approach to narrative construction offers further lessons about the nature of contemporary place, as *Los ingrávidos* proceeds in narrative vignettes that layer together dynamic patterns of experience.

1 • MIGRATION CHRONOTOPES

Imagining Time and Space in Two Brazilian Novels

me desterraron de mi tierra
caminé por la tierra
me deportaron de mi lengua
ella me acompañó
[they banished me from my land
I walked the earth
they deported me from my language
she accompanied me]
—Juan Gelman, "El Expulsado"

Perhaps the reason immigrants worry settled people so much (and often so abstractly) is that they expose the relative nature of certainties inscribed in the earth. —Marc Augé, *Non-places: An Introduction to Supermodernity*

Migration narratives are characterized by an inherent spatial multiplicity: migrant protagonists frequently traverse spaces that are both global and local to them, while negotiating estrangement and belonging. When considering the intimate union between space and belonging, these narratives often unsettle geographies, allowing readers to observe the constructed nature of place-making. More recently, the epistemological question of migration has drawn attention as a means of thinking through identity and meaning. Indeed, Néstor García Canclini has examined the migrant as a "worker of metaphor," linking the displacement of migration and travel with the transition and movement implied in the association of metaphor. He writes, "Migration implies a radical way of experiencing uncertainty, and the passage from one way of naming and speaking to another. . . . These displacements of meaning are habitual in the language of the foreigner because he or she lives among facts that have other names, and names which have lost their facts."[1] Here, Canclini argues that migration as metaphor allows access to new textures of experience, as meanings are constructed and abandoned. If the defining feature of contemporary life is accelerated mobility and hence widespread displacement, as human geographers so often argue, then migration narratives offer a lens to examine not only protagonists' displacement and deterritorialization—the dissolution of their affective attachments to place—but the ways in which those same protagonists remake themselves in new locales and their capacity to reterritorialize and re-create meanings.

In contemporary Brazilian literature, such explorations of the migrant subject preoccupy the works of a variety of authors, including Milton Hatoum (*Relato de un cierto Oriente*), Adriana Lisboa (*Azul-corvo, Rakushisha,* and *Hanói*), Daniel Galera (*Cordilheira*), Bernardo Carvalho (*O filho da mãe*), and Chico Buarque (*Budapest*).[2] Migration narratives provide insight into modes of experience that have frequently been excluded from national histories: to that effect, historian Jeffrey Lesser has noted a tendency among scholars (both Latin American and otherwise) to treat the experiences of immigrants as if they were external to those of their adopted country.[3] At times, the representation of migrant subjects in literature has mirrored the political agendas of the state, as noted by Brazilian literary critic José Leonardo Tonus, who states that "o imigrante tem sofrido um processo de alegorização . . . tem-no privado de sua capacidade de expressar um conteúdo que não seja aquele concedido pelo olhar autoral: conteúdo nacionalista, cosmopolita, regionalista ou transcultural" (immigrants have suffered under a process of allegorization . . . have been dispossessed of their capacities to express content that has not been preconceived by the author's gaze: nationalistic, cosmopolitan, regionalist, or transcultural content).[4] Stories of migration offer an opportunity for an extended evaluation of space and time, as their practices often reveal the plasticity of the local as a territory of belonging constructed on the basis of practice: through shared languages and forays into memory.[5] Furthermore, such narratives highlight the heterogeneous experiences of dislocation: they illustrate inequitable or coerced mobilities as well as the freedom of global movement. As such, textual representations of migration disrupt both flat narratives of national or regional experience and simplistic interpretations of contemporary mobility. In migration-related works, these concerns are mobilized at times to negotiate belonging in response to displacement and, at others, to fracture the dominance of a singular experience of place.

In this chapter, I examine two works that engage language and memory as means of narrating migration from distinct angles: *Estive em Lisboa e lembrei de você,* Luiz Ruffato's contemporary novella about a young Brazilian man's economic migration to Lisbon, and Wilson Bueno's *Mar paraguayo,* the story of a nameless Paraguayan narrator who migrates to Guaratuba.[6] By studying both a transatlantic economic migration and a much shorter journey through the shifting linguistic and cultural territories of the Triple Frontier, I argue that contemporary migration-themed novels disrupt narrative time-space cohesion to reconcile disparate experiences of place. Within this expanded framework, these texts generate alternative realms through their experimentation with language and the weaving of memory into the tangible spaces of the narrative present. To explore the affective dimensions of the migrant experience, I call on Néstor García Canclini's discussions of hybridity in migration and Sara Ahmed's work on estrangement and community formation, particularly the role of memory in inhabiting place.[7] As language—and particularly the textual imitation of spoken language—forms a central tenet of this chapter's contribution, I dialogue my analysis with Alastair Pennycook's work on the power of language to localize the speaker, and Antonio Cornejo Polar's writings on orality in Latin American literature.[8] In the first section of this chapter, I examine the creation of local places through practices of language, old habits, and forays into memory in *Estive em Lisboa e lembrei de você*, noting in particular Ruffato's textual strategies for demarcating territories of language. To follow, I examine the shifting linguistic terrains of Bueno's *Mar paraguayo*, whose protagonist uses a swirling blend of *portunhol* (or *portuñol* in the Spanish)—a combination of Spanish and Portuguese—and Guaraní to narrate her own marginal subjectivity, often inventing words and mediating past and present localities through repeated, rhythmic enunciations of memory.

RESIDUES OF THE LOCAL IN *ESTIVE EM LISBOA E LEMBREI DE VOCÊ*

Fictional narratives of migration often expose the traces and repetitions of formerly inhabited locales in response to global dislocation. As such, this chapter is preoccupied with the myriad socio-spatial configurations that arise in the process of migration. Contemporary literature repeatedly explores the multifaceted power dynamics inherent in traversing multiple geographies, often recounting deeply local stories of protagonists from disparate socioeconomic positions. García Canclini affirms that when discussing the workings of global processes, "one has to speak, above all, about the people who migrate or travel, who do not live where they were born, who exchange goods and messages with distant people, watch movies and television from other countries, or tell stories, gathered together, about the country they left. They reunite to celebrate something remote or communicate via email with others without knowing when they will see them again. In a certain sense, their life takes place elsewhere."[9] Similarly, theorists including Arjun Appadurai and Tim Oakes and Louisa Schein have engaged the concept of translocality to shift the conversation back to that of space: "Translocality draws attention to multiplying forms of mobility without losing sight of the importance of localities in peoples' lives."[10] The notion of translocality emphasizes the persistence of the local, reiterating the link between space and belonging, while acknowledging that movement between two geographies does not erase social relationships sustained across many locales. If we understand the term *local* as a territory of belonging, it is clear that the local is both relative and multiple, unhinged from the constraints of geographic place. Such an understanding of the local reveals the creation of translocal spaces through networking, bonding, and storytelling between migrant protagonists. In this section, I examine the use of memory and language as localizing practices in Ruffato's *Estive em Lisboa e lembrei de você* in order to mediate the sense of dislocation that permeates the short novel.[11]

It is notable that Ruffato himself was born in Cataguases, in the interior of Minas Gerais, Brazil, and came of age at the beginning of Brazil's "lost decade," a period of economic recession that drove many Brazilians to seek work abroad in hope of escaping economic hardship at home. Luiz Ruffato had been to Portugal a number of times before writing the novel, and deliberately chose Lisbon, a city he knew well, when he took part in the Amores Expressos project organized by Companhia das Letras. The original mandate of the project was to send sixteen Brazilian writers around the globe to write a love story.[12] While this task can certainly be interpreted broadly, it is curious to note that the most intimate relationship in Ruffato's work is in fact between the protagonist, Serginho, and his cigarettes. Serginho's vice offers a markedly localizing practice to mediate his transatlantic dislocation and provides a structural framework for the story. This relationship is echoed in the titles of the work's two parts, "Como parei de fumar" (How I quit smoking) and "Como voltei a fumar" (How I started smoking again), the first of which takes place in Cataguases—Ruffato's home city—and leads up to the first-person narrator's decision to migrate to Lisbon in the second part, which details his time there. After a series of personal difficulties, including the loss of his job and the nervous breakdown of his wife, Serginho decides to migrate to Lisbon in hope of economic success, with the eventual plan of returning to Brazil to provide for their son. Following the acknowledgments, Ruffato includes two epigraphs that stress the link between space and memory. The first is from a song by Portuguese rock band Xutos & Pontapés: "Sem me lembrar / De ti eu vivo / Em Lisboa / A Magnífica" (Without remembering / For you I live / In Lisbon / The Glorious).[13] Considering the title of the novel, the epigraph evokes both confusion and perhaps amusement for the reader, who wonders whether Lisbon might be the site for forgetting, rather than remembering. The lyrical association of Lisbon with amnesia also reiterates the intermingling between physical location and psyche in Ruffato's text, foregrounding the link between space and memory that plays a vital role in the work at large. The second epigraph is a poem by Miguel Torga that invokes the uniquely Portuguese word *saudade*—a mix of bittersweet absence and longing—which the poetic voice expresses for Brazil while exiled in Portugal.[14] The liminal territory described at the poem's close—"entre o chão encontrado e o chão perdido" (in between the ground I found and the one I lost)—causes a sense of instability in readers. In his epigraph, Torga investigates this felt instability with regard to the migrant's sense of belonging:

Dois polos de atração no pensamento!
Duas ânsias opostas nos sentidos!
Um purgatório em que o sofrimento
Nunca avista um dos céus apetecidos.[15]

[Two poles of attraction in thought!
Two opposing cravings in the senses!
A purgatory in which suffering
Never saw one of the desired heavens!]

Torga's verses convey the anxiety of living between geographies through the metaphor of purgatory, with the poetic subject trapped in an eternal disjuncture between two spaces to which he is equally drawn.

Through language and stylistics, Ruffato deliberately articulates the fluidity of the in-between in order to capture the novel's dual anchoring in Cataguases and Lisbon. This experimentation is very much in line with his earlier works, as an interest in language occupies *Inferno provisório* and *Eles eram muitos cavalos*.[16] Following the epigraphs of *Estive em Lisboa e lembrei de você*, Ruffato informs the reader that the novella is based on a series of personal testimonies recorded in Lisbon with a migrant worker from Minas.[17] Throughout the short piece, the author strives to replicate the orality of these recordings, often mimicking the rhythm and cadence of a story told aloud through the scarce use of full stops, as on page 17: "O rapaz, bem-falante, óculos escuros, motorista uniformizado, me mostrou o maço preto, caligrafia dourada, 'Conhece?,' respondi que *de-vista*, me ofereceu um, acetei, agradeci" (The young man, well-spoken, sunglasses, uniformed driver, showed me the black packet, gold calligraphy, "Do you know [these]?," I responded that we had seen each other around but never spoke, he offered me one, I accepted and thanked him).[18] This description mimics the flow of a conversation, generating a rhythm evocative of orality. In an interview with the author, I learned that the testimony upon which the novel was supposedly based never took place. "Então assim, o que eu fiz foi uma brincadeira com o leitor" (What I did was create an extended joke with the reader), Ruffato told me, "de propor a ele que aquilo não era uma ficção. Aquilo ali era uma verdade. E como verdade então ele compra essa história de uma maneira diferente de que se não fosse uma verdade, embora no fundo não seja uma verdade" (and propose to him that what he was reading was not fiction. It was the truth. And as the truth, one undertakes a different type of reading than one might if it were known to be fiction, though in reality it is fiction).[19] As Ruffato describes, the reading inspired by a testimony differs from that of a "fictional" account. This revelation is certainly telling when considering the ability of fiction to trouble the notion of authenticity. The reader is compelled to question the textual construction of regionalisms, nationalisms, and other geographical markers, which recalls the porousness of space and place discussed earlier.

However, the text does not rely on the veracity of the testimony, but rather on Ruffato's showcasing of Serginho's local speech patterns grounded in a *português mineiro* (Brazilian Portuguese dialect spoken in the state of Minas Gerais), at once a fabrication of orality and a configuration of the spatial relationships that scaffold Serginho's practice of locality. This all-encompassing task is addressed in the work's very title; rather than *Estive em Lisboa e* ***me*** *lembrei de você*, Ruffato opts to remove the reflexive pronoun.[20] Dropping the pronoun here is an indicator of regional speech,[21] which Ruffato further highlights through the use of italics to underscore those words that form part of the *mineiro* lexicon and its expressions, and the use of boldface for others in order to emphasize words assimilated in Lisbon: "Lisboa *cheira* sardinha no calor e castanha assada no frio, descobri isso revirando a cidade de cabeça-pra-baixo, de **metro,** de **elétrico,** de **autocarro,** de **comboio,** de a-pé" (Lisbon *smells* like sardines in the heat and roasted chestnuts in the cold, I discovered this turning the city upside-down by **metro**, by **tram**, by **bus**, by **train**, by foot).[22] The words "metro," "tram," "bus," and "train" are flagged as those that differ between Brazilian and continental Portuguese. Just as geo-semanticists Ron Scollon and Suzie Wong Scollon remind us that "language indexes the world" and that "much of what we understand depends on exactly where we and the language are located in the world,"[23] the italicized words operate as a portable geography that highlights Serginho's origin. Furthermore, Ruffato's use of typographic emphasis marks the spatial and symbolic territories of Serginho's increasingly multilayered identity. The dance between these two geographies of language recalls García Canclini's assertion that the migrant "is always a translator, someone who constantly lives between his place of origin and his adoptive culture, the experience of what can or cannot be said in another language."[24] This deliberate means of highlighting regionalisms draws attention to the flexible relationship between language, space, and identity, with the first half of the novel characterized by the italicized *mineiro* dialect and the second by a mix of bolded continental Portuguese and regionalisms. As Alcides Villaça notes, this tactic allows for a humorous play on words, without diminishing the painful and complex experience of migration: "Há mesmo a busca da plenitude de uma oralidade, marcada a princípio pelos acentos de um falar mineiro, em que ressoam timbres de quem bem 'proseia,' e depois marcada por incorporações do falar lisboeta, tudo resultando num estatuto híbrido e divertido, que nem por isso apaga as marcas da penosa condição do imigrante" (There is even the search for the plenitude of an orality, marked at the beginning by the accents of a Minas Gerais dialect, where the very 'chatty' sounds reverberate, and later marked by incorporations of Lisboan speech, all resulting in a hybrid and exciting state, although one that does not erase the marks of the painful condition of the immigrant.)[25] Beyond the typographic construction of locality, the first half of the novella includes many geographic reference points that chart the restaurants, bars, street names, and neighborhoods of Serginho's local experience, "bairros da margem esquerda do rio Pomba, Vila Resende, Granjaria, Leonardo, BNH, Vila Domingos Lopes, Vila Reis, Barridê, Tomé, Matadouro, Ana Carrara" (neighborhoods on the left bank of the river Pomba, Vila Resende, Granjaria, Leonardo, BNH, Vila Domingos Lopes, Vila Reis, Barridê, Tomé, Matadouro, Ana Carrara).[26] In the same interview with the author, Ruffato described this mapping as fundamental to the idea of the text as a "testimonial," as it allowed him to gain further legitimacy in his extended *brincadeira* (play) with readers:

> Então, isso é uma coisa assim, que é você criar uma noção de realidade, que, a partir de elementos concretos, mostra uma ilusão. Então assim, esses signos, eles são interessantes pra você poder questionar a própria questão da realidade, o que que é real e o que que não é, né? Ele [o mapeamento] transforma aquilo em real, mas é falso, porque é um falso real, porque o real que não existe! Como pode existir sem Serginho?[27]
>
> [So, it goes something like this: you create a notion of reality, which, though composed of concrete elements, reveals an illusion. So, these signs are interesting for you because they make you question the very notion of reality, what is real and what is not. It [the mapping] makes it real, but it is false, because it is a false real, because the real does not exist! How can it exist without Serginho?]

Throughout the text, Ruffato painstakingly portrays places through the trappings of memory, a tactic that gains prominence as the story moves to Lisbon. In part 1 this can be seen clearly when Serginho reflects on his departure from Cataguases:

> Uma saudade já daquela gente, criados todos juntos, observando o adiantamento do bairro, cafundó pouco a pouco civilizado, o arruamento, a luz elétrica, as redes de água e esgoto, o asfalto, os botequins, as festas pra construção da igreja católica, o erguimento silencioso dos templos dos crentes, os shows no Clube do Cavalo, os comícos, as peladas no campo que tem um marco em ruína.[28]
>
> [A longing for those people, all raised together, watching the progression of the neighborhood, gradually blurring the residents, the street, the light, the water and sewage networks, the asphalt, the bars, the celebrations for the construction of the Catholic church, the silent construction of the temples of the believers, the shows at the Clube do Cavalo, the comedians, the pebbles in the field of a ruined landmark.]

This bustling scene is enmeshed in personal recollection, as Serginho connects the cityscape with its inhabitants in their progressive confrontation with modernity. In contrast with the specificity of these memory-rich references, the narrator's allusions to his imagined future in Brazil are often haphazardly idealist, a dreamlike forecast that pervades the second half of the novel: "[Ia] voltar para o Brasil, comprar uns imóveis, viver de renda, e, esperançoso que sabe, 'Nada é impossível!'" ([I] return to Brazil, buy some properties, live off of the rents . . . expecting that 'Nothing is impossible!').[29] In this way, the spaces of an imagined Brazil are differentiated and pushed forward in time into a fantasy future. In comparison, Serginho's recollections of Cataguases are ever present, tangible, and marked by affect; local places are given shape and form through memory.

In line with this focus on the local, it is important to note that Serginho asserts himself as *mineiro* and not merely Brazilian or Latin American. In the second half of the novella, he is asked to say something in "Brazilian": "Enuncie alguma coisa, ó brasileiro, quero ouvir a música da tua fala" (Sing something, Brazilian, I want to hear the musicality of your speech).[30] Interestingly, Serginho opts to respond with a regionalism, confusing and humoring the Portuguese listener, who from that point forward requests that he speak in his "**dialect**," proclaiming, "Estes brasileiros!" (Those Brazilians!).[31] This exchange emphasizes the geography of language while also highlighting the diversity of migrant subjects, many of whom are lumped together by assumed national origin. In this sequence and in countless others, language serves as its own mobile spatiality, allowing migrant protagonists to move and remain local simultaneously, while connecting transnational subjects through a shared linguistic imaginary. As Alastair Pennycook argues, thinking of language as a practice diminishes the importance of the geographical location in which it is used, in favor of a renewed focus on language's role in configuring social relationships within time and space.[32] Readers clearly observe this when fellow Brazilian migrant Sheila "places" Serginho immediately as a *mineiro*, someone from the state of Minas Gerais: "Você é mineiro . . . só mineiro fala 'aqui'" (You are a *mineiro* . . . only a *mineiro* says "aqui").[33] Here, Serginho's word choice highlights the role of language as both a social and a spatial activity (see Pennycook): his use of *aqui* both indicates his place of origin and configures his position in relation to other Brazilian migrants in Portugal. Later, Serginho inquires as to the nationality of a Brazilian migrant named Rodolfo: "'Você é brasileiro?' confirmou, e, satisfeito, eu [Serginho] disse, 'Puxa vida, que bom encontrar alguém que fala a mesma língua da gente'" ("Are you Brazilian?" I confirmed, and, satisfied, I said, "Gee, it's good to meet someone who speaks the same language as us").[34] Both sequences reveal the relationship between locality and language, and the way that language informs the interplay between the individual and the world he or she navigates.[35] The second interaction, amusing in its insinuation that the continental variety of Portuguese is so distinct from the Brazilian as to form another language, further highlights the role of speech in uniting otherwise dislocated migrant subjects, in this case a poor, undocumented worker from Minas and a fellow migrant from Paraíba.

The novel's treatment of time reifies an understanding of locality that is rooted in practice, rather than geographical location. As discussed earlier in the chapter, Serginho's story is framed by his love affair with smoking, which plays out over the course of several years, as the work's final line reveals: "E foi assim que, depois de seis anos e meio, pouco mais ou menos, entrei numa tabacaria, pedi um maço de SG, um isqueiro, tirei um cigarro, acendi e voltei a fumar" (And this is how, after more or less six and a half years, I went into a tobacco shop, asked for a packet of SG and a lighter, took a cigarette, lit it and started smoking again).[36] Serginho's nicotine habit serves as another metaphor for the residue of personal memory, relentlessly drawing the narrative back to home and the familiar spatial experience of Cataguases and its people. Ruffato portrays smoking as a deeply local affair, punctuating the event with specific temporal and spatial references. Serginho quits smoking the day after the first of April, when he "saí do prédio [do doutor Fernando], atravessi a praça Rui Barbosa, aviei a receita na Drogaria do Povo" (left the building [of Dr. Fernando], crossed Rui Barbossa Square, and filled the prescription in the People's Drugstore).[37] When he ponders taking up the vice again in Lisbon, he recalls not only Dr. Fernando but an entire chorus of local protagonists who would be disappointed in him should his fortitude waver: "Quê isso, Serginho! Vai decepcionar agora as milhares de pessoas que acompanham há anos seus hercúleos esforços?" (What, Serginho! Are you now going to disappoint the thousands of people who have been following your Herculean efforts for years?).[38] Thus, smoking transgresses its marked time and space (i.e., the moment of cessation) and revives the social memory of Cataguases when Serginho resumes the habit in Portugal. Here, Serginho's smoking evokes a sense of familiarity constructed through routine rather than the particularities of geographical place, as the act of lighting a cigarette immediately revives a vivid recollection of Cataguases. The deconstruction of spatial boundaries in contemporary literature often illustrates this flow between local and global planes of experience, allowing readers to move away from strict binaries to examine language, memory, and movement from more intimate vantage points. Rather than the domestic spaces so prominent in other migration-themed novels, such as Milton Hatoum's *Relato de un cierto Oriente*, Adriana Lisboa's *Rakushisha*, and Óscar Nakasato's *Nihonjin*,[39] in *Estive em Lisboa*, Lisbon itself is the platform for the weaving of past and present, local familiarity and global estrangement.

The textual example that best illustrates this weaving of past and present in the urban space is a long Saturday afternoon outing that Serginho takes with fellow Brazilian Sheila. The two begin their day in a Brazilian bistro in downtown Lisbon, where Sheila proceeds to tell her life story through specific spatial markers.[40] She narrates the "tormentos de garota nascida em Maurilândia" (torments of a girl born in Maurilândia), her relocation to a soybean farm in a district of the

Rio Verde, and her school excursion to the capital city of Goiânia, where she completes a project "sobre os monumentos da cidade, ao Bandeirante e às Três Raças" (about the monuments of the city, the Bandeirante and the Three Races).[41] In Goiânia, she is lured into the sex trade by friends bound for Spain and later ends up in Lisbon. Similar to Serginho's, Sheila's tale is rooted in a fragmented series of local points of memory. She succeeds in displacing and drawing out narrative time through extensive sequences of mobility, her story shifting as she transitions from Goiás to the streets of Lisbon, "rua Augusta, rua do Ouro, rua da Prata, rua do Carmo, rua Garrett . . . avenida da Liberdade" (August Street, Gold Street, Silver Street, Carmo Street, Garrett Street . . . Liberty Avenue).[42] Sheila's movements end on the streets of the Portuguese capital, where she encounters barriers due to her social class, immigration status, and profession: "Onde entrava, tratavam ela mal, aos **chutos e pontapés**, como se portasse sida, ou lepra" (Wherever she entered, they treated her badly, **kicked her**, as if she had AIDS, or leprosy).[43] Here, the bolding of the continental Portuguese lexicon echoes the novel's first epigraph and reinforces the sociolinguistic demarcation of space. A number of theorists on space explore this relationship, including Doreen Massey, who has famously proposed that, "social relations of space are experienced differently, and variously interpreted, by those holding different positions as part of it."[44] Despite her transnational migration, Sheila's spatial experience is constrained by her status in Lisbon. Rather than a liberating act, migration to Portugal proves to be restraining in its own fashion for Sheila, ultimately dictated by its internal codes of power. The sequence returns to the narrative present, as Sheila and Serginho chart their way across the city:

> Com ela de-guia, visitamos um monte de **sítios bestiais**, o Castelo de São Jorge, o Elevador de Santa Justa, Belém (para comer *pastel*), o Padrão dos Descobrimentos e o Aquário, na estação Oriente, um negócio onde o sujeito enlabirinta em um nunca-acabar de peixe, uns baitas de tubarões e arraias, e outros, bostinhas de nada, mais parecendo bando de passarinho avoando em-dentro dágua, um troço impressionante, fora a imundice de estrela-do-mar, ouriço-do-mar, medusa etc., e a geladeira dos pinguins **giras** e a piscina das lontras exibidas, mas o mais importante mesmo foi andar no **teleférico.**[45]
>
> [With her as a guide, we visited many **awesome sites**, the Castle of St. George, the Elevator de Santa Justa, Belém (to eat a *pastry*), the Monument of the Discoveries, and the Aquarium in the Oriente station, where the observer gets entangled in never-ending fish, a few wicked sharks and stingrays, and others, little insignificant looking organisms, looking rather like a skein of birds flying in the water, an impressive thing, out of the filth of starfish, sea urchins, jellyfish, etc., and the penguins' **fridge** and the otters' pool, but the most important thing was riding the **cable car**.]

Their route through Lisbon is breathlessly experiential, as Ruffato mingles baked goods, architecture, and sea life into a vividly sensory sequence. In contrast with the confinement of Serginho's cheap hotel room in Lisbon or the café in which he works as an undocumented laborer, or the restriction of Sheila's movement through her nightly prostitution routes, this passage is notably open. Here, the urban realm is portrayed as an arena of new spatial opportunities, brought to life through unrestricted movement and leisure activities. The pair's casual, joyful weekend jaunt departs from the discrimination and social exclusion that otherwise characterize their lives in Lisbon. At the same time, as observed throughout the novel, Serginho's observations of Lisbon are continuously disrupted by other times and other places. As the sequence progresses, Serginho retreats to the slippery territory of memory, to a school trip he took to Rio as a child: "Lembrei da vez que fui no bondinho do Pão-de-Açúcar em-criança, excursão do primeiro colegial da Escola Estadual Professor Quaresma, um deslumbre, o Rio de Janeiro, a baía da Guanabara, o Cristo Rendedor, as praias, a ventania, a tonteira . . ." (I remembered the time that I rode the cable car of the Pão-de-Açúcar as a child, a high school trip from the Escola Estadual Professor Quaresma, a wonder, Rio de Janeiro, Guanabara Bay, Christ the Redeemer, the beaches, the wind, the dizziness . . .)[46] Notably, Serginho uses the word *bondinho* for cable car, whereas earlier in his outing with Sheila he referred to the funicular in Lisbon as a **teleférico**. These memories of Brazil provoke an emotional response in Serginho; he recalls his poor mother repairing his broken backpack after the trip, which would later end up in the trashcan.[47] The intrusion of Serginho's childhood memories into this sequence gives readers the sensation that the past is omnipresent and inescapable, as his seemingly minor word choices highlight the role of language in untangling past and present geographies. The story-sharing between the two Brazilians awakens a type of fluidity between past and present, and thus between Lisbon and various localities in Brazil: a dynamic that unsettles and extends the narrative.

From there, Ruffato shifts focus back to the present, where Serginho and Sheila bask in the afternoon sun in the Parque das Nações. In a moment of intimacy between the deterritorialized pair, they enter a local café, their final destination. It is within the context of this close encounter that their stories shift (temporally and geographically) back to Brazil for the last time; Sheila admits her longing to collect a lot of money in order to "aparecer em Riverlândia por-cima-da-carne-seca, engranada, mandando e desmandando" (show up in Riverlândia at the top of my game, geared up and calling the shots).[48] Her admission moves the narrative geographically full circle, back to the heart of Goiás, while propelling her own personal trajectory forward in time, toward an idealized, uncertain future. This final expression of longing recalls the second epigraph of *Estive em Lisboa*, "in between the ground I found and the one I lost."[49] Yet the tension here is different, the appreciation of Portugal less clear, and the yearning for past locales more evident. The narrative sequence closes in the same destabilized territory that sustains the work at large. Sheila flees the café, abandoning Serginho in a position of renewed vulnerability, immigrants alone in a city that neither belongs to nor legally acknowledges them. Together, Serginho and Sheila remain trapped in a time-space loop of past and future locales, longing to retreat to an imagined Brazil. Yet the Brazil they envision is unstable in its own right, wedged between what was and what might be. In this way, the three temporal points expressed in the novel—past, present, and future—are themselves unmoored, underscoring the volatility inherent to the migrant journey.

In an otherwise destabilizing experience, Serginho's relationships with his Brazilian compatriots provide consistency and provisional solidarity in Lisbon. Toward the end of the work, Serginho takes a walking tour of Lisbon with Rodolfo,[50] and they discuss their mutual experience of dislocation, discrimination, and nostalgia: "'Nós estamos lascados, Serginho,' aqui em Portugal não somos nada, 'Nem nome temos,' somos os *brasileiros*, 'E o que a gente é no Brasil?' nada também, somos os *outros*" ("We are splintered, Serginho," here in Portugal we are nothing, "We do not even have names," we are the *Brazilians*, "And what are we in Brazil?" nothing, we are the *others*").[51] Rodolfo's depiction of the Brazilian migrant reality is bleak yet revealing: migration to Lisbon does not resolve the poverty and marginalization that Rodolfo and Serginho faced in Brazil. In many ways, it increases the discrimination they experience in their being poor, foreign, and undocumented. To that effect, Marco Antonio Rodrigues argues that there is a "precarious mobility" in the novel, which he declares "viabiliza, a princípio, só a passagem de ida, não guarda relação direta com mobilidade social" (makes possible, in principle, only the one-way ticket [to Portugal], which does not guarantee social mobility).[52] As Néstor García Canclini notes in his discussion of migration as metaphor, "A foreigner is not necessarily someone who comes from elsewhere and speaks another language; it is also someone who does not have access to strategic networks, nor takes part in controlling these networks and therefore depends on the decisions of others."[53] Despite the lack of access to strategic networks that García Canclini notes, I affirm that there is a stabilizing camaraderie in the translocal bonds formed between protagonists in Ruffato's novel. Indeed, theorists on translocality have argued that bonds, such as those formed by Serginho, Rodolfo, and Sheila, provide displaced subjects with a sense of being situated during periods of mobility, a supposition supported in migration-themed literature.[54] Indeed, Sara Ahmed argues that the formation of migrant communities provides a sense of rootedness, "a sense of inheriting a collective past by sharing the lack of a home rather than sharing a home."[55] Estrangement presents a gap between memory and place[56] that allows migrant subjects to remake themselves in relation to one another, in order to establish community within unfamiliar locales. Although they may be seen as outsiders by the Portuguese, Rodolfo and Serginho form an entity in their own right by belonging to a subset of the "*outros*" (*others*). In this way, Otherness provides the basis for a shared identity for Rodolfo and Serginho, as well as a means of organizing space and time, as migrants are pushed to the physical margins of the city and forced to live in the in-between, in hybrid and constructed spaces.

Despite the anchoring effect of Serginho's attachments to other Brazilian migrants, these relationships often prove ephemeral, echoing the fleetingness of his time in Lisbon more broadly. Sheila disappears into the dark underworld of Lisbon after selling off their passports, and Serginho is forced out of his hostel and into another, maintaining limited contact with Rodolfo. The novel ends on a particularly defeated note, as Serginho loses his job as a waiter to a blond-haired, blue-eyed, Ukrainian migrant who can speak better English, and finally takes up smoking again. At the same time, Serginho's ability to practice his *mineiro* identity in speech and action makes the act of resuming the habit of smoking almost one of defiance, a willful submission to the longing for memory and the pull of homeland. In spite of the bolded Portuguese words in the text that form part of his speech, Serginho's voice is confidently *mineiro*, and his linguistic practices reveal a notion of language as *doing* (see Pennycook), rather than language as a system that acts within the context of place. Thus, Serginho's speech creates a mobile spatiality: a flexible anchor despite his displacement.

SPEAKING GEOGRAPHIES IN WILSON BUENO'S *MAR PARAGUAYO*

To continue this examination of language as a mobile spatiality, I turn now to *Mar paraguayo* by Wilson Bueno, a text that also experiments with language as means of mapping space and time. The novella does so in innovative ways that extend to the creation and mixing of languages. The question of language in relation to place has particular relevance in Latin America and is embedded in Brazilian history. Since the period of colonization, Spanish and Portuguese have been commonly understood to be the dominant languages of the region. Indeed, the multilingual realities of Latin America's diverse population, traditionally housing large numbers of immigrants, have inevitably left their mark on literary production. Across its history, Brazil has hosted a variety of languages, making this melding, mixing, and borrowing apparent.[57] This is especially significant in states near the border regions of Brazil and Paraguay, such as Paraná, the birthplace of Wilson Bueno, whose coastline includes the seaside town of Guaratuba, the setting of *Mar paraguayo*. Many of Brazil's foundational writers have experimented with language use, including José Martiniano de Alencar, who incorporates numerous indigenous words into *Iracema*.[58] Contemporary Brazilian language crossings are present in a number of texts, such as Lebanese Brazilian writer Salim Miguel's short story "Ponto de Balsa," which combines Spanish and Portuguese; Luis Krausz's *Desterro*, which integrates Yiddish and

German to describe the migration of Jewish subjects to São Paolo; and Luiz Ruffato's *Mamma, son tanto felice*, a work that narrates the tale of a community of Italian immigrants in Brazil.[59]

Written from a poetic, multitemporal, and nonlinear first-person perspective, Bueno's *Mar paraguayo* is the story of a Paraguayan migrant who refers to herself only as "la marafona del balneário" (the seaside resort tramp).[60] The term *marafona* holds a variety of meanings, including a doll with no eyes and no mouth, used in traditional cultural ceremonies and parties in Brazil. It has also been a symbol of fertility, and as such has been used to indicate a prostitute (it is implied throughout the text that the *marafona* might work in the sex trade, and Christopher Larkosh translates *marafona* as "tramp"). However, what is intriguing about the doll-related definition of *marafona* is its focus on the anonymity, facelessness, and lack of identity of this female figure, in line with a reading of the text that focuses on identity. Indeed, the protagonist attempts to assert her identity in an otherwise anonymous and marginalized migrant existence—readers do not learn her name and know little about her origins. As such, one is left only to rely on the polyphonic narrative voice, with its many contradictions and temporal shifts. As a backdrop to these broad-ranging musings, the story is anchored by the *marafona*'s proclaimed innocence regarding the ambiguous death of her male lover, referred to throughout as "el Viejo," and her new infatuation with a young tourist that she sees from her window.

Mar paraguayo is unique in that it supersedes the mere mingling of languages or the use of borrowed words, creating a new linguistic system with its own syntax. The text is written primarily in *portunhol*—along with frequent words in Guaraní and occasional invented words.[61] Curiously, the constant among these is Guaraní, a fact that critics including Jens Andermann have seen as a metaphor for the cultural resistance of the indigenous groups associated with it.[62] The use of *portunhol* is notable for its lack of a standard syntax—the rules of the blended language are invented by each of its speakers. The novella traverses the semantic spaces between Paraguayan Spanish, Brazilian Portuguese, and the dispersed and transnational indigenous spaces of Guaraní, the last of which makes visible the difficulty of attempting to understand language in terms of national borders, as the linguistic and cultural territories of Guaraní existed long before those imposed through colonization. Unlike the Ruffato text, *Mar paraguayo* offers a five-page index of its extensive Guaraní vocabulary with corresponding translations into Portuguese. Indeed, the glossary reveals some of the work's foremost themes, as its varied lexicography often connotes a constant flow and chaos between the extremes of heaven and hell, passion and sorrow, as highlighted by *îtacupú* (boiling water), *tecovembiki* (the fugacity of life), *tupa* (the divine), *añaretamegua* (hell), *porenó* (sex), *morangú* (the imagination).

Graciela Montaldo has likened the text to a type of poetry, arguing that *Mar paraguayo* operates in an interstitial space rather than a third space, in a language "que requiere de la recitación para actualizarse, es decir, que no logra nunca estabilizarse" (that requires recitation for it to be actualized, that is to say, that never manages to stabilize itself).[63] Similarly, in his introduction to the Iluminuras edition of the novel, Néstor Perlongher attests to the linguistic dynamism of *Mar paraguayo*: "Há entre as duas línguas um vacilo, uma tensão, uma oscilação permanente: uma é o 'erro' da outra, seu devir possível, incerto e improvável" (Between the two languages there is a vacillation, a tension, a permanent oscillation: one is the error of the other, its occurrence possible, uncertain, and improbable).[64] However, I would like to move beyond previous readings of the volatility of *Mar paraguayo*, proposing instead that the work's protagonist fuses languages to destabilize existing power hierarchies and inaugurate new geographies. The *marafona*'s language practices mediate the gaps between her phenomenological and physical worlds, highlighting the ability of language to ascribe meaning to place (see Pennycook). As the *marafona* hails from Paraguay, the country's two national languages—Spanish and Guaraní—arrive with her to the beaches of Guaratuba, a territory dominated by Portuguese. Thus, language takes on a trifold function in *Mar paraguayo*, providing the *marafona* a mode for self-assertion, a space for the formation of alternative identity, and a territory for the expression of individual memory.

From a technical perspective, *Mar paraguayo*'s orthography, its syntax, and its blended and invented language further this relationship. The *marafona* engages a kind of syntactic playfulness as she drifts between linguistic codes, mingling Portuguese grammar with Spanish lexica and vice versa: "No voy llorar, no voy me poner toda depranto y soluçante y gelatina en lo travessero" (I will not cry, I will not become weepy and sobbing and wobbly in the stomach)—dropping the Spanish preposition *a*, which normally accompanies *ir*, to mirror the Portuguese syntax in which a preposition is not required: "não vou chorar" (I am not going to cry).[65] On other occasions, the two orthographies are amalgamated, as highlighted by "san cosas de la imaginación" (they are figments of the imagination), with "san" a cross between the Spanish *son* and the Portuguese *são*.[66] Finally, the author offers examples that depart from all three languages, as seen in words with purposeful misspellings, or in the invention of new words, such as "vierbos" (a misspelling of *verbos* [verbs]).[67] Occasionally, the protagonist plays with sound through spelling: "Quiçás, quiçás, quiçás. Chororó, guarará, chororó" (Maybe, maybe, maybe. Murmur, flow, murmur).[68] Here the word "quiçás," rarely used in modern Brazilian Portuguese though still preserved in the continental variety, is meant to signal the Spanish *quizás*, which Bueno simulates phonetically by using a ç in place of the *z*. The excerpt also provides an intertextual musicality by invoking the classic tune by Cuban songwriter Osvaldo Farrés, "Quizás, Quizás, Quizás."[69] Here, once again, readers may refer to the Guaraní glossary for clues regarding the meaning of this fragment: *chororó*, meaning a murmur or whisper, especially the sound of running water, and *guarará*, meaning the sound of rain, and both cascade or flowing water in Guaraní. The words sustain both a phonetic and representational rhythm, as they maintain a uniform cadence in both syllables and intonation.[70] This further reinforces the poetic, melodic quality of the writing and its dreamlike, at times nonsensical, prose.

Similar to other experiments in language from authors such as Junot Díaz and Cristina García, who intersperse untranslated Spanish into their works,[71] *Mar paraguayo* requires readers to accept a certain level of ambiguity. Indeed, Larkosh calls on readers to proceed boldly into the text, "uprooting the impulse for one language alone," and thus to jump into the Paraguayan sea, and "to open one's eyes underwater and read through the shimmering surface of words and phrases without any specific or implied injunction to understanding."[72] The *marafona* oscillates between languages on the core and periphery of Latin America, constructing a narrative that blends the use of a minor language (Guaraní) and major languages (Portuguese and Spanish). Mikhail Bakhtin has interpreted the relationship between language and dominant discourse through the concept of heteroglossia: the coexistence of multiple linguistic codes in a single utterance or text, or the undoing of a single authorial voice.[73] Building on this idea, Bakhtin developed his assessments of hybridization, which underscore how systems of authority can be in conflict with one another in a solitary narrative voice. Although Bakhtin did not base this theory on multilingual texts, both *Mar paraguayo* and *Estive em Lisboa* illuminate this concept in striking ways. Nowhere are these tensions and subjectivities more apparent than in migration-themed narratives, which often house multiple languages and perspectives.[74] By aligning the three languages and their fused variations, Bueno's *marafona* establishes an alternate code, detached from the hierarchies of a single voice. In a way that is impossible in monolingual or bilingual texts, this polyphonic work articulates intersections and crossings, rather than fixed coordinates, contributing anew to its fluid aesthetic and a sense of movement.

The *marafona*'s creation of representational spaces highlights the role of language in scaffolding our presence within the world: as Alastair Pennycook asserts, when we use language to speak, write, interact, and respond, "we make the language, and the space in which this happens."[75] The *marafona*'s use of *portuñol*, of an ad hoc blending and borrowing of multiple languages, follows only the rules she sets out at the moment of enunciation: capturing the world as it was in a singular moment.[76] The confessional nature of the text also returns us to the concept of orality, which is explored at length in *Estive em Lisoba*. Indeed, it is important to contextualize these two works within the broader tradition of orality in Latin America, as explored by theorists including Antonio Cornejo Polar. For Cornejo Polar, much of Latin American literature conveys a "nostalgia our writers feel for orality," coupled with a deep desire to "reconvert the written word to voice" with the hope of resisting the hegemony of analog writing given the fertile landscape of oral narratives that flourish outside it.[77] The testimonial format of these stories gives narrative space to peripheral subjects whose voices infrequently emerge onto the page. Not only does the oral quality of the text reinforce its rendering as testimony, it also reminds readers of the intimate relationship between memory and the testimonial genre broadly. Jens Andermann highlights the performative self-reflexivity of the novella, captured in what he sees as a "constant movement of withdrawal" to which the text responds.[78] Indeed, there is a tension in the novella as the *marafona* asserts herself across a mnemonic landscape that is fraught with trauma and confessions.

The protagonist's assertion of self is inseparable from her forays into memory, which provide readers insight into her world. In this way, memory offers an added layer to what Andreas Huyssen describes as the "mutilated" traditions of the peripheral subject, uttered in a language that is a productive merging of multiple voices, a new and defiant mixed language.[79] The *marafona* recounts the death of el Viejo exhaustively, creating a narrative ebb and flow that mimics the tides of the Guaratuba. His death provides an anchor for the short text, as the narration is repeatedly drawn back to the moment of his passing: "El viejo, que moriria a las siete de la noche, en júnio, mexia-se ainda en la casa e yo podria ouvir, con una nitidez epantosa, sus tosses, sus escarros y escárnios, el viejo, esto traste tan duramente amoroso que me llenô la vida e me puso dama de suerte por puro capricho" (The old man, who died at seven o'clock in the evening, was still in the house, and I could hear, with fleeting clarity, his coughs and sneers and scorns, the old man, this rascal so hard-loving that he filled my life and made me a lucky lady on a pure whim).[80] Indeed, the patterns and amorphousness of water inspiring the work's title are captured textually in its hazy aesthetic, with lengthy digressions into memory and a mixing of linguistic codes. The vastness of the *mar* functions as a symbolic and figurative space for the crisscrossing of language and the junction of past and present, contrasted with the enclosed room in which the *marafona* tells her story. As she sits alone in her room facing the sea, her restricted local life is opened up through her traversal of memory and language, creating a fluid territory of experience.

This flowing terrain creates a microcosm of the intersections that highlight attention to inequalities, absences, and estrangement, reflecting the woman's isolation in her marginal community. She states, "Nací al fondo del fondo del fondo de mi país—esta hacienda guarani, guarânia e soledad" (I was born at the bottom of the bottom of my country—this Guaraní estate, Guarânia and solitude).[81] Similar to Sheila in *Estive em Lisboa*, the *marafona* experiences multiple forms of marginalization based on class, gender, migration status, and profession, an entrapment seen in her relationship to the "Others" of the beach landscape of Guaratuba. She observes the tourists through her window, "al borde de la ventana enquanto los banhistas, con sus esposas gordotas y sus hijos inquietos, llenos de arena, lambuzados de mar y sorvetes con grandes crostas de caramelo, van por el, distarídos, por el camino" (at the windowsill while the bathers, with their fat wives and restless children, full of sand, dirtied by sea and ice cream with large crusts of caramel, pass by, distant, on the path).[82] The text captures aspects of the incommunicability of the marginalized subject in a way that few can. Indeed, in her commentary on *Mar paraguayo* and other migrant narratives in Brazilian literature, Angélica Madeira argues, "As identidades que ali se representam são sempre precárias e deficientes" (The identities represented there are always precarious and deficient).[83] However, I would argue that while the voicing of self and recuperation of the body may be tenuous, the *marafona*'s identity is far from deficient. Through the many flows and intersections of her language, she brings to life a complex experience that is neither easily captured nor easily read. As Rodolfo A. Franconi discusses, the disquietude of the text is made possible by its intersecting languages and geographies, which in turn communicate the way in which the protagonist sees and is seen in the world: "*Mar paraguayo* potencializa variados modos de olhar e ser olhado através de uma complexa teia de insinuações, dissímulos, vaivéns, enfim, transversalidades várias, sendo, até onde sei, um texto inaugurador do cruzamento de falares fronteiriços poeticamente recriados e, por isso mesmo, inquietante" (*Mar paraguayo* makes possible various ways of looking and being seen through a complex web of insinuations, dissimulations, sketches, and finally, various transversalities, being, as far as I know, a text that inaugurates the crossing of poetically re-created frontiers, and, as such, disruptive).[84] It is the *marafona*'s voice in its fragmented language that is vital for the formation of individual truth and declaration of selfhood despite adversity. She states, "No hay idiomas aí. Solo la vertigem de la linguagem. Deja-me que exista" (There are no languages here. Only the vertigo of language. Let me exist).[85] This last statement is complex, as Bueno's "deja-me que exista" can be translated as "Let me exist," or perhaps as "Let it exist for me" (as Larkosh asserts in his partial translation of the work),[86] depending on whether the sentence is interpreted through a Spanish or Portuguese syntax. This brief moment of ambiguity highlights the "vertigo" of the *marafona*'s writing as self-affirmation—a particularly sensory metaphor, in line with the dizzying nature of the narrative. The *marafona*'s narration becomes analogous with the occupying of space and the carving out of linguistic, representational, and cultural margins. She states, "Escribo para que no me rompam dentro las cordas del corazón. Soy mi propria construción e asi me considero la principal culpada por todos los andaimes derruídos de mi projeto esfuerzado" (I write so that I do not break the ropes of my heart. I am my own construction, so I consider myself the one to blame for all the wrecked scaffolding of my project).[87] Here, the *marafona* expresses the challenge of speaking from the margins—and on one's own terms—in her counterhegemonic occupation of narrative space. Concurrently, her story is deeply connected to the body: "Sei que escribo y esto es como grafar impresso todo el contorno de un cuerpo vivo en el muro de la calle central" (I know that I write, and this is how to print the outline of a living body on the wall of the high street).[88]

As in the Ruffato text, Bueno's experimentation with language in *Mar paraguayo* troubles the alignment of spatial and temporal geographies. While the story's action plays out on the Brazilian coast, the language of the "marafona del balneário" is drawn from multiple times and spaces, revealing her immigrant roots. Like the amorphous flow of a body of water, the story does not have a clear ending: the reader does not ascertain whether the *marafona* killed el Viejo, nor is there any inkling as to what might happen next. On the contrary, the novel begins and ends with a simple assertion of self and place. In the opening line the narrator states, "Yo soy la marafona del balneário. Acá, en Guaratuba, vivo de suerte" (I am the *marafona* of the resort town. Here, in Guaratuba, I'm alive by sheer luck).[89] In her last line, she utters, "Mi mar? Mi mar soy yo. Íyá" (My sea? I am my sea. Íyá).[90] A referencing of the glossary reveals that Íyá is the Guaraní goddess of water, ending the story not only with an imagery of the sea but also in the linguistic territory of the indigenous language.[91] However, read aloud, "Íyá" also mimics the Spanish *y ya*, or "and that's all." Not only is the *mar* of *Mar paraguayo* a metaphor for self, but it *is* in fact self, as seen in her closing statement—a self that, while conflicted and peripheral, unequivocally declares its presence.

CONCLUSION

In both of the Brazilian migration narratives I explore in this chapter, language and memory emerge as powerful tools with which to pattern the experience of new locales. In the twenty-first century, territories of language are further complicated by contact zones, accelerated movement between spaces, and virtual realms that have altered the linguistic landscape of writing, reading, and publishing. Similarly, the twentieth century saw a renewed focus on memory in the context of global modernity. The rise of the testimonial genre and the attention paid to subjective memory provide evidence for our attempt to circumnavigate our own lives in the face of fragmentation. As such, exile writing and other narratives of displacement actively negotiate a mismatch between memory and place, while also providing a means of recognizing situatedness within movement. The return to an abandoned or perhaps imagined homeland is an enduring spatial trope within the region's literature—see, for example, Patricio Pron's *El espíritu de mis padres sigue subiendo en la lluvia,* whose narrator traverses physical and psychological landscapes in ruin in order to piece together his father's life, and Tatiana Salem Levy's *A chave da casa,* whose narrator ruminates on remembered and embodied trauma as she journeys from Rio de Janeiro to her grandfather's old house in Turkey.[92] Andreas Huyssen argues that this return to memory reveals our collective societal attempt to "anchor ourselves in a world characterized by an increasing instability of time and the fracturing of lived space."[93] Based on my readings of the configurations in this selection of migration narratives, both novels allow migrants to attach themselves, however provisionally, to deeper roots and bonds, aiding in the often tumultuous experience of displacement. Curiously, among the alternative space-time configurations in these works, those established via language are the most durable and consistent. Where memory and networks waver or dissipate, language proves to be a consistent yet mutable marker of locality and identity carried into foreign locales.

Revisiting Michel de Certeau's assertion that every story is a spatial practice, how might we extend this argument to understand time? Undoubtedly every story is also a practice in time, a framing. Fiction, thus, is the isolation and chaining together of moments along a narrative trajectory. These moments play out at their own velocity, prolonged to cover vast chronological territory, or made to stand still in order to draw out the significance of specific events. This tendency reiterates the treatment of narrative temporality broadly in contemporary Brazilian literature, as literary scholar Regina Dalcastagnè comments: "Muito longe de toda teoria sobre a realidade e a nossa percepção dela, prosseguimos, na vida cotidiana, criando narrativa lineares, cronologicamente estruturadas, para darnos conta de nossa presença no mundo. Uma presença que envolve, basicamente, a experiência do tempo" (Far from all theory on reality is our perception of it, we go about our daily lives, creating linear narratives, chronologically structured, to make ourselves aware of our presence in the world. A presence that encompasses, basically, the experience of time).[94] Dalcastagnè's emphasis on the experience of time contextualizes the prominence of subjective memory in contemporary literature. Indeed, while narrative time may progress forward in *Estive em Lisboa* and *Mar paraguayo*, both time and space are extended, disrupted, and drawn out through the intertwining of memory, allowing readers to observe migratory experiences via their fragments, overlaps, and absences.[95] Above all, these two works tell us that the experience of migration is manifold, shifting, and often contradictory. Race, class, gender, and legal status shape the local experience of global processes, showing us how borders can be softened, made flexible or even indiscernible. When contemplating the question of origin of migrant protagonists, this appears often to fall in a dynamic negotiation between memory and imagined future—of that which was and that which might be. Similarly, migration narratives remind us that locality and globality are not mutually exclusive but are rather woven together in the fabric of our day-to-day lives: in what we eat, where we live, with whom we spend our time, how we speak. Just as language inscribes a journey across space and time, migration narratives expose the many markers of self that migrants negotiate through their grounding and concretizing practices of locality. They are inherently linked to belonging, making language locally bound as it travels globally.

2 • SPEED CONTROL

The Politics of Mobility in Roberto Bolaño's *2666* and Its Theatrical Adaptation by Àlex Rigola

> The U.S.-Mexican border es una herida abierta where the Third World grates against the first and bleeds. And before a scab forms it hemorrhages again, the lifeblood of two worlds merging to form a third country—a border culture. —Gloria Anzaldúa, *Borderlands: The New Mestiza*

> We are in the epoch of simultaneity: we are in the epoch of juxtaposition, the epoch of near and far, of the side-by-side, of the dispersed. We are at the moment, I believe, when our experience of the world is less than that of a long life developing through time than that of a network that connects points that intersect within its own skein.
> —Michel Foucault, "Of Other Spaces: Utopias and Heterotopias"

Contemporary Latin American narratives often connect stories that take place in disparate locations, spanning vast timeframes and uniting seemingly unrelated protagonists. Indeed, twenty-first-century artistic production often makes visible the complex interfaces in which our lives play out, whether in the intimacy of the home, the subjective realm of the psyche, or transnational journeys that defy geographical boundaries. These themes have preoccupied film for quite some time, as seen in works such as Steven Soderbergh's *Traffic*, Alejandro González Iñárritu's *Amores Perros*, Edward Zwick's *Blood Diamond*, and Stephen Gaghan's *Syriana*.[1] In these films, threads as diverse as the transnational drug and diamond trades and the global oil exchange draw varied stories together along a common plotline. In contemporary fiction, Roberto Bolaño's *Los detectives salvajes* and *2666* illuminate the interplay between global processes and local places in a single work.[2] Both novels navigate vast swaths of territory and time, highlighting links between multiple plotlines that are broken up into narrative vignettes, or micronarratives woven together to form larger stories.[3]

The micronarrative structure has become a defining characteristic of twenty-first-century literature's preoccupation with polyvocal narration and multiterritoriality. Numerous contemporary Latin American authors, including Patricio Pron (Argentina), Tatiana Salem Levy and Luiz Ruffato (Brazil), and Valeria Luiselli (Mexico), explored in chapter 4, have been associated with a similar form. Yet Bolaño's use of the vignette gives him a fine-tuned control of narrative time, in the context of both speed and temporal setting: he can propel the plot forward at a crawl as much as a gallop. A nuanced engagement with speed and stasis pumps blood through the work's plot, sweeping the narrative focus across geographies before screeching to a halt to perseverate over minute details.

Bolaño's final novel, *2666*, was published posthumously in 2004. It comprises five parts, which the author requested be released individually, acutely aware of his looming death, and in the hope of maximizing profit for his children. Eventually, it was decided that the work be published as a single volume in order to preserve continuity.[4] The novel is a 1,100-page tour de force likened stylistically to the much shorter *Los detectives salvajes*. The work's vignettes span seven decades and a geographical range from rural Germany to cosmopolitan metropolises and the industrial sprawl of a fictionalized Ciudad Juárez. However, this vast novel resists regional attachments, opting instead to layer many spatial imaginaries by drifting freely between narrative settings.[5] The plotline of the five-part work—whose sections may be read independently or as part of a whole—proceeds as follows: part 1, "La parte de los críticos," details five academics' hunt for a mysterious German writer, Benno von Archimboldi, a search that lands them in Santa Teresa, Mexico, a city troubled by uneven industrial development and a series of violent murders. Part 2, "La parte de Amalfitano," recounts the tale of Chilean professor Oscar Amalfitano and his daughter, Rosa, both of whom become increasingly involved in the crimes, leading Rosa to eventually flee to the North with an American journalist. The third section, "La parte de Fate," is the tale of said journalist—a man named Quincy Williams who goes by the pen name Oscar Fate. Fate arrives in the city to cover a boxing match and later becomes intrigued by the femicides in Santa Teresa. The fourth section, "La parte de los crímenes," describes the victims of the crimes and the investigation surrounding them, including the story of Klaus Haas, the presumed murderer, and the man eventually revealed to be Archimboldi's nephew. Finally, in "La parte de Archimboldi," the fifth and final part, readers return to Benno von Archimboldi as they follow his trail from his birthplace up until his arrival in Santa Teresa.[6] Spatially, the novel maps a web of connections emanating from its epicenter, Santa Teresa, the fictional substitute for Ciudad Juárez. In this way, the work continuously returns to a local place as an anchor, a gravitational force. However, the narrative interrelationships that are drawn back to Santa Teresa illuminate the violence that underpins the structures of contemporary life, drawing attention to the relationship between visibility, movement, and power.

In this chapter, I examine the interplay between speed, mobility, and power in Bolaño's *2666* and its 2006 theatrical adaptation by Spanish director Àlex Rigola, which was first performed in the 2007–2008 theatrical season of Teatre Lliure in Barcelona.[7] In both the novel and the stage production, the strategic use of speed and stasis reveals disparities between the interconnected and heterogeneous textures of the global. Rigola's play provides a valuable foil to the novel in its use of film sequencing as a mode of visually simulating micronarratives. In this way, I propose that this theatrical adaptation is uniquely suited to exploring some of the broader themes of this book, including rapid modernization, uneven economic development, and the spatial multiplicity that characterizes contemporary life. Although *2666*'s novelistic structure and thematic leaps compress vast geographies across fragmented time, speed is not portrayed in a linear fashion, instead manifesting in complex and often unexpected ways that highlight power differentials between contemporary actors. While adapting the work to the stage, Rigola stated, "The narrative requires me to look for new methods, different narrative forms within a single production—the conference format, or the use of images at a particular point, or the use of objects."[8] Although the play remains remarkably loyal to the text in script and characters, the staging is ultimately a visual transformation that interweaves film, music, and projections to curate *2666*'s engagement with movement and stillness as tools of narrative temporalization. In a 2006 interview, Rigola discusses the inventive nature of modifying the work for the stage, a process that he undertook with playwright Pablo Ley: "A play has a life of its own, it's not really the novel anymore, the materials are very different. The type of poetry you can produce in a novel is completely different from the poetry of the stage. In an adaptation you start with one material, one set of contents and an underlying story, but the way of telling it is very different."[9] Thus, as I elaborate here, the use of projected visuals and distorted timing in Rigola's adaptation serve as calculated, theatrical devices for visually staging the incongruences of speed inherent to the novel.

To begin this analysis, I approach the inequitable mobilities of *2666*'s desert borderlands in dialogue with contributions from the fields of human geography, anthropology, and sociology—namely, the works of Rita Laura Segato, Martin Albrow, Doreen Massey, and Milton Santos.[10] While many previous studies of Bolaño's work (see, for example, those by Grant Farred and Sharae Deckard)[11] have primarily focused on the femicides and maquiladoras as representations of the structural violence of neoliberal economic policy, I engage mobility as a vector for understanding a broader range of disparate experiences of global life in *2666*. From there, I devote the next three sections of this chapter to comparative readings of movement, acceleration, and immobility in the novel and stage production. As a counterpoint to speed, I examine the role of stasis and its implications as a state of restricted movement and an opportunity for rest, mediation, and internal reflection. Bolaño's work often cuts across vast expanses, moving from Europe to the borderlands of a fictionalized Ciudad Juárez within a series of two pages, then focusing, for example, on particular narrative moments such as a book dangling from a clothesline. Indeed, the manipulation of speed also plays a vital role throughout the stage performance of *2666*: some scenes incorporate a tachycardic collage of mixed-media visuals, as in the strobed images projected over the stage, where the actors throw a raucous party. On other occasions, the work is literally carried out in slow motion via film and exaggerated bodily movements by the actors onstage. Is this form of stasis a remnant of the local amid rapid, large-scale movements in space and time? How does contemporary cultural production untangle the differences between restricted movement and the luxury of stasis, coerced migration, and unfettered mobility? Moreover, what does the narrative production of time and mobility say about the control of speed in contemporary life?

INEQUITABLE MOBILITIES

Before commencing a close reading of the text and its stage adaptation, it is useful to outline a few observations regarding the role of speed, and thus of mobility, within globalization. Often deemed one of the defining features of modernity, speed plays out as both an architecture and device in *2666* and its adaptation. To quote critic Hermann Herlinghaus, *2666* portrays "a planetary state of affairs, pointing to the heart of everyday existence as a figure in which the uneven development generated by global capitalism translates into particular pathological scenarios."[12] In the late twentieth and early twenty-first centuries, a rise in policies promoting laissez-faire economics on a global scale has complicated the link between speed and the body in the context of Latin America. An influx in technology, coupled with loosened state controls, deregulation, and privatization of formerly state-owned capital, has made individuals within the region more vulnerable, exposing them to an often invisible wheel of transnational phenomena. This process can be meaningfully interpreted through human geographer Milton Santos's understanding of the flows and fixed objects that configure globalization. Today's world, Santos argues, is characterized by the twin forces of velocity and fluidity. He proposes a reading of speed as a political force—rather than a technical one—citing the "incompatibilities" between velocities that arise between territories.[13] The ideological impulse of speed, Santos explains, can be enforced in certain contexts—namely, in the operations of multinational corporations, for whom speed and efficiency are near synonymous with capital gain. Santos describes this state of affairs as *velocidad hegemónica*: speed is rendered as an imperative, as a template for human progress and the continued development of civilization. In light of this emphasis on productive output, this definition exists in tandem with Santos's understanding of fluidity (the possibility of circulation), a state of movement that affords unequal benefits to people and places (see Lucas Megaço and Carolyn Prouse).[14] In his commentary on Santos's work, Jesús Martín Bárbero writes of the "new motor"[15] that propels globalization through unprecedented competition between enterprises for greater connectivity and efficiency: both metrics that rely greatly on speed. In many cases, readers of *2666* observe the victims of this time-space compression, seen in the violent effects of the arrival of multinational industries to the desert landscape of the U.S.-Mexico border.[16] Such corporations, Santos argues, compel all that existed before their arrival to adapt to their norms of practice, regardless of the broader social impact of such changes: "The bearers of extreme velocities look to induce the rest of the actors to accompany them, seeking to disseminate the infrastructure essential to the desired fluidity in the places that are considered necessary for their activity."[17] Many (though not all) of the victims of femicide portrayed in *2666* are workers in the maquiladoras, manufacturing operations in the free-trade zone on the border between Mexico and the United States. Here, I refer to Argentine anthropologist Rita Segato's reading of the U.S.-Mexico border near Ciudad Juárez, a space characterized by conflict between "excess and lack," noting particularly her emphasis on movement and power: "It is the frontier that money has to cross, virtually and materially, to reach the firm land where capital finds itself finally safe and gives its rewards in prestige, security, comfort, and health . . . the frontier beyond which capital gets moralized and reaches worthwhile, sound banks . . . where great entrepreneurs 'work' on one side and live on the other . . . the frontier of the great expansion and fast valorization, where terrain is literally stolen from the desert each day."[18] Segato's description of a hungry, devouring multinational capitalist trade system evokes the carnivorous economic and interpersonal violence that dominate Bolaño's fictionalized border city. His apparent fascination with Ciudad Juárez draws all points of gravity back to the fictional Santa Teresa—a border city in Latin America whose multiple economic, gendered, and racialized marginalities occupy the central role in his symphonic novel. Indeed, critical examinations of Ciudad Juárez have permeated literary studies of Bolaño's work. Patrick Dove devotes a chapter of *Literature and Interregnum* to *2666*'s critique of structural violence in globalization and closes his work with a lengthy rumination on Ciudad Juárez as allegory. He characterizes Ciudad Juárez not as an isolated tragedy—the result of breakneck economic growth, inadequate protections, and widespread corruption—but as a microcosm of a world whose very functioning is sustained by a network of excess-lack relationships: "What calls out to us in the name Ciudad Juárez also affects how we think about our world. The two are inseparable: we cannot talk about the world today or even make reference to something called 'our world' without also bringing up—even if it goes unspoken—the violence and suffering that are named metonymically by Ciudad Juárez."[19] The violence Dove refers to takes many forms, all of which speak back to the disruption of neoliberal globalization, the impunity and violence that sustain the cross-border trade in narcotics, and the structural inequalities that underpin the uneven acceleration of industrial development on the basis of maximum profit and cheap labor. Fittingly, Bolaño has long examined violence in his writings, in works such as *Estrella distante, Amuleto,* and *Nocturno de Chile.*[20] However, although these works do connect individual-level instances of violence to broader contexts, such as neofascism and authoritarian regimes in *Estrella distante, 2666* goes a step further, and thus implicates all contemporary actors in the violence of the Santa Teresa femicides, which are not merely a consequence of the women's murderers or the exploitative conditions of the maquilas but a symptom of neoliberal capitalism. Critics have often pointed to Bolaño's friendship with Sergio González Rodríguez, author of *Huesos en el desierto,*[21] a journalistic account of the femicides in Ciudad Juárez, as an aesthetic inspiration, given that the author had himself never traveled to Juárez. However, González Rodriguez's contribution extends beyond that of aesthetic influence: according to Marcela Valdés (and as cited by Dove), González Rodriguez was a primary source for information about the femicides and was also the person responsible for dissuading Bolaño from pursuing a story of a single serial killer, encouraging him to look instead toward structural failures and systems of corruption.[22] Rather than a person or persons responsible for the killing, González Rodriguez pointed to the impunity of those in charge of narco-trafficking, the widespread corruption in the state and city governments (and consequently the police forces). Perhaps it is for this reason that Bolaño says of the femicides in the novel, "Nadie presta atención a estos asesinatos, pero en ellos se esconde el secreto del mundo" (No one pays attention to these killings, but the secret of the world is hidden in them)—once again, an interesting assertion given that Bolaño himself did not visit Juárez.[23] Regarding this statement, Dove responds, "If the 'secret of the world' lies concealed in the crimes of Santa Teresa, as one of Bolaño's characters asserts, this may be because those crimes illustrate a mortal danger that accompanies globalization: that the unification of the globe does not yield 'One World' but instead unleashes an unworlding through which life is tendentially reduced to the status of detritus and disposability."[24] However, despite the repeated associations of the women's deaths and the detritus of production—a point that is particularly brutally emphasized when Bolaño describes the trash collected in the factory waste receptacle where the foreman finds the body of one of the murdered women—the femicide victims are not simply collateral damage of neoliberalism and rampant economic growth. In discussing the femicides of Juárez as "crimes of the second state" (the paralegal bodies that exert power in the absence of state control), Rita Segato deems the femicides both "producers and re-producers" of impunity as they sustain the regimes of fear and control that permit the "extreme asymmetry" of the rampant extraction of wealth.[25] In the fictional urban sprawl of Santa Teresa, it is clear that power lies in the hands of a select few shadowy figures who traverse the city with ease, presumably narcos and corrupt cops who operate outside the law. They are, to paraphrase Farred, a constitutive element of the maquiladora's everyday operations or, in Segato's view of Juárez, a crucial demarcation of a territory of control maintained by a second state to preserve its relentless extraction of resources:[26] the frontier between excess and lack is maintained by the bloody exercise of violence.

In the following sections, I illustrate how access to movement in *2666* reflects imbalances of power and multifaceted social inequalities. The novel distinguishes itself for its portrayal of heterogeneous trajectories through a globalized world, serving to contradict the many globalization theorists who might homogenize and condense the experience of life in the twenty-first century as popularly proposed in Thomas Friedman's *The World Is Flat*.[27] While *2666*'s characters collide through instances of coincidence and are variously entrapped within structures of violence, they hardly function together in harmonic synchronization. As a group, *2666*'s protagonists might find themselves variously confined to prison cells or casually crossing the border into the United States and back in a single afternoon to drive a friend to the airport. The most privileged among the novel's globally fluid protagonists cover vast geographical territory without sacrificing the ability to stop and wait. The notion of mobility as a form of power harks back to Martin Albrow's theory of time-space social stratification, which attributes imbalances of power and privilege to inequitable control over one's position in time and space.[28] The elusive writer Archimboldi, for example, uses his privileged control of temporal and spatial resources to move through the world almost invisibly while managing lengthy stays in European cities. More than a reflection on speed, these cosmopolitan figures testify to the mobility politics articulated by human geographer Doreen Massey, who writes prolifically on how we experience space in an era of globalization: "Social relations of space are experienced differently, and variously interpreted, by those holding different positions as part of it."[29] Indeed, some privileged actors are capable of defining the compression of time and space at their discretion. As such, it is plausible to interpret the degree of choice one has over their mobility as a proxy for their social and economic capital. Time and space are compressed for the privileged few, who are able to not only speed life up but also hold it in place, or even slow it down by altering spatial routes. The selective use of stasis serves both to magnify a particular narrative moment and to reflect on the socioeconomics of time within *2666* at large. In line with this notion, some moments of stasis in the novel are less an entrapment in the local than they are a holding pattern, a space for contemplation in the form of memory, flashbacks, dreams, and desires. This can be seen clearly in the lengthy correspondences between the four academics of the first part of the novel, each of whom goes into great depth on their thoughts, interactions, and memories about one another.

Yet the underside of these affluent experiences of globalization is the countless people whose labor—as physical bodily movement and the pace of their output—is used as fuel for the free movement and enjoyable leisure time of privileged contemporary actors. Conversely, within the rigged mechanism of free trade and structural violence, the maquiladora workers are not afforded the luxury of stasis. Among these actors, Bolaño portrays the female victims of the neoliberal violence of the maquiladoras, whose bodies are literally stopped in their tracks. When considering the impoverished female workers of Santa Teresa more broadly, this physical immobility ultimately reflects a lack of social mobility. Although many of them are migrants from southern Mexican states, these women do not have the privilege of at-will transnational movement or voluntary exile. They are not jet-setters zipping between European and North American cities via car, train, or plane. On the contrary, their world is often structured by the deeply repetitive routine of factory work, or in Bolaño's representation, the ceaseless cycle of violent death and forensic investigation. This restriction of mobility can be read as the quotidian violence of having to work in substandard conditions—but it manifests most jarringly in the women's murders. In *2666*, these crime portraits are integrated into more developed stories, from haphazard police investigations to the peculiar love affair between the detective, Juan de Dios Martínez, and the psychologist, Elvira Campos. Bolaño also incorporates news reports, commentaries from feminist activists, and oral testimonies on the deaths, thus situating the crimes within multiple discourses—personal, institutional, and public. The novel's interlacing of stories has a dual effect: it interrupts the narratives on the periphery of the femicides, drawing each of the section's protagonists back to the scene of the crime, while also disturbing the very incidences of violence around which the work revolves. Critic Scott Esposito comments on this intermingling, stating that "although Bolaño's final novel is nothing if not fecund with the tiny reservoirs of horror that lurk within and perversely dominate otherwise mundane lives, in *2666* Bolaño is most successful at realizing this horror when finding it in the landscape."[30] Indeed, this narrative strategy serves to establish a grid onto which to (partially) map the scope of the crimes, linking the banal and the mundane with the horrid, the violent, and the unfathomable. Thus, *2666* is less a work about a jet-setting group of academics and writers in a shared global network than it is a commentary on interlinked yet disparate mobilities and violence in the age of globalization. Let us turn now to textual examples that highlight some of these incongruences.

IMMOBILITY AND ACCELERATION IN *2666*

The vignette-based structure of *2666* not only creates narrative snapshots but also forces readers to pause and reflect between the fragments they encounter. The first instance of the snapshot structure can be seen in the initial pages of the novel when French academic Jean-Claude Pelletier first engages Archimboldi's work.[31] This vignette is separated by a three-line gap in the text from the following vignette, a deliberation on his economic status during that period: "Pelletier pudo recordar el día en que leyó por primera vez a Archimboldi y se vio a sí mismo, joven y pobre, viviendo en una chambre de bonne, compartiendo el lavamanos, en donde se lavaba la cara y los dientes" (Pelletier could think back on the day when he first read Archimboldi, and he saw himself, young and poor, living in a *chambre de bonne*, sharing the sink where he washed his face and brushed his teeth).[32] From that point forward, Bolaño creates an uninterrupted set of micronarratives across each of the sections. This textual fragmentation serves to disrupt and multiply narrative time and space, while also slowing down the rhythm of the text by compelling readers to linger momentarily between each vignette. Throughout the novel, Bolaño goes on to develop many key threads introduced in these initial stories, often transitioning rapidly between two or three narratives, as seen at the close of "The Part about Fate." Observed individually, these micronarratives rarely occupy more than a handful of pages; more often than not, they are a page or less in length. Consequently, readers move through the work with its pauses and intermissions, connecting narrative snippets that often overlap and regress in time.

Beyond the technique's particular significance in part 4, the use of micronarratives affects the pace of reading, which can be plot-rich and rapid-paced before decelerating significantly to recount seemingly minor details at length. Through this careful time-space manipulation, Bolaño is able to span a vast geographic territory while meticulously documenting the local. Furthermore, his detailed emphasis on the local provides a means of playing narrative stasis and acceleration against one another. In the first section, for example, extended narrative time is dedicated to describing local activities, such as where the academics dine and converse:

> Comieron goulash y puré de garbonzos con remolacha y pescado macerado en limón con yogur, una cena con velas y violines, y rusos auténticos e irlandeses disfrazados de rusos, desde todo punto de vista desmesurada y desde el punto de vista gastronómico más bien pobretona y dudosa, que acompañaron con copas de vodka y una botella de vino de Burdeos.[33]
>
> [They ate goulash and chickpea puree with beets and fish macerated in lemon with yogurt, a dinner with candles and violins and real Russian waiters and Irish waiters disguised as Russians, all of it excessive from any point of view, and somewhat rustic and dubious from a gastronomic point of view, and they had vodka with their dinner and a bottle of Bordeaux.][34]

The level of detail in this excerpt focuses the reader's attention on gastronomic particularities that seem to be absurdly, and perhaps extraneously, specific. The sweeping transnationality of the novel's many locations, including leaps between Madrid and London, seems to be purposefully juxtaposed to a minute attention to detail, in terms of both the physical settings and the characters' inner thoughts. This strategy allows Bolaño to demonstrate the collision of universal and particular within a globalized world (see, for example, the work of Roland Robertson),[35] countering the idea of globalization's "homogenizing" effect on the local through elaborate (if rapid-fire) illustrations of local-global intersections.

From a thematic perspective, lingering plays an equally important role in communicating the spatial and temporal inequalities between the characters of *2666*. An interesting example of this is in the fourth section, where readers gain insight into the life and imprisonment of detained German expatriate Klaus Haas, who is suspected of committing the murders recounted earlier in the section. It is soon clear that despite his detention in Santa Teresa's prison, Haas has great agency, as he moves about the jail with ease, obtaining a cell phone and even arranging journalists to stage press conferences: "En junio Klaus Haas convocó mediante llamadas telefónicas una conferencia de prensa en el penal de Santa Teresa a la que asistieron seis periodistas" (In June, Klaus Haas made some phone calls and convened a press conference at the Santa Teresa penitentiary, attended by six reporters).[36] While his spatial route may be confined, he has much greater flexibility in where he moves about the prison than his fellow inmates. This seemingly contradictory set of circumstances shows how mobility goes far beyond physical movement and applies also to freedom of communication and hierarchal position. As Albrow notes, social stratification in the age of globalization often manifests in individuals' ability to move and communicate freely within their respective spheres.[37] Bolaño characterizes Haas as a quiet observer of sorts, an outsider in Mexico, silently watching his surroundings: "A Haas le gustaba sentarse en el suelo, la espalda apoyada contra la pared, en la parte sombreada del patio. Y le gustaba pensar. . . . Después abría los ojos y contemplaba, como desde un sueño, a algunos de los Bisontes que daban vueltas" (Haas liked to sit on the ground, against the wall, in the shady part of the yard. And he liked to think. . . . He opened his eyes and contemplated, as if in a dream, some of the Bisontes, who were moving around the sunny part of the yard).[38] Haas is an expatriate in Mexico and thus situated in a higher position of power due to his status as a white male foreigner of economic means. His membership in social groups with greater command over temporal and spatial resources (see Albrow)[39] provides him a very different experience of incarceration compared with that of his fellow prisoners. The jail offers a valuable point from which to observe constraints on Haas's mobility, given that he is neither entirely free nor under the same scrutiny as the other inmates. In a confrontation over Haas's innocence, he asks another prisoner whether he thought he (Haas) had committed the murders: "Cabrón me dijo no, no, tú seguro que no, gringo, como si yo fuera un jodido gringo, que puede que lo sea en el fondo, aunque cada vez lo soy menos" (The bastard said no, not you gringo, as if I was a fucking gringo, which inside maybe I am, although I'm becoming less and less of one).[40] Indeed, although Haas is confined in a local space, he is not necessarily a local subject. The ease with which he accesses the outside world and his ability to set his own rules show how his residence in the local is conditioned by his global mobility.

The case of Oscar Amalfitano is a fitting gateway to the discussion of the theatrical adaptation. Like Haas, despite his status as an expat, Oscar Amalfitano (played by Andreu Benito) does not spend his time globetrotting, but rather in his backyard swimming through memories and pondering a geometry book hanging from his clothesline, a position of privileged immobility in light of the events happening outside his door. To be clear, it is not *being* mobile or immobile that grants Amalfitano privilege, but rather his ability to choose between these two states: the *control* of his position in time and space, to recall Albrow's discussion of time-space stratification. Bolaño slows down the narrative through descriptions and inner monologues and, in doing so, contrasts the speed of global life with the stasis of the local place. In contrast with his fixed geographical positioning, the professor's dreams, flashbacks, and internal voices form a significant part of his narrative: "Aquella noche la voz no volvió a manifestarse y Amalfitano durmió muy mal, un sueño turbado por saltos y respingones" (That night there were no further manifestations of the voice and Amalfitano slept very badly, his sleep plagued by jerks and starts).[41] These pauses allow *2666*'s characters to make transnational phenomenological journeys through recollection and imagination, despite restrictions on their geographical movements. Àlex Rigola's stage adaptation of "La parte de Amalfitano" offers a unique means of engaging Amalfitano's propensity for inner monologue. The entire scene is staged in the desert landscape of the professor's backyard, devoid of obvious signs of the city, hemmed in by a large fence that extends across the stage (figure 2.1).

FIGURE 2.1. Oscar Amalfitano (with Rafael Dieste's *Testamento geométrico* hung on a clothesline, left) in his backyard with his fence extending across the entire stage and beyond. © Ros Ribas, MAE, Teatre Lliure, 2010.

In this scene, the fence serves as a powerful spatial cue by quarantining the private space of the yard from the surrounding public area of the city. Beyond the fence, little is visible, only the sandy terrain and the bright-blue desert sky of Santa Teresa, described in the novel as "una flor carnívora" (a carnivorous flower).[42] Though Amalfitano is primarily alone onstage, his daughter, Rosa (played by Cristina Brondo), enters early on, as well as Decano Guerra and Joven Guerra (Manuel Carlos Lillo and Ferran Carvahal), with whom Amalfitano shares the notorious Los Suicidas mezcal.[43] This setting calls attention to Amalfitano's internal musings as he lingers spatially and temporally between Barcelona, Chile, and Santa Teresa. The professor is caught between geographies in a mind-set of unsettled immobility. Similarly, his voluntary exile from Chile is described in the novel by one of the literary critics as "lleno de inconvenientes, de saltos y rupturas que más o menos se repiten y que dificultan cualquier cosa importante que uno se proponga hacer" (full of inconveniences, of skips and breaks that essentially keep recurring and interfere with anything you try to do that's important).[44] In this section of both play and novel, memory serves as a platform for transnational crossings between Santa Teresa and other geographies, testifying to the ease with which the protagonists defy the constraints of geographical place within their phenomenological worlds. These intersections play out first with Lola (played by Alícia Pérez), Amalfitano's estranged wife, who descends from his remembered Barcelona to give an extended performance onstage, sitting in the plastic chairs in his yard in Mexico and conveying an informal, domestic effect. As in the novel, Amalfitano hears the voice of his deceased Chilean father, entering into an altered psychological state, which the play highlights through casting a spotlight on him and obscuring all else onstage. In his adaptation, Rigola effectively demonstrates that despite Amalfitano's stationary position, he has the time and the solitude to engage the various spaces of his past through memory. This rendering reminds viewers of the fluidity of space for protagonists like Amalfitano who have the privilege of stasis. This also provides a contrasting representation to the restricted mobility of the maquiladora workers, who are given very little time and restricted spaces, at mercy to their working environment and a society that repeatedly denies their agency and right to mobility without the threat of violence.

BODIES, IMMOBILITY, AND REPETITION IN "THE PART ABOUT THE CRIMES"

Throughout Bolaño's *2666*, bodies are viewed and then transmuted into the desert landscape like flora and fauna. As an extended and brutal enumeration of femicides, "The Part about the Crimes" is the work's longest section and has also received the most critical attention from scholars. In her essay "Globalized Philomels," Laura Barberán Reinares examines the dehumanization of this section's subaltern victims within the context of neoliberalism, while Ángeles Donoso

Macaya looks at the aesthetics of violence and serial repetition in the portrayal of the victims' bodies.[45] This infamous section spans 1993 to 1997, amid a repetitive violence that seems to stifle the progression of time as the victims' bodies are scrutinized in harrowing detail. There is a grotesque and unrelenting visual character to this part of the novel, particularly its cyclical depictions of the crime scenes. Indeed, returning relentlessly to the crimes converts the bodies into fixed points amid a whirlwind of investigations that lead nowhere. In reconstructing the deaths, Bolaño demonstrates the restriction and commodification of the women's agency over their own bodily movements under an umbrella of power hierarchies. With the arrival of North American companies to the borderland during the heyday of the North American Free Trade Agreement, the women of Santa Teresa (Juárez) became part of a larger commodity chain that prioritizes profit margins over human life, often taking late-night buses to work, laboring long hours in low-paid manual labor, and dwelling in precarious shantytowns near the factories.

Despite their spatial confinement within the microenvironment of Santa Teresa, the maquiladora workers are actors within global circuits (see Saskia Sassen)[46] whose marginalization, exploitation, and deaths are consequences of broader processes beyond the immediate locale. In the novel, the workers become cogs in the machine of the transnational maquiladora industry, trapped in the perverse and pervasive web of violence and misogyny permeating the city. In the description of a body found in the waste receptacle of one of the factories, it is mentioned that only one of the maquiladoras had a cafeteria for the workers, whereas in the others, "los obreros comían junto a sus máquinas o formando corrillos en cualquier rincón. Allí hablaban y se reían hasta que sonaba la sirena que marcaba el fin de la comida" (the workers ate next to their machines or in small groups in a corner, talking and laughing until the siren sounded that signaled the end of lunch).[47] Here, Bolaño once again relies on the contrast between speed and stasis to evoke both the relentless, inhumane pace of manufacturing work and the abrupt stop-and-start of the factory schedule. This is particularly pertinent when considering the system of mass production and consumption that spawns *2666*'s fictionalized border town, reminding readers of the dehumanization of its female subjects and the process through which certain bodies and forms of labor are deliberately rendered expendable. The similarities between the commodification of the women's work in the global labor market and their physical objectification are difficult to ignore; the women's bodies (and work) are given little value, and their deaths are systematically overlooked. This speaks to the complex bond between their bodies as tools of production within the neoliberal capitalist system inherent to the maquiladora culture and sites on which violence is inflicted within a climate of pervasive misogyny. This commodification is also highlighted by the victims' involvement in forms of devalued labor in the multinational industries of manufacturing and sex work: in addition to the maquila workers, several of the women whose murders are recounted as forensic reports in "La parte de los crímenes" are described as sex workers, or suspected of being prostitutes on the basis of dubious evidence like red lipstick, nail polish, or condoms:

> En octubre se encontró el cuerpo de otra mujer en el desierto, al sur de Santa Teresa, entre dos pistas vecinales. El cuerpo se hallaba en estado de descomposición y los forenses dijeron que iba a llevar días determinar las causas de la muerte. El cadáver tenía las uñas pintadas de rojo. Por las prendas de vestir dedujeron que era joven: pantalón de mezclilla y blusa escotada.[48]
>
> [In October the body of another woman was found in the desert, south of Santa Teresa, between two country roads. The body was in a state of decomposition and the forensic scientists said it would take days to determine the cause of death. The victim had red-painted nails, which led the first officers on the scene to think she was a whore. By the clothes—jeans and a low-cut blouse—they deduced she was young.][49]

On that note, the relationship between the body, production, and desire is of equal significance. At the whim of a misogynist hyperculture enveloping the city, the women are raped and often sexually mutilated—including the removal of their nipples—before they are killed. In Gilles Deleuze and Félix Guattari's *Anti-Oedipus: Capitalism and Schizophrenia,* the authors analyze the relationship between desire and society, modeling the unconscious connection between human bodies and production through the metaphor or model of "desiring machines."[50] The idea of the body-as-machine removes free will from the human experience, as subjects are converted to consuming and producing devices trapped in a cycle of unconscious, mechanical desire.

The descriptions follow a consistent pattern: the date the body was found, the name (if there was one), the appearance of the body and the clothes of the dead woman, the cause of death, and a (typically unsuccessful) attempt to puzzle together the pieces of her disappearance. Some of the women are suspected to have been killed by their partners or in seemingly random acts by strangers, but for most, the killers are never found, and many of the suspects flee the city before being detained. In the compression of narrative time and space through the repetitive structure and unrelenting brutality of these stories, everything coalesces into a single act of violence for the reader, and hundreds of acts merge into a horrific stream that courses through the section in a multifaceted yet singular representation of gendered violence. The detached and unflinching attention to detail and documentary-like descriptions present in "La parte de los crímenes" have the succinctness of a police report. Several scholars—among them, Julia Monárrez Fragoso and Alicia Gaspar de Alba—have noted the close resemblance between Bolaño's descriptions of the femicide victims and the forensic reports published by Casa Amiga, a crisis center and advocacy group for women who experience gender violence.[51] Monárrez Fragoso and Gaspar de Alba are among those who have criticized Bolaño's uncredited use of these descriptions and the names of the victims, particularly given the prominence of *2666* among literary representations of femicide in Juárez. The novel's reflections on the female body as expendable commodity—and more conceptually, as the place where violence comes to rest—invoke contemporary dialogues among activists and collectives that aim to combat gender violence in Latin America.[52]

The systematic and repetitive description of the murders lends an exponential character to the text. At the same time, the brevity of the vignettes is weighed down by their duplication, as they are repeated and revisited for over three hundred pages. Hundreds of victims become thousands, perhaps even more, as narrative lines blur for the reader, moving through countless crime scenes, all strikingly similar. Notably, Bolaño gestures at the unknown number of murdered women whose deaths were not recorded: "Otras que quedaron fuera de la lista o que jamás nadie las encontró, enterradas en fosas comunes en el desierto o esparcidas sus cenizas en medio de la noche, cuando ni el que siembra sabe en dónde, en qué lugar se encuentra" (Other girls and women who didn't make it onto the list or were never found, who were buried in unmarked graves in the desert or whose ashes were scattered in the middle of the night, when not even the person scattering them knew where he was, what place he had come to).[53] Although it is uncertain whether this is a holdover from the use of Casa Amiga's reports, Bolaño sticks to a limited vocabulary when describing the physical appearance of the victims, intensifying the sense of repetition in "La parte de los crímenes." Many of the women are described as having "pelo largo hasta la cintura" (long hair down to her waist), "pelo negro y lacio hasta más abajo de los hombros" (straight black hair past her shoulders), and being "delgada, morena [con] el pelo de color negro" (thin, dark-skinned, [with] black hair).[54] These descriptions and their variations give an almost robotic quality to their bodies, which are grouped together by commonalities, reinforcing anonymity. Similarly, the repetitive, generalizable nature of these descriptions leads the reader to understand the murders as multiple instances of broader forces acting at the local level, rather than isolated incidents. The speed of this section is nuanced in this regard, both brief and impactful in its snapshots, while also lengthy and cyclical in scope. To exacerbate matters, the novel's depiction of the crime investigations is characterized by haphazard follow-up, with the attention of local police easily diverted to comparatively trivial matters, such as the vandalism of churches, and the bodies of many women eventually interred in communal graves.

To fully evaluate these crimes and continue this chapter's discussion of mobility, it is necessary to note some similarities in the circumstances of the many deaths enumerated in "La parte de los crímenes." The mobility of women of color is a central focus of the scant information that the police are able to gather about the victims immediately before their deaths. Many of the bodies are discovered near highways, many of the girls are abducted on their way home from school, and innumerable others disappear as they walk home from work: in one report, Bolaño writes by way of explanation, "Alguna parte del trayecto algo ocurrió o algo se torció para siempre su madre después le dijeron que cabía la posibilidad de que se hubiera fugado con un hombre" (Somewhere along the way something happened or something went permanently wrong and afterward her mother was told there was a chance she had run off with a man).[55] Speed—as sudden abduction and relentless factory production—plays a significant role in this last report, as Bolaño notes that the victim in question, Margarita Lopez, disappeared on her fifty-minute walk home from an overnight work shift that lasted from nine o'clock at night to five thirty in the morning.[56] Another woman is killed by her boyfriend after refusing to immigrate with him to the United States, one is shot while taking out her car keys, one is found dead with a bus ticket to Tucson in her purse, a bus "que la mujer ya no iba a tomar" (that she would never catch).[57] In each of these instances, a woman's mobility is brought to a sudden stop, and stasis is created through the brutal silencing of a living body by murder.[58] This form of coerced stasis accompanies questions about the agency that Bolaño grants the femicide victims in his representation: they enter the narrative as silent cadavers whose histories are gathered through police interviews and forensic clues. Indeed, Bolaño does not afford these women the ability to speak their own truths; readers must fill in the gaps as they take in uneven portrayals of encountered bodies and constructed stories.

Àlex Rigola's theatrical treatment of the fourth section offers enlightening engagement with the question of victim agency through the director's use of repetition and corporality. Nuala Finnegan has noted the importance of the body in Rigola's oeuvre, broadly stating, "Rigola's more recent work . . . seems to want to move to a space beyond language, a privileging of the body as narrative as well as the body in narrative."[59] "La parte de los crímenes" has the most recognizable portrayal of Santa Teresa's desert scenery in the entire play. Here, the director uses projected texts and lighting on a center-stage backdrop. In contrast with the novel, which gives brief accounts of the assassinations and the corpses using fictionalized names, Rigola opts to focus on one dying body onstage, while later projecting a scrolling list of the names of the real-life victims of Juárez onto the back of the stage. As the scene opens, actors emerge from behind the sheets that line the walls of center, left, and right stage. Amid tumbleweed, sand, small bushes, and newly dug graves, the blood-soaked cadaver of a woman (played by Alba Pujol) lying on a plastic sheet is situated downstage right, with the sound of buzzing flies and barking dogs heard in the distance. The body lies face-down—underscoring the woman's anonymity—as the three investigators, Pedro Negrete, Lalo Cura, and Juan de Dios Martínez (played by Manuel Carlos Lillo, Ferran Carvajal, and Julio Manrique, respectively), examine it and ask, "¿Se sabe quién es?" (Do we know who this is?). Their response is invariably a negative, and this lack of recognition draws attention to the obscurity of the victims. After a series of exchanges, the body is abandoned when another cadaver is discovered: Lalo Cura states, "Jefe, aquí hay otra muerte" (Boss, there's another dead one here). The actors exit from under the screens and the stage turns dark blue while the dead woman, forgotten, falls into the shadows. Immediately, the backdrop becomes a projector for the display of two important texts. First, a modified version of the oft-cited quote by *2666*'s psychic, Florita Almeda, appears. As a clairvoyant, Almeda offers a particular testament to the invisibility of Santa Teresa's femicides, given her ability to see what is hiding in plain sight:

> Estoy hablando de visiones que le cortarían el aliento al más macho de los machos. En sueños veo los crímenes y es como si un aparato de televisión explotara y siguiera viendo, en los trocitos de la pantalla esparcidos por mi dormitorio, escenas horribles, llantos que no acaban nunca. . . . Estoy hablando de las mujeres bárbaramente asesinadas en Santa Teresa, estoy hablando de las niñas y de las madres de familia y las trabajadoras de toda condición y ley que cada día aparecen muertas en los barrios. . . . Estoy hablando de Santa Teresa.[60]
>
> [I'm talking about visions that would take away the breath of the bravest of brave men. In dreams I see the crimes and it's as if a television set had exploded and I keep seeing, in the little shards of screen around my bedroom, horrible scenes, endless tears. . . . I'm talking about the women brutally murdered in Santa Teresa, I'm talking about the girls and the mothers of families and the workers from all walks of life who turn up dead each day in the neighborhoods. . . . I'm talking about Santa Teresa.][61]

The projected quote disappears, replaced by perhaps the most memorable sequence of the five-hour performance, the projected scrolling of the real-life victims' full names and years of death. This contributes to the staging of the novel's focus on the continuity, magnitude, and simultaneous ephemerality of the victims. Rigola cites deaths from 1993 and extending beyond the dates included in the novel, leading up to 2003. The decontextualized appearance of each woman's name in some ways mimics the repetitive quality of the novel's forensic snapshots. However, the continuity of the scrolling list highlights the murder of each woman as symbolic of a more extended instance of violence. Through this setup, Rigola visually captures the repetition and ephemerality of the victims in a way that is shorter-lived than the text's portrayals of the same. At the close of the scrolling, the remaining bodies are summarized only as: "Y 75 cadáveres sin identificar" (And 75 unidentified corpses).

During this sequence, text and performance collide as the body situated downstage right comes to life, seemingly in a wrenching re-enactment of her

FIGURE 2.2. The light-pink crosses reflect the victims' names in a double projection. © Ros Ribas, Teatre Lliure, 2010.

death. The female victim writhes in her own blood, screaming and panting, whispering, then shrieking "por favor" (please). Meanwhile, from behind the screen come nameless women and men who stake the infamous pink crosses into makeshift graves (figure 2.2). Because of the widespread publicization of the femicides in Juarez, the crosses—which began as a local practice of memorialization in Juarez—have gained prominence in the Mexican and international imaginaries surrounding gender violence.[62] The crosses quickly take over the panorama of the stage and create a sense of permanence, remaining fixed in the desert soil after being staked and offering a longer-lasting—although more individualized—testament to the women's deaths than their vanishing names. Indeed, the real crosses of Ciudad Juárez endure after the bodies have been removed and the investigations have been abandoned, a lasting material marker contrasted with the systematic and violent erasure of the women's deaths.

Repetition offers a vector for understanding the role of brevity and erasure in the execution of this section. This dual projection is effective because the women's names appear in the skies and on the landscapes of Santa Teresa, while the stage lighting meanders between dark hues of red, green, and black. Only the names are illuminated in white, with the sole additional light source a series of spotlights shining horizontally from the stage floor. This low lighting illuminates the action while preserving the ambiguity and obscurity vital to the sequence. Individual actors are indistinguishable as their bodies flow on- and offstage. Darkness shrouds the resurrected woman, while a spotlight streams in a parallel direction a few meters from her body (figure 2.3). The audience's attention is drawn to the ephemerality of the victims, and also to the broad scope of the violence that literally engulfs the stage. Although the portrayal of the bodies differs between novel and play, the robotic quality of the projected names is evocative

FIGURE 2.3. Community members leave the pink crosses, iconic of Ciudad Juárez, in a constant stream as the names continue to scroll on the screen of center stage. © Ros Ribas, MAE, Teatre Lliure, 2010.

of how the victims are presented in the novel. Both depictions are matter-of-fact, cyclical in their repetition, and lacking affect. With that said, for viewers, encountering one body after the next in sequence is a powerful experience, one that provokes anguish and a sense of deep outrage given how little time and space they are allotted on-screen. At the end of the sobering sequence, the blood-soaked woman lets out a final scream, the last crosses are staked, and the names continue to scroll on a tranquil stage.

Notably, this scene's deliberate manipulation of movement and stillness provides a valuable moment for reflection to close this section with a discussion of the role of the body in communicating violence. As in the text, the audience encounters one victim after the next, in sequence. However, the presence of the woman onstage brings a poignant quality to the scene that is largely absent in the novel, as audience members hear her screams and watch her struggle until her death. However, although Pujol screams and writhes, she never leaves her general positioning, simultaneously shaping the narrative of her death while nonetheless remaining fixed in the representation created for her onstage. To that effect, Finnegan has written about the role of excess, and in particular the representation of excessive death in Rigola's adaptation of *2666*.[63] Although Finnegan finds that the screaming body in some ways "re-inscribes" the doubly Othered body of the impoverished Mexican woman as spectacle,[64] she also interprets Pujol's sacrificial screams as an effective means of disrupting Bolaño's narrative representations of victims devoid of voice and agency. "This gendered expression of horror in sonic terms while highly mediated in this in-between chaotic, frequently incoherent space, may well be the vehicle through which the feminicidal horrors of Juárez are best approximated. At the very least, we can perhaps see how the body of Alba Pujol and the sounds she emits foreground questions of agency and resistance as it tells its own story of pain, wounding and sacrifice."[65] Similar to Finnegan's interpretation of the body as a text from which to read signifiers of violence, Rita Segato explores the ways in which female bodies operate in the environment of the borderlands. In her contribution to Rosa-Linda Fregoso and Cynthia Bejarano's *Terrorizing Women*, Segato argues that the corpses of victims serve as canvases for "messages," immobile bodies that circulate within an information network. She writes, "If we listen carefully to the messages that circulate there, we can see the face of the subject speaking through them. . . . In other words, the femicides are messages sent by a subject/author who can be identified, located, and profiled only by rigorously 'listening' to these crimes as communicative acts. . . . In its enunciation we can find the interlocutor's trail, his imprint, like a photographic negative."[66] In a subsequent essay, "Las nuevas formas de la guerra y el cuerpo de las mujeres" (New forms of war and the body of women), Segato directly engages the violence against sex workers and maquila employees as a manifestation of contemporary power struggles and conflicting claims to sovereignty. She interprets women's bodies as sites of "reterritorialization," proposing that the gendered body offers a site for marking claims to territory in a globalized world, particularly—as Dove later elaborates—inscriptions of paralegal sovereignty.[67] Following Segato's argument, victims' bodies become message boards onto which visual and discursive notes of misogyny and control are cataloged and recorded. These bodies circulate in the material world, via corporal and photographic evidence, as well as digitally, forming part of a web of impunity, brutality, and the rewriting of local identities by global forces. Studying the play in juxtaposition with the novel thus expands our understanding of coercive movement and immobility, while also posing the question of how to ethically engage with representations of violence.

FRENZY, SLOW MOTION, AND STANDSTILL: RIGOLA'S USE OF FILM IN *2666*

Rigola's use of film further extends textualities into the visual realm, bolstering our understanding of how the novel moves across space and time. Bolaño's fascination with film is well documented. Marking the tenth anniversary of his death, the first-ever public exhibition of his personal and professional artifacts, *Arixiu Bolaño: 1977–2003* (Bolaño archive), was displayed at the Centre de Cultura Contemporània de Barcelona.[68] The collection, a product of the collaboration between the center and Bolaño's widow, Carolina López, provides numerous indications that film played a significant role in the author's creative process, highlighting the fact that many influential filmmakers had an impact on the writer.[69] In line with this fascination, references to cinema pepper the pages of *2666*, including the snuff film industry associated with the murders of Santa Teresa; Chucho Rodriguez, the film buff and video store owner introduced in the "The Part about Fate"; and references to director David Lynch, with whose work Bolaño's has been frequently been compared. Rigola also cites Lynch as an aesthetic inspiration for his adaptation.[70] At the narrative level, the use of vignettes has an undeniably visual quality that resembles a series of film stills. Exploring the visual nature of the text is an appropriate point of departure for studying the manifestations of speed in the play, as Rigola's patchwork aesthetic interweaves vignettes, highlighting fragmentation, multiple perspectives, and discourses. The narrative ruptures and transitions express the uneven nature of globalization, revealing the heterogeneous experiences and local manifestations of global processes. Similarly, Rigola's use of film in the theatrical production supports exercises of compression and expansion, as the director reframes the action on stage and screen, forcing multiple representations to occupy the same visual plane. As such, Rigola's staging reflects the complex trajectories of *2666*'s protagonists, who are charged with reconstituting time and space in their locally lived experiences of the global.

Rigola first incorporates video footage in the form of projected scenes of Santa Teresa in "La parte de los críticos." In this scene, Oscar Amalfitano jots notes on a large whiteboard, which is converted to a screen for the projection of mixed scenes of the city and its outskirts with its gritty, austere desert landscape and urban buildings. The continuous stream of footage appears to have been filmed from a moving vehicle, and the landscapes of Santa Teresa pass by rapidly with a velocity that disorients and decontextualizes the footage: the viewer cannot physically place what he or she is seeing. At the same time, the inability to ground the scenes has a universalizing and even estranging effect; it is as if Santa Teresa (Juárez) could be a number of places and nowhere at all, at once familiar and strange. This dizzying sensation is heightened by the visual overlap of the film's scenes of the border town and the academics' notes, as their scribbled hunt for Archimboldi is literally mapped onto the landscape of Santa Teresa (figure 2.4). This transposition disrupts the visual dichotomy between the fixed writings and the moving footage, giving the audience the sense that both text and image are in motion.

By laying the world out on a screen, Rigola links the ambiguous, transnational journeys of Archimboldi with the very present, local places of Santa Teresa. Much of what is known about Archimboldi's origins and position remains elusive, giving readers the sense that he is nowhere and everywhere at once. Indeed, it is not until the end of the novel—when readers learn that Archimboldi is in fact Hans Reiter (played by Joan Carreras), born in Prussia in 1920—that they begin to get a sense of the geographical trajectory of his life. In this way, both the stage performance and the novel provide exemplary moments in which to contrast mobility and immobility as a visual cue for contemplating the interplay between the global and the local.

Throughout the play, Rigola's use of film distorts the audience's understanding of what is or is not a frame. His projections convert the stage into a type of

FIGURE 2.4. The whiteboard and notes onto which scenes of Santa Teresa have been projected. © Ros Ribas, MAE, Teatre Lliure, 2010.

frame itself, a desert sky into a film display, or a whiteboard into a screen for projected footage. The projected and performed scenes often comingle, thus fragmenting and unsettling time, a technique evocative of the primary text's temporal and spatial jumps between vignettes. These techniques allow Rigola to stage the phenomenological processes of globalization within *2666* before his audience, highlighting interconnections and fractures. The temporal distortion wrought by distanciated influences is rarely visible to the globalized subject,[71] who has naturalized the systemization of time zones and the uniform measurement of hours and minutes: yet in Rigola's production, the manipulation of time is so overt as to disorient the viewer. As noted by Jara Martínez Valderas and Javier J. González Martínez, this distortion of time plays part of Rigola's body of work on a panoramic scale, "En distintas ocasiones Rigola pone al público en la tesitura de elegir el canal, zapping, por el que quiere seguir la representación: la pantalla, el movimiento o la palabra. Este efecto sigue acentuando la sensación de búsqueda, de pérdida, de descontrol" (On several occasions, Rigola puts the audience in the position of zapping and choosing the channel with which it wants to continue the performance: the screen, movement or words. This effect accentuates a feeling of search, loss, and lack of control).[72] The pace of the stage performance and the internal time of projected images are at times contrasted, at others forcibly synchronized. Occasionally,

FIGURE 2.5. The seated boxer at the beginning of "La parte de fate." © Ros Ribas, MAE, Teatre Lliure, 2010.

the screen displays a real-time projection of the action onstage. This bewildering effect creates a sense of motorized movement among the actors, in line with the dialogue between contemporary theater and film.[73] The conflicts between chronological dissonance and simultaneity reinforce the plasticity of time, as the temporal progression of Rigola's staged world is repeatedly disassembled and reconstituted.

In "The Part about Fate," Rigola's use of film and projected images serves a variety of ends: the director is able to create a sense of frenzy, to mimic the fast pace of travel, to slow down and even suspend the work in time. "The Part about Fate" begins with the projection of a green frame in which a male figure (played by Julio Manrique) is seated, wearing a luchador mask, boxing gloves, a suit jacket, shorts, and leather boxing boots that extend to midcalf. The edges of the stage within a stage are visible on all four sides, and the title of the piece is projected above on a black backdrop similar to a movie theater (figure 2.5).[74]

A few moments later, a second box of equal dimensions is projected above the green frame. Here, film and performance merge; for the first time, the projection becomes the lead narrative, a filmed conversation between Oscar Fate and Barry Seaman. Both Seaman and Fate are covered in sweat, back-dropped by a blazing sun. Meanwhile, the action onstage diverges; the boxer figure remains seated and then later exits, followed by the provocative entrance of Rosita Mendez (Alba Pujol), with Chucho (Féliz Pons), Fate, and the journalist. Given the equal proportions of stage and screen, the viewer has the sense of watching two narratives unfold simultaneously (figure 2.6). This disrupts any sense of linearity and confuses the distinction between recorded and live performance.

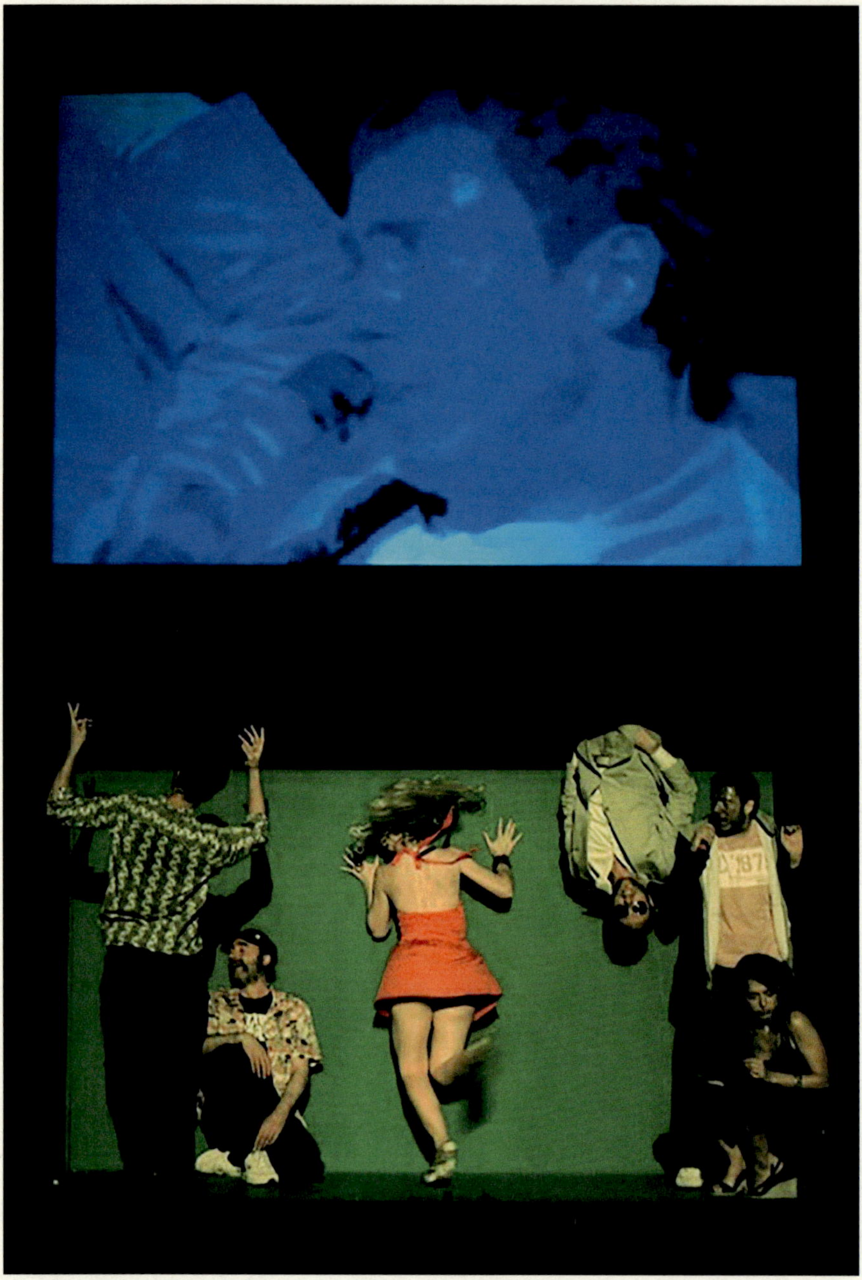

FIGURE 2.6. Simultaneous action on stage and screen. © Ros Ribas, MAE, Teatre Lliure, 2010.

FIGURE 2.7. The actors cluster together in the green box. It is of note that Rigola cast white actors to play roles in a novel set in Mexico, particularly given the dynamics at play in a European adaptation of a Latin American work, and even more so given the multiple forms of violence inflicted on women of color throughout *2666*. The use of a white actor in blackface to play the part of Fate, the black American detective, is a particularly problematic decision. © Ros Ribas, MAE, Teatre Lliure, 2010.

The screen then goes black, and the action plays out on the stage below within another frame, the actors' bodies crammed together as they lean against its eerily green walls, shadows stretching behind them (figure 2.7). Video projections come in many varieties in the theatrical version of "The Part about Fate," including the boxing match and ambiguous sexualized scenes in the novel's infamous house party. In the initial projection, the footage proceeds at a frantic pace, zooming from a scene of a group eating Mexican food to a scene of them doing shots of tequila, while the actors below dance together to the popular reggaeton melody "Gasolina" by Puerto Rican artist Daddy Yankee. Their bodies reproduce the frantic nature of the tune and footage, capturing the escalating hyperactivity of the night, which becomes increasingly violent.[75]

At one point, the recorded dancing and the performance are in sync; later, the stage is projected in real time, blurring the lines between reality and fiction, and between cinematographic and performance time. Later, the projected video continues to play as several characters disperse from the stage. In this Dionysian scene and throughout the play, Rigola uses video footage to test and problematize human experiences of time. The use of slow motion heightens the audience's attention to detail and produces a strained effect as the actors contort their movements to try to replicate the pace of the footage. Rigola's occasional halting of the action feels jolting, contributing to the bizarre aesthetic. Thus, the manipulation of speed and the use of video allow the piece to re-create the strange underworld of Santa Teresa, where violence and mania lurk just below the surface. Rigola's staging practices construct visible representations of Bolaño's multilayered narrative by using speed to configure local settings in relation to global forces.[76]

Lastly, Rigola's use of film in the fifth and final scene accelerates to depict the life of Benno von Archimboldi (Hans Reiter), the elusive writer pursued by the academics in the first part of the novel. The backdrop remains a large screen projecting multiple images—such as black-and-white war photos—punctuated by empty frames. Similar to earlier sequences, there are minimal props, and the stage is cast in black.[77] A beam of light illuminates Señora Bubis, the writer's longtime editor, as she sits on stage left, smoking and narrating much of the story. The set is shrouded in darkness, save for a large treadmill that bisects the stage. Archimboldi enters from stage right and steps onto the treadmill. Behind him, projected images change continuously, generating a sense of constant motion. As actors enter the scene, they join Archimboldi on the treadmill, then dismount when their narratives end, occasionally lingering at the edge of the stage. Juxtaposed to this show of mobility is Señora Bubis, who remains a fixture on stage right. Bubis gazes into the audience as Archimboldi journeys on, shoeless and bare-chested. As the scene comes to a close, the pace of the treadmill increases, bringing the actor to a fast walk, which escalates to a light jog, and finally a breakneck run. At the climax of the five-hour performance, Archimboldi sprints to center stage, his body projected in real time on the video screen behind him. The projected image splits and multiplies, fracturing Archimboldi's discrete presence. Once again, Archimboldi is rendered not as a physical, situated being but as the intangible, omnipresent figure of the writer (figure 2.8), ever open to interpretation. Thus, Archimboldi comes to embody the same transnational cosmopolitanism critiqued in the novel at large, moving through hierarchies, processes, and spaces, commanding time and space, and always in control, undeterred by the protagonists who join him temporarily to affirm the interconnection of their narratives with his. Archimboldi's position as a writer allows him to make visible the very dimensions of the local and the global that he navigates with ease, while the hunt by the four academics becomes a race against this elusiveness and a disambiguation of time and space.

CONCLUSION

In this chapter, I have strived to illustrate the ways in which speed and stasis act as narrative and staging devices for the depiction of heterogeneous and conflicted processes of local-global interaction. The novel and theatrical adaption of

FIGURE 2.8. Archimboldi sprints in front of his real-time projection. © Ros Ribas, MAE, Teatre Lliure, 2010.

2666 highlight tremendous interconnectivity and stark disparities of contemporary life through linked narrative arcs and visual overlays. As the relative and multifaceted configurations of local experience play out in narrative snapshots, the novel emphasizes the lack of insularity between visual and literary arts, and the importance of considering the former in dialogue with the latter in form, structure, and theme, particularly in the twenty-first century. Many continue to associate the panoramic envisioning of the world not with literature but with film, as discussed in this chapter. However, works that are structured by the use of micronarrative, such as *2666* or the writings of Argentine Rodrigo Fresán, indicate that this trend may be changing. Bolaño's *2666* soars across vast spaces without sacrificing intimate and subjective regressions into memory and situated events, revealing the heterogeneous, multiscalar processes of local-global interaction. The use of memory in particular testifies to literature's ability to create narrative space through the complex terrain of the human psyche, and to the importance of such space in salvaging lost time and geographies. These leaps and pauses challenge us to recognize the simultaneity of many flows within globalization and the ongoing reconstitution of the local through its embedment in global networks (see, for example, the work of Saskia Sassen).[78] In both the novel and its stage adaptation, the reader/viewer bounces back and forth between detailed, "visible" localities and broad, abstract (often global) processes. In the lingering spaces of immobility, our complex spatial experiences create narrative and cultural disjunctures, spaces where the uneven impact of globalization becomes visible, along with the disparate privileges afforded by such development.

These hierarchies are best examined in the novel's ruminations on speed as a concept that unites our understandings of time and space, traversing multiple places and perspectives and distributing narrative attention between the novel's speaking protagonists, its victims, and its secondary figures. Both manifestations of *2666* reveal the ways in which each contemporary actor's command of time and space configures the experience of global, phenomenological forces that transform local settings. The most marginalized of these figures are captured in an ephemeral manner, as if descending into the black hole to which the work has been likened. In that vein, in reference to the real women who have been murdered along the U.S.-Mexico border, Segato writes that "from the small scale of their situation and localization," the murdered women of Juárez "wake us up and guide us into a more lucid rereading of the transformations the world undergoes nowadays."[79] In this context, the presence of Bolaño's work as one of the most widely known representations of gendered and economic violence in the free trade zone poses difficult questions about the ethics of representation, and about the power of literary works to reinforce power imbalances and, in this case, to further brutalize and further silence marginalized subjects. Though the height of

Bolañismo may be behind us as we progress into the drifting spatial experiences of the twenty-first century, Bolaño's body of work continues to reveal itself in complex and subtle ways; it is our task to reapproximate and re-engage it. Indeed, texts such as *2666* force us to think critically about the relationship between literature and globalization, making visible the multiple processes of interconnection, disjuncture, and violence between local and global lives.

3 • AMBIVALENT SPACES

Allegories of Ruin in Bernardo Carvalho's *Teatro* and Gilberto Noll's *Harmada*

> Ruins, past and present, are bracketed from everyday life, *as if* from another era that only incidentally touches our own; nonetheless, they are bound up with nationalist discourses of power, identity, and memory. Not just "proof" of human existence and past practices, the crushed rocks become the measure of who "we" are now.
>
> —Diana Taylor

In contemporary Latin American literature, both the delineation of spatial markers and the conspicuous absence thereof reflect the changing fabric of local and global contacts. Geographically ambiguous literature provides a unique platform from which to ask two crucial questions: What spatial tropes linger in these works, and what do they tell us about their protagonists' confrontation with global forces? The removal of narratives from the confines of local specificity allows space to take on a powerful allegorical role, as the deliberate construction of ambiguous space recalls the tension between universal and local themes in writing.[1] At the same time—and as explored in chapters 1 and 2—as our globalized world distorts place-specific identities and geographic fixedness, writers increasingly defy borders, transforming the framework of local experience. This plasticity of identity preoccupies Bernardo Carvalho's *Teatro* and Gilberto Noll's *Harmada*, the two Brazilian novels that are the focus of this chapter.[2] Indeed, Latin America's contemporary authors trouble the link between place and belonging, revealing the complexity of navigating multilayered spatial imaginaries that intermingle past and present.

This chapter explores tropes of ruin and spatial ambiguity in *Teatro* and *Harmada*. Both works are products of the 1990s that reflect on a particular historical moment in Latin America during which the region continued to struggle with underdevelopment while becoming increasingly imbedded in global processes. In Brazil, the early 1990s were marked by significant changes to policy in order to combat economic troubles and social unrest, termed the "reform decade" by economists. New international circumstances and policy changes led to the loosening of state control over the Brazilian economy, which in turn opened the market to outside influences, including imported goods. Although these novels rarely provide a direct commentary on historical events, they use allegorical modeling to highlight the sentiment of unrest ripe in the region during this period, the impact of global political and economic forces. The two works feature fictitious nationally undefined settings: the city of Harmada in Noll's novel, and the *país das maravilhas* (country of wonders) and its bordering land in Carvalho's *Teatro*. Both novels' renderings of place bring to the fore a deep sense of ambivalence, an uneasy tension that ties together belonging and displacement, past and present, universal and particular. This tension flourishes in the authors' depiction of narrative worlds as ruins populated by protagonists who struggle to mediate experience in fractured languages, and in the vertigo communicated by unreliable narrators who operate in undefined settings. Indeed, there is a sense of being nowhere and everywhere at once in the urban decay of *Harmada* and the desolate borderlands of *Teatro*, whose settings comingle familiarity and estrangement. At times, these fictive realms are portrayed as sites of nostalgia, decadence, and even marvel; on other occasions, they are dilapidated and decaying, remnants of what once was. Through their engagement with spatial tropes common to Latin American literature—the journey to a capital city and the borderlands—Noll and Carvalho illustrate how the immediate settings of contemporary Latin American literature become at once intimate and distanciated as global forces penetrate local lives. The protagonists of their works are confronted with the disquieting feeling that the most familiar characteristics of their day-to-day lives are constructed by outside forces and networks.

Despite their differences, both Noll's and Carvalho's novels share a dichotomous structure and reflect deeply on the ambivalence of modern life. The narrative settings of *Harmada* and *Teatro* often take the form of ruins and decaying places, whose very deterioration endows them with powers of temporal and spatial disruption. Indeed, ruins persist in the present-day landscape while also recalling other moments in the broad arc of history, making them a powerful framework for studying space. Ruins do not emerge out of nothing; they are always and immediately the artefacts of another era. In my reading of the texts, ruins serve two primary functions: as a physical cue for failed modernization processes in Latin America, as seen in crumbling cities, streets, and ghostly borderlands, and as a spatial metaphor for the expression of loss and transformation in an era of globalization. As Andreas Huyssen comments, "We are nostalgic for the ruins of modernity because they still seem to hold a promise that has vanished from our own age: the promise of an alternative future"[3]—ruins have the unique ability to embody the past, the present, and an incomplete projected future at once, making them powerful conceptual tools. In this way, ruins act as a direct affront to the homogenizing and flattening processes of global phenomenological forces. As the products of other times and spaces, ruins represent a spatial and temporal irregularity in the "flat" landscape of globalization: they hint at the other locales that once occupied a given place.

Harmada and *Teatro* contradict the portrayal of globalized spaces as aesthetically clean and detached from signs of previous eras, in narratives that challenge the nonplaces famously theorized by Marc Augé. Augé defines nonplaces as homogeneous and transient in nature, sites that are replicated globally, such as supermarkets, airports, high-end hotels, and shopping malls.[4] He stresses the lack of place-bound identity in nonplaces and the disconnect one feels in them. In juxtaposition to the nonplace, the sites I discuss in these spatially ambiguous novels are hinged on memory and belonging, creatively and thoughtfully universalizing the particular. While many of the portrayals of *Harmada* and *Teatro* may be geographically ambiguous, they are also deeply laden with meaning. Amid memory-rich narratives, there is an overarching feeling of alienation, an incomplete sense of knowing and not knowing. This feeds into the cycle of rehashing memory, in novels that are vague but also filled with traces of human activity. Both works provide just enough detail to sketch out generalities about where they occur without allowing readers to place them fully. In my study of *Harmada* and *Teatro*, ruins offer a means of evaluating conflicts between times and spaces, particularly with regard to the tension between familiarity and estrangement that dominates the texts. The centrality of performance in *Harmada* and the notion of the stage in *Teatro* remind readers of the ruin-and-rebuilding cycle of the theater, a context in which one staged reality must be demolished for another to take its place. It is with this ambivalence in mind that I parse the ruins and invented realms of *Harmada* and *Teatro*, focusing on the novels' portrayal of deterioration and reconstruction of modes of knowing and inhabiting the world.

PLACING RUIN: UNEARTHING LITERARY ALLEGORIES IN THE RUBBLE

When considering the many ruins of Latin America, we may first envision ancient indigenous sites or artifacts of a pre-Columbian era. Indeed, the landscape of Latin America is rich with visual reminders of its precolonial past: the Incan ruins of Machu Picchu in Peru, Bolivia's Tiwanaku, the center of Mesoamerica in Mexico's sprawling Teotihuacan, or Brazil's Parque Arqueológico do Solstício, known also as the Amazon Stonehenge and located in the northernmost Brazilian state of Amapá. However, these examples are—as I will elaborate—highly particular forms of ruin, whose histories of restoration and preservation illustrate very specific priorities and ideological projects. More conceptually, these sites illustrate specific modes of thinking about the relationship between time and space—thought processes that are useful for understanding ruin as a frequent component of the human geography and history of Latin America, and as a disruptive spatial trope from which to examine the region's literary engagement with modernity. The physical form of a ruin occupies space in a present-day locale without necessarily *belonging* to it. This intrusion of an unfamiliar past into the present—conjoining temporal distance and spatial proximity—instills a sense of ambivalence in the observer. As such, ruins disrupt the tissue of temporal experience, conjoining the familiar *here and now* of a ruin's visible present-day form with the foreign *there and then* of what it once was.[5] This chapter investigates the profound ambivalence that ruins in narrative can evoke—in its aesthetic, conceptual manifestations, as well in its attention to physical decay.

As sites equally amenable to stagnation and transformation, ruins offer a means of examining changes in the way Latin Americans inhabit the world: whether it is the expiry of ways of being that predate the distanciated interactions of globalization, or perhaps the rapid boom-and-bust cycle of construction and demolition that has accompanied the industrialization of the region's economies. We might understand ruin as physical deterioration, or perhaps abandonment of a site after the dissolution of links between a place and its purpose. The process of ruination might take place as the gradual decay of neglect fueled by economic migration or industrial collapse, or the sudden destruction of an earthquake or explosive-aided demolition. In the novels I study in this chapter, the trope of ruin is most usefully understood in tandem with spatial ambiguity, as both conjure an uncertainty, a desire on behalf of the reader to excavate the real settings and structures from the rubble of uncertainty. What further links these conceptual devices is the ambiguous role of absence, a vacancy that can be variously interpreted as freedom to reinvent or devastating loss.

Yet Latin America's postindustrial and colonial ruins differ from their pre-Columbian counterparts in significant ways. In contrast to the regulated use of restored pre-Columbian sites, which are largely confined, protected, or residing in museums, many Latin Americans live alongside and interact with ruined or otherwise abandoned structures from the twentieth and twenty-first centuries.[6] Modern-day ruins provide powerful spatial narratives of the socioeconomic and political transformations of Latin America, particularly in the context of Brazil. Although Brazil is not known for massive restored ruins like those that dot the landscapes of Mexico, Guatemala, and Peru, the country has its own preoccupation with multilayered ruins. Indeed, in his essay "Ruins of the South," Alfredo González-Ruibal declares, "Brazil is a country in ruins and obsessed with its own ruination."[7] He refers not only to the ruins of indigenous civilizations but also to the new ruination of those same sites through the deforestation of agrobusiness, the crumbling failed ideological projects of modernity so evident in Brasília, and the postindustrial detritus wrought by endless cycles of expansion, decadence, and collapse. Although the derelict landscapes of Noll's *Harmada* and Carvalho's

Teatro are not specifically marked as Brazilian, both authors continue a long tradition of ruin as a central preoccupation of Brazilian literature and cultural production. Indeed, as González-Ruibal writes, "in real or imagined derelict buildings, writers see the life of individuals or of the nation as on a distorted mirror."[8] Latin American literature is rife with literary engagement with ruin, including Pablo Neruda's poems on Machu Picchu, the real and metaphoric ruins of Mexico in Carlos Fuentes's *Cambio de piel*, and selections of poetry by Carlos Drummond de Andrade on cemeteries and decay.[9] Perhaps the most well-known literary musing on ruin is Juan Rulfo's midcentury Boom novel, *Pedro Páramo*,[10] in which the ruinous ghost town of Comala acts as a metaphor for the destructive and violent aftermath of the Mexican Revolution. *Pedro Páramo*—whose ruins provide thematic fuel for Noll's *Harmada*, as I will discuss later in this chapter—and other works shed light on many of the region's challenges, including poverty, cyclical violence, failed development, and political tyranny.

The topic of postindustrial ruin offers an enlightening lens through which to explore many of these themes. In *Nostalgia for Ruins*, Huyssen reminds us, "As a significant conceptual and architectural constellation that points to moments of decay, falling apart, and ruination[,] [ruins were] already present in the beginnings of modernity in the eighteenth century."[11] Ruins reveal irregularities in official (often state-sponsored) narratives of progress, modernity, and unified development. They point to the expiration or forcible eradication of ways of life, the ill-fated plans of ideological projects, refusals of hegemony, and counterrevolutions. During this period, the metaphor of ruin provided a reminder of some of the limitations of humankind's plunge into modernity, which was associated with catastrophe, forming an important component in the aesthetic of the sublime.[12] The time stamp of ruin is particularly significant when contrasting contemporary ruins with their ancient counterparts, as they are often constructed, lived, and abandoned in a viewer's lifetime. The breakneck pace of construction and deconstruction of modern-day structures has inevitably changed the velocity at which places come undone.[13] Indeed, industry drives the rapid cycle of construction, decline, demolition, and redevelopment, in which the "unutilized" ruin is demolished and rebuilt anew to communicate new visions of the future. To understand the legacy of postindustrial development in Latin America, we must turn our attention to the trail of detritus left in the wake of the acceleration of global exchange and its hegemonic stratification of economic outcomes. Perhaps most significantly, the emergence of postindustrial ruins illustrates "structural inequalities often global in character and therefore with no easy local solution."[14] Social inequality, uneven development, hegemony, and the legacies of empire run deeply through the works of Noll and Carvalho. Indeed, as a marker of decline, ruin often serves as a visible discriminant between those who have profited immensely from industrial growth and those who have not.

The question of postindustrial ruin in literature demands an explicit focus on select concepts within human geography: notably, national borders and the metropolis. Some Brazilian literary critics have focused specifically on the city and its ruins as a representative geography of contemporary experience. In her recent work *Contemporâneos: Expressões da literatura brasileira no século XXI*, Beatriz Resende examines cityscapes as a central preoccupation of contemporary Brazilian literature, portraying the metropolis as a microcosm of globalization: citing the constant remaking of the here and now, Resende writes that "espaço toma novas formas no diálogo do cotidiano local de perdas e danos com o universo global da economia" (space takes on new forms in the dialogue of the everyday, local-level losses and harms with the global universe of the economy).[15] In her comments on Resende's work and on the broader landscape of contemporary Brazilian literature, Leila Lehnen writes, "Nowhere more than in the globalized metropolis can we observe the acceleration of time and the multiple tragedies of everyday life. Nowhere but in this territory are the personal and public tragedies more evident, but also more invisible, in the anonymous flows that transverse its arteries of concrete and steel."[16] Lehnen's comment on the stark anatomy of the city calls to mind the immaculate ruins of Brazil's modernist capital, Brasília, whose soaring public monuments of midcentury urban planning are slowly succumbing to tall grass and crumbling concrete. Though Clarice Lispector passed away in 1977, the prolific author had the opportunity to provide a few telling comments on the city: "Olho Brasília como olho Roma: Brasília começou com uma simplificação final de ruínas. A hera ainda não cresceu" (I see Brasília as I see Rome: Brasília started with a final simplification of ruins. The ivy has not yet grown).[17] Here, Lispector gestures at the ideals of modernism on which the capital was founded, yet she also presents it as a failed ideological project in a state of ruin before the city was ever inaugurated.[18] The city, itself a monument of sorts to the ideals of modernity and progress, is predominantly designed to be navigated by car, with its business, entertainment, and residential districts cleanly divided to represent separate spheres of life. Scholars of architecture and anthropology have noted the dearth of sidewalks and street corners where the local can be patterned at a pedestrian pace, citing the lack of informal public gathering spaces in the city center as a driving force behind the lack of communal affective attachments in the city (see, for example, the work of James Holston). The city—originally built to support a population of about 500,000—is now home to about 2.5 million inhabitants, whose modes of traversing and inhabiting space have naturally spilled over the boundaries drawn by Lucas Costa. Well-worn pedestrian footpaths crisscross the grassy expanses between the broad motorways of Brasília's cloverleaf interchanges. Even in the most modernist zones, Brasília's residents reconstruct meanings through their informal uses of place. One of Brasília's most famous amphitheaters in the southwest of the city now provides a skateboarding site for young folks unperturbed by tall

FIGURE 3.1. The Plaza de las Tres Culturas in Mexico City. In the foreground, the reconstructed, "official" ruins of Tenochtitlan. Midground, a colonial church. In the background, the "unintentional" ruins of one of the buildings of the Tlatelolco housing project. © Carlos Valenzuela, August 3, 2019, Wikimedia Commons, https://commons.wikimedia.org/wiki/File:Plaza_de_las_3_cultruas_p3.jpg.

grass or crumbling concrete and, more likely than not, unaware that they are skating atop a modernist monument to public congregation in designated spaces. This type of spatial repurposing forces us to question the very notion of ruin as a nonfunctional space, and also highlights the ingenuity of local actors who re-enlist formerly unoccupied structures into active use within contemporary life.

Perhaps most importantly for this discussion of Latin American literature's interface with the disorienting forces of modernity, ruins reveal the multilayered nature of the spatial imaginaries that constitute a locale. The visible form of a ruin speaks to past time-space configurations that are often alien to the observer, and thus compels us to recognize the contingent nature of our experiences of the local. Indeed, ruins often transcend their original place-bound specificity as they undergo a process of abandonment and destruction followed by repurposing and rebuilding: as such, the presence of ruin in the contemporary landscape highlights the ways in which the local is repeatedly woven and reworked over the warp threads of geographical place. Many well-known sites are ruins built on ruins, as observed in the Plaza de las Tres Culturas in Mexico City (figure 3.1). The plaza is home to a carefully restored section of the Templo Mayor[19] that once provided the administrative center of Tenochtitlan. Next to the ruins is a seventeenth-century Catholic church—Santiago de Tlatelolco—that was built by a Franciscan order during the early stages of colonization. The plaza was conceived as a monument to the three cultures of Mexico, a synthesis of ruins and new development that would fuse disparate spatial imaginaries into a unified representation of the Mexican mestizo identity. The plaza is framed by the Conjunto Urbano Nonoalco Tlatelolco, Mario Pani's midcentury functionalist housing project, constructed on the remnants of the pre-Columbian Aztec city and then the colonial city that followed. Here, each preserved culture is allotted its ruin—the indigenous, and specifically Aztec, civilization and the Spanish colonization—while the projected identity of contemporary Mexico is distinguished as nonruin, the culture of the future rather than the one of the past. Although damaged severely by the 1985 earthquake, the Conjunto Urbano Nonoalco Tlatelolco continues to house over fifty-five thousand residents in Mexico City. However, this tale of reinhabiting ruined spaces is not a straightforward narrative of local resistance and inventive repurposing: in the legacy of the Conjunto, extreme poverty, government inaction, and municipal neglect have contributed to the deterioration of the buildings and a high crime rate throughout the complex. The gradual ruination of the towers—the failure of Pani's project to operate as planned—illustrates the downfall of a midcentury functionalist modernizing vision: after all, "ruins work as a purulent wound in the urban fabric that poisons the monuments of progress and exposes its falseness."[20] For now, the apartment complex houses some of Mexico City's poorest inhabitants and gradually sinks into the lakebed that once supported the Aztec capital of Tenochtitlan.

When faced with a ruin, one may strive to reconstruct past imaginaries, to preserve (or in many cases, to restore) ruins so that they remain frozen in time. Indeed, conservation efforts often focus on restoring colonial architecture or pre-Columbian ruins. This prompts us to consider that the task of reconstructing ruins may often be less a matter of restoring what once was—an impossible task—than of projecting a desired future.[21] The designation of a site as a preserved ruin engenders further questions about who has access to a place, to its memories and its present uses. This selectivity has prompted a rethinking of ruin by scholars, including Gastón Gordillo, who makes a case for the disruptive potential of rubble. Rubble, Gordillo argues, is "matter that belongs to no one and to everyone"—an affirmation that will gain significance in this chapter's study of spatially ambiguous realms as universal property.[22] In his important distinction, Gordillo argues that ruins are often fetishized by elites and elitist official histories, or those who determine which spaces to celebrate as ruins and which to not. In contrast, the rubble generated by imperial and capitalist development is often averted or overlooked.[23] Similarly, it is for this reason that González-Ruibal argues that places turned to rubble offer *archein*, the freedom to begin again.[24] Indeed, contemporary ruins in particular illustrate Henri Lefebvre's spatial framework, which states that spaces must be constantly remade and actively produced in order to exist.[25] The abandonment of ruins is a necessary element in their reconfiguration; their falling into neglect a requisite for their transformation into something new.

As contemporary ruins are often repurposed to suit new ends, they function as texts from which to interpret the link between space and memory, particularly collective memory. Some of the varied ruins of contemporary Latin America include the remains of Villa Grimaldi, the torture chambers of the Pinochet regime located on the outskirts of Santiago. In her study of Villa Grimaldi—the original structure razed, and part of the site now converted into a memorial park for the victims—Diana Taylor discusses a visit to the ruined site through the lens of performance: "These stones—the 'real' thing—materialize the past. . . . We populate the space with peoples and actions as we reenact past practices, conscious that others climbed these stairs and sat where we are now sitting. . . . Physically being in the place . . . can summon up visceral connections to lives lived and lost, even to lives about which the visitors know little. But as we conjure them up, we know that they're gone, and remain there forever as gone. They allow us to forget that we too are present and absent at the same time. We come and go; the ruins (and the ghosts) remain in their still-there-ness."[26] As Taylor's comment highlights, the question of what to do with a ruin is also a question of what (and how) to remember. Indeed, in their introduction to *Telling Ruins in Latin America*, editors Michael Lazzara and Vicky Unruh write, "What might be 'our' individual and collective responsibility in the face of a ruinous past and its human fallout, particularly when complete understanding is paradoxically impossible and imperative?"[27] In this vein, it would be neglectful to discuss this topic without highlighting the positioning of these novels vis-à-vis the Brazilian military dictatorship and other authoritarian regimes that took hold in Latin America during the latter half of the twentieth century, particularly with respect to the question of collective memory and contested versions of events. Indeed, Noll's work has been examined extensively as an example of postdictatorial fiction, most notably by Idelber Avelar,[28] who identifies within *Harmada* a tortured imperative to mourn, an impetus that highlights Latin American postdictatorial literature's need to determine its position relative to the neoliberal present, while also broaching the conflicted task of grieving a traumatic dictatorial past without acquiescing to hegemonic forms of memory. As a spatial trope, ruin reminds us that confronting history is also a matter of confronting modernity: deciding what (and how) to remember while remaining afloat amid the disorienting flows of contemporary life.

The two novels I analyze in this chapter follow their protagonists across fragmented territories of memory as they struggle to lay claim to familiarity and heritage. Narrated from the in-between, both works are rife with the precarity of memory and spatial imaginaries in conflict. Indeed, these two works are scaffolded by mismatches between past and present, power imbalances, conflicting accounts, and disparate spatial imaginaries. It is in this thicket of opposing affects and inequitable forces that "bodies and buildings succumb to the same fate"[29]—hence the abandoned cars of *Teatro*'s borderlands and the impoverished, often disfigured nameless inhabitants of Harmada. Beyond the physical settings of their novels, Noll and Carvalho depict their main protagonists in a state of decline amid the rubble of identities and expired ways of life that no longer suffice. Indeed, both novels are preoccupied with their narrators' practices of excavation and reconstruction as they strive to remake personal and historical truths.

THE AMBIVALENT SPACES OF NOLL'S *HARMADA*

From the first lines of *Harmada*, readers enter a series of interconnected episodes mediated through sensory perception rather than defined geographical anchors. The unnamed main protagonist is situated outdoors, reclining on the earth: "Aqui ninguém me vê. E eu posso enfim me deitar na terra. Aproveitar a terra que virou lama depois do temporal" (Nobody sees me here. I can finally lie down on the ground. Enjoy the soil that became muddy after the storm).[30] Thus, the novel begins in a moment of solitude and contact with the organic world, significant in that it gives priority to the earth over a specific locale, the universal over the particular. These first lines also emphasize the body, which will come to play a vital role throughout the novel, as Noll highlights the deeply sensory and subjective nature of personal experiences of place. Indeed, the spatial ambiguity of this scene contrasts with its sensory specificity; the protagonist feels the ground underneath him, and the muddy earth is tangible. This moment of solitary intimacy is interrupted when a ball hits the narrator's shoulder: his first encounter with other subjectivities. The protagonist exchanges a few words with the young boy who retrieves the ball. As the story progresses, the reader learns that the two are located on the bank of a river devoid of spatial markers, entitled simply "um rio qualquer" (any river).[31] They walk along the course of the luminous body of water, eventually stopping to bathe. The narrative then moves between a series of unnamed locations, with the narrator drinking in a bar, then accompanying a lame man toward another unspecified river. These initial scenes set the stage for a story that unfolds in indistinct places, giving preference to the senses and fluid memory sequences: "Fiquei assim por algum tempo, parado pensando nos últimos acontecimentos, tentando fazer um balanço sucinto daquilo que acabara de ocorrer" (I remained like this for a while, thinking about the latest events, trying to give a short account of what had just happened).[32] Similar to the turbulent, effusive flows of the *marafona*'s narration in *Mar paraguayo*, the internal, drifting narrative of *Harmada* sweeps readers up in the ex-actor's mnemonic world.

Harmada is a largely internal work, drifting into the realms of its protagonist's consciousness without regard for the constraints of temporal or spatial linearity.

As Fermín Rodríguez eloquently notes of *Harmada*, "No hay transiciones; no hay ningún nexo narrativo entre escenas que se hacen y se disipan sin dejar rastros, como borbotones de materia líquida estallando en un caldo biótico de fuerzas elementales" (There are no transitions; there is no narrative nexus between the scenes that are made and dissipated without any trace, like gusts of liquid matter bursting into a primordial soup of elemental forces).[33] While the lack of transitions between paragraphs challenges readers, the varied episodes share an epicenter, the magnetic capital city of Harmada. It is in Harmada that the narrator comes into contact with Amanda, his short-term lover, and her newborn daughter Cristina (Cris), who will reappear later on. The hotel in which the two reside bears no specific name, nor does the street on which it is located: "Ao chegar na estrada notei lá no fundo uma construção bem iluminada nas janelas, trazendo na fachada em letras fluorescentes a palavra hotel" (When I reached the road, I noticed a well-illuminated building at the back of the windows, with the word "hotel" in fluorescent letters on the façade).[34] Here, the names of the other characters—Sandra, Amanda, Cristina, Sônia—are generic. Readers might assume they belong to a romance language, but only the circumflex accent over the letter *o* of Sônia points to Portuguese. In contrast to this nonspecificity, Noll includes pointed cultural references in this first section: for example, César Franck, a French composer whose music is mentioned in his encounter in the hotel room, and Yuri Dupont, supposedly a Russian author whose work is to debut in the theater. In this way, Noll intermingles truth and fiction, as Franck is a real-life historical figure and Dupont is not: Noll gains credibility with the reader through these factual references, only to cast a veil of mystery by fabricating other details.

Given these incongruences, the narrator is another vector of unreliability as readers are unable to trust the cultural, social, political, and spatial references that craft the intricate narrative world of *Harmada*. In constructing the novel's landscape, Noll weaves a sense of palpable ambivalence into the settings by painstakingly mingling the fictitious and the real. Readers may feel safe in assuming that the story takes place in a Latin American country, but the novel's references shed little light on a specific location. These events are coupled with place-laden geographical cues, including a soccer team called Eldorado from a city known as Chaves, one a clichéd reference to the fictional lost city of the colonial Latin American imaginary, and the second a common surname in Spanish. Importantly, Harmada's exact location is never specified. Along with the title of the work and its characters, these deliberately vague references evoke a Latin American imaginary, generalizing a few spatial markers to stand in for an entire region. In doing so, Noll problematizes the notion that globally embedded life has washed away place-bound cultural specificity, and points instead to the multiscalar, distanciated nature of ostensibly local features: as Anthony Giddens points out, the place-based permutations of the local—a shopping mall or, in this case, a soccer team—are often manifestations of distant, global processes that exist across many localities.[35] Taken in combination with his commitment to vagueness—the river is "um rio cualquier" (any river), and a bathroom is an "privada desconhecida" (unknown lavatory)[36]—Noll's narrative setting questions the basis on which local actors form affective attachments to place. This construction of a specific locale through generalizable terms fosters a disquieting mixture of familiarity and estrangement. If anything, *Harmada*'s themes provide an allegorical regional commentary on globalization, rather than a specifically Brazilian one. To reinforce this sentiment, Noll does not point to Brazil, but invents a generic set of attributes associated with a Latin American rather than a purely Brazilian imaginary. In addition to the naming practices and references just discussed, the author mentions earthquakes, pointing to possible locations including Chile and Mexico rather than Brazil (where earthquakes are rare)—a decision that further destabilizes the plot, conjuring images of rubble and devastation. Rather than conveying a unified sense of place, the novel remains staunchly nonspecific, its pages dappled with markers that signal the region's embeddedness in global phenomenological processes.

Meanwhile, Noll provides a cursory impression of the narrator's background by interspersing the narrative with various biographical reference points: his time working in the capital city of Harmada, his failed marriage to a woman named Jane, his infertility, and a homosexual encounter. In each of these mnemonic sequences, the narrative of *Harmada* is centrally focused on individual experience interpreted through physical senses and forays into memory—both mediation tactics in the face of the disruption of global modernity. This cyclical pattern is highlighted by the narrator's tendency to repeat statements throughout the novel, as if he were merely spinning his wheels in an attempt to rebuild his life. In this meandering, an unmoored internal journey, the ex-actor often evokes a boom-and-bust rhythm, as seen in his reference to a friend whose father was a man of financial highs and lows.[37] At times, the narrator brushes off tremendous losses in a single sentence. Referring to the death of his boss and departure of his wife, he notes, "Em questão de horas perco o emprego e a mulher" (In a matter of hours, I lost the job and the woman).[38] At others, he endlessly rehashes his misfortunes and errors. To that effect, David Treece writes that the ex-actor's internal and literal voyages through memory and landscape play out "as if repeated journeys were leading him via crooked paths to tread the same ground or to arrive from different directions at the same crossroads."[39] The sense of spatial ambiguity intensifies as the narrator reaches an eerie asylum for the homeless and mentally ill, in which the bulk of his story unfolds: "Depois de rondar e rondar por cômodos daquele prédio sem fim, acabei encontrando os indigentes todos que habitavam aquela casa num vasto refeitório, sentados um de cada lado junto a compridas mesas" (After prowling around rooms of the endless building, I finally found all the people who inhabited the house in a vast cafeteria, seated on either side of the long tables).[40] The asylum serves as a holding center for lives in shambles, and indeed the narrator pauses to reflect on his own "gasta meia-idade" (wasted middle age).[41] There is a sterility to this sprawling place, as the narrator is stripped of his own identity, converted into a number: "Eu usava uma pijama verde com um número no peito" (I wore green pajamas with a number on my chest).[42] Upon donning this uniform, the narrator becomes a John Doe of sorts, one patient among many. Indeed, regarding the anonymity of Noll's protagonists, Idelber Avelar writes that the absence of the proper name serves to "dissolve" the facticity of the subject, thus universalizing the ostensibly private, subjective experiences of the narrator.[43] This allegorical projection of experience is further helped by the narrator's chosen role of storyteller within the asylum, a performative tendency that I will further analyze after assessing the landscapes of *Harmada* and *Teatro*.

THE URBAN WASTELAND OF *HARMADA*

In *Harmada*, the city serves as a point of convergence for spatial ambiguity and ruin. The novel ends in a symphonic denouement that highlights the decline of both the city and the narrator. In contrast with the first part of the work, the narrator's experience in the capital is filled with affect and references to personal history, which serve to anchor an otherwise fluid narrative. The narrator configures locality through personal experience in both sections of the novel, but it is his memories of the city that further enmesh him in spatial routes from the past. At the same time, his experience in Harmada is entrenched in a sense of ambivalence about his identity, his position in the city, and his ability to survive his own literal and figurative collapse, as well as that of the capital. Indeed, critic José Castello notes that the protagonist "afoga num pântano linguístico: como entre os esquizofrênicos, seu espírito está fendido e os pensamentos o asfixiam. Harmada, a capital, vem ampará-lo nessa vagueação" (drowns in a linguistic swamp: as among the schizophrenics, his spirit is split, and his thoughts stifle him. Harmada, the capital, comes to support him in this).[44] Amid this crumbling backdrop, both the narrator and his adopted daughter, Cristina, who comes to join him in the mental hospital, encounter a sense of purpose in recovering their lost identities. They arrive by bus at night, slowly filling in the contours of Harmada, and observe "a beautiful stretch of beach" initially from a high-rise apartment.[45] From this same vantage point, the characters observe the silhouette of a crumbling city on the sea, broken and rugged: "Da área de serviço se tem uma vista ríspida de Harmada: a enseada Sul, onde o mar é oscuro, cor de barro e se abre para um horizonte rasgado, despido de ilhas" (From the service area one has a coarse view of Harmada: the south cove, where the sea is dark, mud-colored and opens to a torn horizon, stripped of islands).[46] This passage conjures a pervasive aura of austerity, as if the city with its jagged edges were a mere profile of its former self. Signs of physical decay are near ubiquitous, from the narrator's very first ventures into the capital, where he notices drug addicts congregating around the theater where Bruce and Cris later perform.[47] This narrative focus on social problems and economic stagnation persists when the narrator witnesses, for example, a long line of job applicants queuing outside a factory from the apartment window: "Vejo uma fila enorme que dobra a esquina, pelo jeito candidatos a algum emprego de uma fábrica de cofres, onde a fila começa" (I see an enormous queue, which goes around the corner, it must be candidates for some job at a safe factory, where the line starts).[48] These signs of decline—both the drug addicts and the unemployed—extend beyond material decay and speak to the social ills of economic stagnation. The city illustrates an economic deterioration that supersedes its immediate settings, linked to phenomenological processes of a failed modernization endeavor during the 1990s that permeated much of Latin America. In Harmada, supply far exceeds demand, given that the city struggles with uneven economic development and poverty. There is an eerie feeling to the nameless masses of restless bodies not dissimilar to the specters that inhabit Rulfo's Comala. Indeed, although these images of decline might be superficially read as local social problems, they inevitably speak back to global processes of industrialization that leave heterogeneous traces on the physical and phenomenological landscapes of Latin America. The scene of the queue outside the factory necessarily reminds the reader of the world outside Harmada: the city is an allegorical collision point of the forces of modernity on a particular locale, whose inhabitants emerge disoriented and unhinged, barely recognizing the once-familiar settings of the city.

Certainly, many of the descriptions of Harmada are evocative of *Pedro Páramo*, and the city appears to be haunted, filled with ghostly buildings from yesteryear, empty and dilapidated.[49] Upon viewing one of the buildings at sunrise, the narrator states, "Era madrugada, o prédio parecia morto" (It was dawn, the building looked dead).[50] At the same time, he narrates his past in Harmada as one of uninhibited decadence, reminiscing about participating in theatrical activities with Cristina and spending long nights drinking with Bruce, an old friend, while engaging in random sexual encounters. The ex-actor sits with Bruce, who recalls the day that he went into a frenzy during a long walk across the city, stripping off his clothes and covering himself entirely with soil, as if to return the rubble of his body to the earth. In their conversation, many lines of dialogue begin with repeated references to memory, as they dig up their pasts and parse the events that have led them to reunite in Harmada after years of separation.[51] In the narrative present, the ex-actor repeatedly notes the vacant state of many of the rooms and apartments he enters.[52] The barrenness inherent to unoccupied spaces is an isolation that mirrors the protagonist's emotional state. He comments to Bruce, "Ficaremos ilhados aqui" (We'll be stranded here), repeating again, "Ilhados" (Stranded).[53] Later on, in a last-ditch effort to revive himself from his shambolic life, the narrator rejects his seclusion, stressing his need to return to society in hope of self-preservation: "Eu precisaria aprender a me incluir no mundo em volta, só isso não deveria se chamar de covardia, era a única forma de me preservar" (I would have to learn to include myself in the world spinning around me, this alone should not be called cowardice, it was the only way to preserve myself).[54] Here, we notice that the narrator sees a need to revive his attachments to place in order to forcibly localize himself amid the vertigo of a world that spirals around him.

He finds stability in preserving his physical self as a means of reconciling the conflict between his decadent past life in Harmada and the state of decline that has come to bear on both the city and his own body. The corporal decline of the narrator's unkempt body is emphasized throughout, and he repeatedly mentions the sweat that drenches his clothes and the growth of his beard stubble. Upon arriving disheveled in Harmada, the ex-actor wishes to repair his teeth and purchase new clothes, discarding the clothes he received at the asylum: "Desta vez eu falo como se estivesse decidindo pela minha restauração total" (This time I speak as if I were deciding upon my total restoration).[55] Here, the narrator interprets change as a complete transformation of the self, one of body, mind, and spirit. His desire to excavate a better version of himself from the past calls on the promise of ruin as *archein*,[56] and the narrator's decline is reframed as an opportunity to begin anew. The ex-actor's need for renewal also shows his desire to connect again with others in an attempt at combatting loneliness. He goes to the dentist with the hope of allowing "novamente a [sua] língua entrar em outra boca, uma outra língua entrar na [sua] boca sem encontrar agora cáries, ruínas, falhas" ([his] tongue to enter the mouth of another again, and for another tongue to enter [his] mouth without finding cavities, ruins, flaws).[57] In this way, even the narrator's body is cast as a type of ruin to be restored. Here, the ex-actor constructs a self-portrait akin to that of a preserved ruin: like the stagnating urban landscape of Harmada, he is trapped in a state of partial decline. In one scene, the narrator watches in the mirror as a stream of blood drips from a cut on his face: "Tenho a sensação de que a minha vida parou. Aqui, sentado nesta privada desconhecida, com a cabeça para trás para estancar o sangue, tenho a sensação de que a minha vida parou" (I have the sense that my life has stalled. Here, sitting in this unknown lavatory, with my head tilted back to staunch the bleeding, I have the sense that my life has stalled). The city draws him into its web, giving him a sense of hope: "Depois de tanto tempo eu estava novamente em Harmada, e precisava fazer com que a minha vida continuasse a se dar por lá, como se ela fosse de um certo cultivo para conseguir a agilidade de se desbordar em outras ocorrências" (After all this time I was in Harmada again, and I had to continue to make my life there, as if the city allowed me to cultivate an agility that affects other happenings in my life).[58] Unlike the sterile, depersonalized stage of the mental asylum, Harmada is at the very least a place rich in human life and personal history, although these multilayered histories never match its present condition.

When the short novel draws to a close, the narrator's personal and physical decline coincides with that of the crumbling city. In the end, his efforts at self-reconstruction prove futile in the face of heavy drinking; incidences of bleeding, nausea, and vomiting; sexual exploits, including bestiality; and sleeping on the streets. These behaviors seem to be symptomatic of a more intractable problem plaguing not only the narrator but the city at large—namely, that of unemployment, poverty, and mental illness—leading the narrator down the pathway of addiction as he struggles with dangerous behavior exacerbated by his homelessness. In the end, even the magnetism of Harmada proves insufficient to support his resurrection. In the short work's final sequences, the city's decay is magnified: "As ruas pareciam ainda mais sujas do que de costume. As vezes eu precisava contornar sacos de plástico como lixo, dilacerados no meio da calçada. Em vários deles, cachorros e mendigos faziam a festa" (The streets looked even dirtier than usual. Sometimes I had to work around plastic bags and garbage tearing up the middle of the sidewalk. In several of these trash piles, dogs and beggars would party).[59] This poverty even intrudes into his personal space when the narrator finds a mute, vagabond boy sleeping in his apartment. He takes pity on the child and allows him to stay the night. Indeed, signs of decline permeate every level of space in the novel, from the phenomenological and global to the very local and intimate.

The close of this short work presents a ruination as a means of beginning anew. Gazing out the window as the sun rises over the ruined city, the narrator lets out a thin, reverberating cry, that of a ruin begging not to be abandoned: "Não me abandona, eu quero mais" (Don't abandon me, I want more), he pleads repeatedly.[60] In a clear critique of Latin America's colonial past, the novel ends shortly thereafter on the day commemorating the city's founding, which is boldly described as "a data em que um homem chega de barco numa praia" (the date on which a man arrives by boat on a beach).[61] The same young boy squatting in his apartment leads the narrator to the center of Harmada to meet the ghost of Pedro Harmada, the city's founder. The narrator imagines the founder as he stumbles onto the shore, wounded and bleeding, and decides, "Nestas terras daqui vou fundar uma cidade" (I'll found a city in these lands).[62] This scene, Noll's most unequivocal reference to Juan Rulfo's work, fittingly takes place in the old part of the city crowded with crumbling colonial buildings: "Até o fim de uma rua sem saída, na parte velha da cidade. Havia no local um prédio de três andares, escuro, muito antigo, espantosamente úmido—de algumas fendas na era vertida uma água rala e vagrosa, mas contínua" (At the close of a dead-end street, in the old part of town. There was a three-story building, dark, very old, astonishingly damp—a thin, vague but continuous stream of water leaking from the cracks in the wall).[63] Though the description of this particular building is vague at best, its location within the old town evokes images of colonial architecture and decomposing facades, and the presence of Pedro Harmada only heightens the sense that it is haunted. The water that drips from the masonry returns readers to the first lines of the story with the narrator sitting on the banks of the river, a juncture at which nature is inevitable and continuous, and the material world temporary and susceptible to decay. In the face of nature, humankind is impermanent, just as the city and the protagonist slowly crumble. In this concluding sequence, Harmada conjures images familiar to many Latin American cities, evoking the Mexico City sidewalks cracked by seismic activity, the stillness of Havana's Teatro Verdun, and the slow regrowth of the rainforest as it reclaims land cleared for rubber harvesting. This indeterminate ending reinforces the imperfect, fragmented, and cyclical nature of the novel, which has an almost centrifugal fixation on Harmada. As the wheel of the plot completes its rotation, the final lines highlight the role of ruin as the product of demolition to make way for new construction, in which the past is razed to accommodate an ahistorical present where free market economics will come to reign. Through its many fractured uncertainties, *Harmada* gestures at a particular moment in the last decade of the twentieth century, one in which Latin America is fully moved by global capital.

THE RUINED BORDERLANDS OF *TEATRO*

Rather than a pilgrimage to the capital, Bernardo Carvalho's *Teatro* focuses on an equally important spatial trope in the Latin American literary imaginary: the borderland. Carvalho engages the border as a conceptual framework to explore the division between socioeconomic and political realities, the tension between developed and developing countries, privileged and marginal languages, and the pervasive structural and interpersonal forms of violence that permeate this geopolitical space. Although readers might associate the setting of *Teatro* with U.S.-Mexico border relations, the allegorical relationships set up in the novel could serve to represent the relationship between any two countries sharing a border while facing an extreme power imbalance. Viewing *Teatro* from the lens of the U.S.-Mexico border can be helpful in engaging some of the broader discussions of this book, however. Indeed, many of the themes explored in Roberto Bolaño's fictionalized Ciudad Juárez in chapter 2, including the demonization and politicization of the border space in the era of neoliberal capitalism, continue to be relevant to our exploration of space in this novel. As Bolaño does in *2666*, Carvalho sheds light on an often disregarded demographic, those on the "wrong side of the border," making visible an often marginalized sector of Latin Americans (regardless of which border one chooses). Gloria Anzaldúa is perhaps most well known for her conceptual reworking of the border space in her now-canonical text *Borderlands*.[64] In this piece, Anzaldúa ponders the multilayered borderland between the United States and Mexico, defining the border area as one of regeneration, melding, mixing, and a complex process of acculturation. She describes the border as the product of "emotional residue of an unnatural boundary," a space constantly in flux.[65] At the same time, the borderland often fosters the emergence of new cultures, languages, and political views that are distinct from those on either side of the divide. Like all spaces, borders are not only physical but also psychological and symbolic. When speaking to the identities formed along the U.S.-Mexico border, Anzaldúa comments, "The struggle has always been inner and is played out in outer terrains."[66] This psychological component of the borderland is explored at length in *Teatro*. Carvalho uses the space of the border to ruminate on questions of identity and battles for language, voice, and power. In doing so, he investigates the complex and often contradictory experience of the dislocation that accompanies migration—an experience whose ties with ambivalence recall Sara Ahmed's assertion that returning home entails a failure of memory to match the present, "of not being inhabited in the same way by that which appears as familiar."[67] The physical space of the border thus comes to embody the displacement felt on both sides, with the protagonist of *Teatro* lacking a sense of rootedness to his place of origin, and also to the developed country in which he was raised, fitting at times into both spaces and, at times, into neither. In this way, borderland and ruin intermingle to form a spatial platform from which to explore a conflicted farrago of estrangement and belonging felt by those coming from the "wrong" side of the tracks and living in the in-between.

Much like *Harmada*, *Teatro* is a novel steeped in ambiguity, as Carvalho leaves his geographical locations largely undefined. Readers are not aware of the site of the action, and the often abbreviated names of the protagonists provide no definitive clues to their national origin: Daniel, V., N., and Ana C. As Noll does in *Harmada*, Carvalho intersperses his novel with a scant handful of real-world references, primarily locations in Europe: France (Puivert, Mirepoix, Toulouse, and Montségur), Bosnia, and Serbia. These places are portrayed as foreign and distant from the space of the borderland, allowing readers to assume that the tale does not take place in proximity to Europe. While *Harmada* constructs a series of generic indicators pointing to Latin America, *Teatro* leaves the setting of the novel unspecified save for a few general references. In fact, Carvalho eschews spatial definitions based in reality, inventing two fictitious countries, one that exists by name and another that exists by proxy: the *país das maravilhas* (country of wonders), a developed state, and its unnamed neighbor, which is described as a destitute place whose inhabitants speak a less prestigious language. *Teatro* thus takes on an allegorical quality without entering into the genre of fantasy, as local settings are constructed in generalizable terms, which leads to a sense of spatial vertigo in places that seem to be devoid of anthropological markers.[68] The erasure of geographical identifiers also removes the story from the context of Latin America or any other place, allowing for broad associations. Here, Carvalho succeeds in universalizing the particular by building the local on the back of generalizable spatial markers. The spatial nonspecificity of the novel extends beyond the ambiguous setting to the generic naming of *Teatro*'s characters: the reader rarely learns characters' last names, including that of the protagonist of the first section of the text, Daniel. Indeed, the author uses this ambiguity as a backdrop from which to explore universal themes including terrorism and the impact of trauma on the fragmentation of the psyche, as well as binaries such as sanity-insanity, poverty-wealth, and departure-return. At the same time, and in line with *Harmada*, *Teatro* engages the liminal zone between belonging and estrangement as a reflection of the experience of the ills of globalization, as its characters struggle with social isolation and extreme poverty in their nameless countries.

Like the borderland the novel explores, *Teatro* is divided into two parts: "Os sãos" (The beings), followed by "O meu nome" (My name). The novel's first part tells the tale of a retired police officer, Daniel, who claims to have verified information on a series of terrorist attacks in the *país das maravilhas*, the country to which the narrator's parents fled before his birth. In the initial sequences, readers learn that the *país das maravilhas* is also the "centro do império" (center of empire),[69] stressing the issue of hegemony in cross-border relationships. This reinforces the tale's likening to the Mexico-U.S. border, as does the description of the desert landscape between the two. In contrast with the "center of empire," the unnamed country is economically depressed and peripheral: "Atravessou a fronteira, fugindo da miséria e da insanidade de um mundo à margem" (He crossed the border, fleeing from the misery and insanity of a world on the margins).[70] Significantly, the bordering country has a ruinous, ghostly quality to it, later described as the "outro cemitério" (other cemetery).[71] As Noll does in *Harmada*, Carvalho extends this imagery at length, populating the borderland with specters, destruction, and decay: "Já aqui, do meio dos mortos, nesta imensa lata de lixo, onde despejam os restos e as misérias, posso falar" (Already here, from the midst of the dead, in this immense garbage can, where the remains and miseries are poured, I can speak).[72] Describing the country in such a state—essentially a landfill—creates a stark contrast between the developed country of wonders and its unnamed neighbor. In the land of origin, things are falling apart and death touches everyone. In the other land, marvels (*maravilhas*) are possible. At the same time, the deliberate spatial ambiguity of *Teatro* reminds us that borders, like rubble, are sites of possibility, tension, and renegotiation. Borders signify the invention of a new space with new modes of being, cultural norms unbound by the burden of strict or singular national paradigms. By freeing *Teatro*'s borderland from the constraints of local, regional, or national markers, Carvalho endows his setting with the potential for universality. The novel's borderland is made to stand in for every borderland, a strange and eerie space between wealth and impoverishment, nowhere and everywhere, the ruinous space of a region in crisis.

Readers are thus aware of the severity of the protagonist's forced return to his homeland: he must go back because of the risks associated with the information he has on the attacks, undertaking the reverse journey of his parents, an act he describes as a "volta para a periferia" (return to the periphery).[73] Here, readers receive yet another spatial reference to the core-periphery relationship as it reflects territories of empire and nonempire. The area directly along the border is desolate, laden with wreckage. As he crosses, he opts to blow up his car, erasing any trace of his journey: "Viajei durante dois dias até a fronteira, onde abandonei e explodi o carro, não antes de adulterar o número do chassi. . . . E comum encontrar carros explodidos na fronteira" (I traveled for two days to the border, where I abandoned and exploded the car, not before adulterating the number of the chassis. . . . It is common to find exploded cars on the border).[74] Not only does this explosion contribute to the devastating image of the "other side" of the border as a place in decline—in this case scattered with abandoned vehicles—but the act of erasing the number on the car's chassis eliminates its link to the protagonist. While Daniel's decision to blow up the car *proceeds from* place, following that of other actors on the borderland, his action also *creates* place: he contributes another wrecked chassis to the ruinous landscape that borders the *país das maravilhas*. Physical space and identity are intertwined, implying that crossing the border could offer up a possibility for renewal. At the same time, this section of the text reminds readers of the mutualistic relationship between place and practice. Daniel desperately clings to the limited capacity of self-enunciation to foster belonging: reinhabiting his own territory of language and retracing his parents' spatial route to the borderland (albeit in reverse).

TERROR, CONFUSION, AND THE UNRELIABLE NARRATOR IN *TEATRO*

Exploring themes similar to those of previous chapters, *Teatro* reflects on the use of writing as a way of creating, occupying, and taking up space for our marginalized narrator. Writing allows Daniel another means of building space, a way of creating and sustaining alternative versions of reality. In this way, he strives to reinscribe his subjective, local voice onto the often disillusioning experience of global, phenomenological processes. The socioeconomic disparity between the two countries in *Teatro* is impossible to ignore. Carvalho uses the spatial trope of the borderlands to highlight the connection between power and space, which is seen most clearly in the writing practices of *Teatro*'s narrator. At its core, *Teatro* recounts the story of those responsible for a series of terrorist attacks, a pair of outcasts who send a lethal powder to influential members of society in an attempt to combat the ills of neoliberal capitalism. These acts take place in the developed *pais das maravilhas*, but given the state of affairs in the country bordering it, the attacks serve as a political statement on the discrepancies between the two places, as the narrator's homeland struggles with the impact of an uneven modernization process. Thus, *Teatro* ruminates on the imbalanced nature of globalization as seen through the lens of tense border relations. Moreover, the global and local dialogue with each other through expressions of violence in the novel. The two terrorists are described as Western insiders, reclusive intellectuals on a crusade to bring justice to a systematically unbalanced power hierarchy. Curiously, the narrator is tasked with reproducing the letters from the supposed culprits. Given the challenge of identifying the terrorists, after the first attack, he is told by the police to write letters justifying the events from the perspective of the terrorist. In other words, he is tasked with reconstructing the motivations of individuals through the traces they leave on global processes. At the same time, writing offers the narrator a mechanism for ordering the world around him in order to create alternative realities and to situate himself amid them:

> Conheço todas de cor. Pesei cada frase, cada palavra. Sob as ordens dos superiores, tentei imaginar os motivos, e criei um personagem por trás dos atentados. Fui buscar no fundo da minha imaginação tudo o que não havia utilizado no meu projeto abortado de tornarme um escritor. Inventei aquele homem revoltando, louco, só. E conforme novos atentados iam occorendo, com intervalos por vezes de dois, por outras de três e até cinco anos, sem uma única palavra do verdadeiro 'terorista,' sem nenhuma manifestação daquele homem que provavelmente nada tinha a ver com o que criava, ia compondo sua personalidade em novas cartas, dando-lhe maior complexidade psicológiaca, colocando-o no centro de um teatro.[75]
>
> [I know them all by heart. I weighed every sentence, every word. Under the orders of the superiors, I tried to imagine the motives, and created a character behind the attacks. I went into the depths of my imagination of everything I had not used in my aborted project of becoming a writer. I made up that man in revolt, mad, lonely. And as new attacks took place, with intervals of sometimes two, others of three or even five years, without a single word of the true "terrorist," without any trace of that man who probably had nothing to do with what he created, I would compose his personality into new letters, giving him greater psychological complexity, placing him in the center of a theater.]

Teatro considers the notion of authorship and the lines between fact and fiction, seen here in readers' uncertainty as to whether the narrator is crafting or imitating the letters. His attention to detail regarding the psychology of the terrorists, their motives, and even the timing of the intervals between the attacks hits disturbingly close to home. The reader is left wondering whether the police may have staged the attacks and taken advantage of the imagination of a failed writer. Not only does this further confuse the lines between truth and fiction, but it also reflects the unreliability of authority (the police) in finding the true culprits. This also has consequences for the trustworthiness of the narrator, as readers are made aware of the fabrication of the letters. The final line of the passage returns readers to the title of the work and its overarching theme, the theater. Interestingly, the theater—completely manufactured, staged, and curated—is the ultimate ambivalent space, a fabrication of reality that the audience recognizes as fake but must accept as real. The stage acts as a type of borderland itself, between reality and unreality, audience and actor.

The troubling of authorship as representation is a persistent concern within Carvalho's work. Anderson da Mata has commented on these issues, stating, "As reflexões estão a todo tempo apontando para a questão da autoria, da escrita e da leitura como mecanismos de entendimento, mas frágeis a ponto de expor seu autor à confusão" (The reflections point continuously to the question of authorship, writing and reading as mechanisms of understanding, but are fragile to the point of exposing its author to confusion).[76] This fragility provides a valuable means of interpreting the delicate, shadowy world that Carvalho constructs. Readers often feel perplexed about what they are reading within a narrative structure that is disordered or mirrored. Indeed, there is a familiarity to the two-part novel, coupled with an estrangement that is not dissimilar to the destabilizing of the familiar that occurs through globalization, as the local becomes inscribed with global tensions. This sense of delirium and placelessness has profound narrative consequences. Such confusion is not exclusive to *Teatro* and can be seen in Carvalho's other works, including *Nove Noites* and *Magnólia*.[77] Similar to *Teatro*, these latter novels mirror their plotline in two halves with inverted protagonists, an inversion that allows Carvalho to ruminate on the question of narrative reliability and the subjectivity of truth. In this way, Carvalho uses writing as a means of exposing the constructed nature of all truths, and the elusive and slippery character of facts. As the line between reality and fiction blurs, narrative voices are multiplied and fractured as Carvalho describes events only to later expose their fabrication. This sense of confusion is heightened in the second section of *Teatro*, when another narrator named Daniel, a photographer, tells the story of Ana C., who has become a famous transvestite porn star with a legion of fans while residing in an insane asylum. The end of the second section leads readers to believe that Ana C. is *himself* residing in an asylum and is in fact the author of the first section, "Os sãos." This flips the story on its head, placing into question the authorship of both halves. In the end, Carvalho succeeds in creating a narrative universe in which no voice can be trusted, and in which everything, including space, is in a state of flux. In her analysis of Carvalho's work, Stefania Chiarelli describes this technique as a type of game designed to obfuscate the boundary between reality and fiction in the minds of readers to create a fictional environment in which it is impossible to establish a singular truth amid the many fabrications.[78] Pushing this argument further, I propose that Carvalho leads readers into a labyrinth in which they begin to question their own sense of logic in a story likened to a hall of mirrors. From a spatial perspective, this furthers the feeling of dislocation and estrangement, as readers are led from one ambiguous reality to another.

In an exchange that recalls themes from the first half of *Teatro*, Daniel discusses the acts of terrorism with Ana C., his ex-lover, re-encountering her in his homeland many years later. They discuss the events in detail along with the corresponding speculations in local media. Himself an aspiring author, Daniel connects writing with the creation of space, stating, "Mas as coisas vão mudando e, quando você percebe, já ultrapassou os limites que tinha estabelecido, as regras mais fundamentais, e está perdido num lugar totalmente desconhecido, para além das fronteiras, onde ainda estão para ser inventados o Norte e o Sul, o Leste e o Oeste" (But things change, and when you realize it, you have already crossed the borders you have established, the most fundamental rules, and you are lost in a totally unknown place, beyond the borders, where North and South, East and West are still to be invented).[79] Here, Carvalho speaks to the arbitrary nature of these markers, understanding geography as both written and unwritten, a metacommentary on the politics of the border spaces. The border functions as a "written" boundary between two otherwise fluid geographies, which returns us to Anzaldúa's assertion of the undetermined, transnational nature of the borderland.[80] Amid the confusion related to truth and authorship, the presumed terrorists create yet another fictionalized world: "Já tinham reinventado por completo a realidade do mundo, numa espécie de pacto implícito, estirando os limites da verossimilhança e da lógica, com o possível intuito de subvertê-la, pelo menos na cabeça de V" (They had already completely reinvented the reality of the world, in a kind of implicit pact, stretching the limits of verisimilitude and logic, with the possible intention of subverting it, at least in V's head).[81] This world becomes the microcosm the narrator reads about on the other side of the border via newspaper articles, allowing Carvalho to further multiply (and confuse) narrative perspectives.

Ultimately, the narrator resigns himself to life on the periphery, amid rubble and misery: "Embora nesta cidade tudo pareça agora tão distante, como se eu estivesse protegido, estou no meio da guerra, da miséria do mundo, que foi banida pela 'metrópole' para esta periferia onde meu pai nasceu e onde vou passar provavelmente as minhas últimas horas" (Although in this city everything now seems so distant, as if I were protected, I am in the middle of the war, the misery of the world, I was banished by the "metropolis" to this periphery where my father was born and where I will probably spend my last hours).[82] This quote highlights the complex fate of the protagonist amid the decline of the borderland that both protects him and confines his fate. Daniel recognizes that he is safeguarded within the ruins from an imminent death on the other side of the border. However, there is a sense of unrest as he is quarantined in this space, his fate sealed. As in *Harmada,* Daniel's return home does not signify a renewal; he is forced to live in the ruins of a slippery past that was never fully his. In this way, borderland and ruin work in a complementary fashion, reminding readers of the fluidity and tenuousness of identity. The novel's positioning within the borderland speaks to the relativity of truth and authoritative claims: the narrator is able to speak his truth only from the other side of the border, a space upholding an alternative set of values.[83]

LANGUAGE AS PRECARIOUS SELF-ENUNCIATION IN *HARMADA* AND *TEATRO*

The fragmentation of language in both novels contributes to the model of ruin in its many dimensions. Both main protagonists relay their stories in internal thoughts and memory sequences, and there is little dialogue with secondary figures. This entrapment in subjective experience is reflected in the structure of the works; *Teatro* and *Harmada* are both relatively short and do not contain chapter divisions. While *Teatro* is divided into two parts, each of which is essentially an uninterrupted narrative, *Harmada* is a singular story with no pointed breaks. This organization contributes to their disjointed aesthetic, which in turn bolsters the link between the conceptual construction of ruin and the fragmentation of personal histories. In his study of *Teatro,* Paulo Thomaz discusses how disintegration of language troubles our sense of narrative time and causality, leading to implausibility: "Constituem resíduos, ruínas de sentido, que intoxicam de tal maneira os vínculos de temporalidade e causalidade da narrativa que, para o leitor, acaba por colocar em risco a própria plausibilidade dos textos" (They are residues, ruins of meaning, which intoxicate the relationship between temporality and causality of the narrative in such a way that, for the reader, endangers the very plausibility of the texts).[84] The residues to which Thomaz alludes characterize both works, with the sense of narrative disintegration heightened by protagonists who spend a significant amount of time in insane asylums. Throughout Carvalho's work, readers are forced to grasp for meaning and piece together the larger puzzle. In *Teatro,* Daniel struggles to communicate in his parents' mother tongue, a language he does not fully command. As a heritage speaker, he finds his language of origin to be rudimentary, and he is unable to articulate detail. Ironically, however, Daniel is reliant on this fragmented tongue, as it allows him to tell his story without fear, protecting him from the politics of the *país das maravilhas,* where he aids police in investigating the crimes. Although the narrator stresses his poor command of the language, it ultimately works to save his life. After faking his death, Daniel decides to protect himself by telling his own story from the other side of the border in a language no longer his own:

> Nasci e cresci do outro lado da fronteira que o meu pai atravessou na calada da noite com a minha mãe grávida para viver no "centro do império," ela dizia, e agora eu entendo. A mesma fronteira que tive que atravessar de volta para falar essa língua que ele havia abandonado ao decidir viver lá, embora comigo ainda tentasse usá-la, e que aos poucos compreendeu ser a sua única esperança e o último vestígio da sua identidade, a única herança que podia me deixar.[85]
>
> [I was born and raised across the border that my father crossed in the dead of night with my pregnant mother to live in the "center of empire," she would say, and now I understand. The same border that I had to cross back to speak the language he had abandoned in deciding to live there, although I still tried to use it, and that little by little he understood to be his only hope and the last vestige of his identity, the only heritage that he could leave me.]

Daniel's return to his heritage language highlights his struggle to resist linguistic, cultural, and political hegemony. Recalling the role of language in the texts explored in chapter 1, Daniel's mother tongue serves as a territory of belonging, mapping his experiential paths across space and time. However, Daniel's tenuous and imperfect grasp of the language highlights his conflicted perspective on the estrangement that accompanies transnational migration. The narrator mentions on numerous occasions that, at least on this side of the border, "posso falar" (I can speak).[86] Language also comes to mark the border between sanity and insanity in *Teatro*, as the narrator remarks that his words will be perceived as heresy or even lunacy, words that would "cairia no ridículo e no vazio" (fall into ridicule and emptiness), ultimately transforming him into a sedated, walking dead man.[87] Language is frequently inaccessible and cumbersome in *Teatro*: to that effect, Chiarelli notes that language operates as a metaphor for the impossibility of integration in the text.[88] Indeed, concluding *Teatro* in the strange space of an asylum reminds readers that insanity is perhaps the place of ultimate isolation, as it makes reliable human communication impossible.

Language use is linked to performance, with the role of the theater—the stage itself an ambiguous, malleable space—providing a means of reconstructing the ruins in both *Harmada* and *Teatro*. Indeed, there is an austerity in the settings and dialogues of both novels that is evocative of contemporary performative realms with spaces that feature an economy of artifacts, as if they are what might remain after a storm, after all embellishment is removed, not unlike Àlex Rigola's staging of *2666* explored in chapter 2. These items might include a bed, an empty apartment, a barren room. This same economy of things is mirrored in the language of the texts, which are often written in short declarations, fragments lacking elaboration and with deliberately vague lexicography. The concept of the stage is further echoed in the structure of *Teatro*'s plot: the entire novel operates as a stage, and the second section is narrated as an inversion of the first. The work's title does not disappoint, given that readers enter into the performance of this dialectic in the two halves of the work. If we consider the text as a theater in and of itself, the protagonists are converted into actors and all language becomes performative. In *Harmada*, the space of the stage is also fundamental, playing out in unofficial narration and storytelling, and also in the literal stage of theatrical performances. Aside from the main protagonist of *Harmada*, several of the novel's secondary characters—such as Cristina and Bruce—are also actors. Even when not intentionally acting, the narrator's speech has a playful spontaneity to it that emphasizes its performativity. Particularly in the asylum, where he gives his daily performances, the jobless actor becomes a type of puppet, a showman.

The barren setting of the asylum contrasts with the narrator's desire to perform, and his subjective voice becomes a powerful cue for the specific amid the ambiguous. Shortly after his arrival, he conducts daily performances for fellow inmates, recounting lengthy stories and personal tales. Interestingly, these monologues often burst forth from the narrator as if he had no control over his own words, revealing the limits of language:

> Eu, bem na verdade, jamais preparava as narrativas que desembocavam pela minha boca. O rumo do desenrolar das tramas se dava só ali, no ato de proferir a ação. Aliás, detestava pensar previamente acerca do que teria a contar. Eu me deixava conduzir pela fala, apenas isso, e esta fala nunca me desapontou, ao contrário, esta fala só soube me levar por inesperados e espantosos episódios.[89]
>
> [I, in fact, never prepared the narratives that flowed through my mouth. The course of the unfolding of the plots occurred only there, in the act of uttering the action. In fact, I hated to think about what I would have to say in advance. I let myself be led by speech, just that, and this speech never disappointed me, on the contrary, this speech only managed to lead me through unexpected and astonishing episodes.]

Here, the reader is startled by the involuntary quality of these performances, whose impulsive spontaneity suggests the speaker does not have full control over his words. Regardless of the ad hoc nature of these tales, the narrator hints at his underlying desire to voice his experiences and connect with those around him through spontaneous play.

> Pois é, eu fui um artista, um ator de teatro. E, de lá para cá, desde que abandonei ou fui abandonado pela profissão, não sei, desde então já não consigo mais fazer

> qualquer outra coisa . . . tudo aquilo que eu faço é como se estivesse representando, entende? Se pego uma pedra aqui e a levo até lá me dá um negócio por dentro, como se fosse trilhões de vezes mais pesado carregar esta mentira de carregar a pedra do que a própria pedra, não sei se você me entende, mas o caso é grave, acredite. . . . Eu e você aqui sabe?, tudo isto que estou a te falar, não acredite em nada, é uma repelente mentira, eu não sou de confiança, não, não acredite em mim.[90]
>
> [Well, I was an artist, a theater actor. And from then on, since I left or was abandoned by my profession, I don't know, since then I cannot do anything else . . . everything I do is as if I were acting, you see? If I take a stone here and put it there, it gives me a business inside, as if it were trillions of times heavier to carry this lie of carrying the stone than the stone itself, I do not know if you understand me, but the case is serious, believe me. . . . I and you are here, you know? All this I'm telling you, don't believe any of it, it's a repellent lie, I'm not trustworthy, no, do not believe me.]

In this fragment, readers are struck by the burden that speech becomes for the narrator. He likens his own voice to the carrying of a heavy stone, as he must constantly perform a lie. In fact, even as he is speaking, he tells readers to discredit him. The disassociation between language, identity, and voluntary thought further marginalizes the narrator, as he becomes trapped in his own performance. The narrator's performances have a quality of fabrication, as if in his forays into memory he tries to claim pieces of the rubble and reassemble them into a coherent narrative by telling stories: "que eu dizia serem episódios vividos ou testemunhados por mim" (that I said were episodes lived or witnessed by me).[91] Here, the ex-actor acts as an unreliable curator, preserving the ruins of the past through memory-laden performances while betraying the shaky scaffolding of his expressive project.[92] In his analysis of Carvalho's work through a Walserian interpretation of history, Caio Yurgel's description of Carvalho's protagonists recalls the ex-actor's desperate attempts at self-enunciation in Noll's *Harmada*: "These individuals are pure language. Their actions are doomed. . . . The landscape upon which they walk is undoing itself, and they have no control over it. If the sun cannot be rushed across the globe, if every day is destined to start five or six hours too late, then maybe a few well-placed words might buy them some extra time. But even at their very best words can only mitigate a problem, delay so slightly the inevitable."[93] Yurgel's comment highlights the relentless struggle of Noll's and Carvalho's protagonists to construct a world in which they fit comfortably, or at least one in which they have some semblance of control over their fates: yet in both novels, these attempts are marred acquiescence and hopelessness. In this way, in both *Teatro* and *Harmada*, the reader is tasked with sifting through contradictory information at every turn in a hunt for fragments that might piece together a comprehensible story. Thus, even our reading of the texts can be likened to the reconstruction of a ruin, sifting through the rubble of disparate accounts and ambiguous places. Indeed, in line with this performativity, the novels become theaters of their own making, austere and ruinous structures for the staging of lives in flux.

CONCLUSIONS

The spatial ambiguity of *Teatro* and *Harmada* fosters a profound feeling of ambivalence for both the protagonists and the reader, who remain caught between a sense of familiarity and foreignness, a reflection of local lives increasingly shaped by global processes.[94] On the one hand, the lack of place-based particularity leaves the settings of *Harmada* and *Teatro* sufficiently open so as to belong to anyone, but for this same reason they are imbued with a sense of estrangement: everyone could belong there, but nobody does. There is a familiarity to these strange narrative worlds, but also a disaffection, an inability to truly connect or relate with them. In his writing on the role of nonspaces in the ideological construction of globalization, Eduardo Grüner writes,

> Es el movimiento "alegórico" que corresponde a sociedades como las nuestras, a las que la colonización hizo perder su sentido originario y al mismo tiempo impidió la construcción de uno nuevo, propio y autónomo, y que ahora es necesario reconstruir, incluso inventar, sobre el paisaje ruinoso.[95]

> [It is the "allegorical" movement that corresponds to societies like ours, those that colonization robbed of their original meaning and simultaneously interfered with the construction of new, autonomous signifiers, and that now must reconstruct, and even invent, such meanings onto the ruinous landscape.]

The invisible yet profoundly affective forms of ruin arise at the expiration (or even destruction) of a way of life, or more specifically, of a mode of inhabiting a place. When confronted with the disorienting forces of modernity, local protagonists return to subjective experience and self-enunciation as they strive to rebuild themselves amid the rubble. Perhaps it is for this reason that both *Harmada* and *Teatro* present protagonists trapped in cycles of ruination and attempted reconstruction, as the anonymous narrator of *Harmada* digs through shared memories with old friends and performs stories from his past in front of the residents of an asylum, or the narrator of *Teatro* forges the underlying motivations of terrorist attacks committed through the postal service.

These novels reflect their timeframe in Latin America during the 1990s, a decade in which the region would be increasingly confronted with the discontents of neoliberalism, as it was further thrust into the global marketplace. Both the metropolis of Harmada and the land bordering the *país das maravilhas* are places challenged by boom-and-bust cycles of economic growth and collapse. Perhaps for this reason, critically interpreting ruin presents a task of layering instabilities to expose the dynamic destruction and reconstruction of intangible and physical places. This ruin is mirrored in the works' main protagonists, both of whom struggle with isolation and perhaps even delusion, translating to a steady erosion of narrative reliability. However, it is significant that this overwhelming struggle with dislocation and ambivalence is most often mediated through language: much like the polyphonic narrative of Wilson Bueno's *marafona* in *Mar Paraguayo*, performance (in the case of *Harmada*) and writing (in the case of *Teatro*) become mechanisms for the expression of marginalized bodies and voices, as the narrators attempt to fit their subjectivities within new and unstable worlds.

4 · ANOTHER CITY AND ANOTHER LIFE

Writing Multitudes in Valeria Luiselli's *Los ingrávidos*

Nueva York es una teoría de ciudad construida sólo en función del tiempo, Manhattan es una hora, o un siglo, con la polilla de los *subways* barrenándola, comiéndosela segundo tras segundo.

[New York is a theory of a city built on the foundation of time alone. Manhattan is an hour, or a century, with the woodworm of the *subways* boring through it, eating it away, second by second.]

—Gilberto Owen to Celestino Gorostiza, 18 September 1928

Like an old house, the narrative structure of Valeria Luiselli's novel *Los ingrávidos* is filled with trapdoors and crawlspaces. In her playful literary world, the author ruminates on familiarity, belonging, and home as well as the importance of writing as a mode of occupying other spaces and temporalities. Given that the central goal of *Latin American Literature at the Millennium* is to illuminate narrative engagements with contemporary experiences—local musings on global processes—it is apt to end the book with a novel overtly preoccupied by textual practices. *Los ingrávidos* offers an extended commentary on the role of language in constructing worlds through writing, reading, and translating. The struggle for self-enunciation—a core preoccupation of the ruined protagonists of chapter 3—comes to the fore in *Los ingrávidos,* since writing is cast as a means of producing and occupying space. To discuss the spaces of Luiselli's novel is to highlight the careful construction of its architecture: the novel operates as an accordion with narrative pleats for readers to unfold.[1] Throughout, Luiselli ruminates transparently on the process of constructing textual worlds, offering glimpses into the painstakingly scaffolded architecture that gives readers the impression of serendipity. Readers encounter spatial and temporal coincidences that draw the translator closer to the ghostly figure of the poet Gilberto Owen, while the narrators' metatextual reflections serve as disclosures of their own unreliability. *Los ingrávidos* is dense with the multitudes referenced in this chapter's title—a word that here encompasses the fracturing and multiplying that emerges from the novel's plurality of narrators, narrative truths, and geographic settings. Beyond the physical locations of Mexico City, New York, and Philadelphia, the spatial construction of the novel unfolds in textual games that Luiselli designs to integrate her protagonists' lives together across shifting localities. Beyond the significance of its urban settings, *Los ingrávidos* is not about a specific locale, but rather a treatise about the experience of inhabiting place—and creating reality through narrating place—in a world populated by other people. Luiselli's readers, like her protagonists, transit the shared space of the subway with hundreds of other people, each of whom enters and exits the platform with a vastly different worldview, having patterned their own subjective experiences onto the affective canvas of public space. It is here that Luiselli's work reckons with the multiple and iterative nature of locale, as her characters write and rewrite their presence in the world as they cobble together stories about their own lives and those of others.

In a work that travels back and forth across space and time, writing becomes a means of taking up space as well as a mode of constructing possibilities. Luiselli establishes a mutualistic relationship between her musings on locality and textuality within the novel, thus creating polyvocal representations of urban life that remain open to further intervention. In this way, writing operates as a means of layering experiences of place and parsing their inconsistencies, revealing an understanding of the local as an open, multilayered process rather than a bounded space of interaction. These deeply affective engagements with what it means to inhabit a city highlight the impact of mobility, liminality, and heterogeneity in configuring contemporary representations of place. In order to engage these questions, I call on the works of Doreen Massey and Yi-Fu Tuan to theoretically orient questions of space and place inherent to the novel. There are few metaphors better suited to describe these narrative tropes than those that Luiselli herself weaves into the text: the aftershocks of an earthquake, the shuttling back-and-forth of a subway train, the reconstruction of a stranger's life through biographical factoids scribbled on sticky notes. This is part of the challenge of studying a text like *Los ingrávidos*, whose narrators are so disarmingly willing to reveal the novel's secrets that literary critics may find themselves at a loss. Reaching the dense, porous heart of the novel seems an impossible task hindered by the sinking realization that an analysis of this text may suffer the same fate as any attempt to represent the totality of contemporary life: an incomplete portrait akin to the blurry reflection of one's face in a train window, superimposed over the visage of another person passing on another train. With these reservations, however, this chapter offers an examination of the narrative scaffolding of *Los ingrávidos*, followed by a study of Luiselli's techniques for opening textual space to allow multiple perspectives to accumulate in the formation of narrative place. I conclude with an examination of *retelling* as a vehicle for constructing malleable representations of the local as a heterogeneous process. The novel is a joyous hide-and-seek, and its focus on textual mediations of reality provides a resonant conclusion to my study of contemporary narrative's engagement with unprecedented global connectivity.

SCAFFOLDING MULTITUDES

Los ingrávidos is a polyvocal narrative in which two protagonists are split into four narrators. The first voice is a writer and mother working on her novel while seemingly confined to a house in Mexico City, who quickly writes another narrator into the story. We understand this second narrator to be the former's younger self, a translator working for a small publishing house in Harlem. At the core of the plot is another game of sorts, as the young woman hunts for traces of Gilberto Owen, a little-known Mexican poet and member of the Los contemporáneos group, whose work she wishes to translate and thus rescue from literary obscurity. Eventually, Owen enters the work as a protagonist in his own right and assumes the primary narrative voice. However, even this voice is fractured, as there are in fact two Owens speaking: a young clerk working for the Mexican consulate in New York during the Harlem Renaissance, and a much older Owen grappling with cirrhosis, divorce, and poverty in Philadelphia. The splitting of narrative voices and micronarrative format of the novel allow Luiselli to layer multiple iterations of place, while the presence of disparate narrative voices evokes the vignette style of other works examined in this book, particularly *2666*. Luiselli's life, much like her body of work, has often centered on transnational movement, as she moved from Mexico City to several different countries and back again before settling in New York City. At its core, *Los ingrávidos* is also a tale of migration, that of a young Mexican woman who seeks work in New York, eventually returning to Mexico City and looking back on her life abroad. Similarly, Owen's spatial routes from New York to Philadelphia, as well as his recollections of Bogotá and his Mexican origins, provide ample context for this chapter's discussion of spatial and temporal movement. The spatial representations of *Los ingrávidos* allow us to reflect on the task of translation, of a self as much as a text, across contexts in a globalized world, leaving multiple versions—former selves—behind in other locales. In her study of the novel, Regina Cardoso Nelky writes, "Nada es estable ni definitivo, la movilidad es una característica del ser humano contemporáneo"

(Nothing is stable or definitive, mobility is a characteristic of the contemporary human being).[2]

It is safe to say that hypermobility was on Owen's mind when he arrived in New York just before the stock market crash of 1929. His letters from the period—some of which make their way into Luiselli's novel—reflect a profound concern for the rapid pace of urban life, and a sense of disorientation in his surroundings, as the epigraph of this chapter highlights. In an early fragment of *Los ingrávidos,* the narrator notes that Owen's poetry gave the impression that he hated New York, that he was on the margins of the literary and cultural boom of the Harlem Renaissance.[3] In short, she attests that Owen was, or at least that he felt like, a person out of place. *Los ingrávidos*' narrator juxtaposes Owen's sense of placelessness with her own displacement in her process of narrative recuperation. As she struggles to write the story of her own pursuit of Owen, the novelist-narrator admits, "No puedo escribir esta historia como yo quisiera—como si todavía ahí y fuera sólo esa otra persona—. Me cuesta hablar de calles y de caras como si aún las recorriera todos los días. No encuentro los tiempos verbales precisos" (I can't write this story the way I would like to—as if I were still there, still just only that other person. I find it difficult to talk about streets and faces as if I saw them every day. I can't find the correct tenses).[4] By offering this unveiled commentary on her craft, the narrator places her own reliability into question, forcing the reader to grapple with the very textuality of the novel and sparking a general mistrust of the narrator—the reader knows, ostensibly, what she is up to, yet is at the mercy of what she chooses to disclose. Indeed, Luiselli's novel is rife with metatextual reflection, as she reveals the deliberation of her practices to the reader through her narrators' digressions and amendments.[5]

The key to the permeable, multilayered local renderings of Luiselli's narration lies in piecing together this *elaboración posterior* (later elaboration). In crafting her story of Owen's years in New York, and her own time spent pursuing him, the narrator calls repeatedly on other times and places, opening the text to distant influences and allowing other voices to filter into the places of her narratives as she gathers the details from Gilberto Owen's documents and letters, fragments of which are interspersed throughout the novel. Although the translator's curiosity is piqued by the little that is known about Owen's time in New York, rather than limiting herself to these historical events, she collects his personal notes, poetry, and biography, which she fabricates, rearranges, and exaggerates.

To illustrate this process, it is helpful to examine the young translator's approach to approximating Owen's experience of New York in line with recent work in the field of human geography on the experience of place. During a conversation with her neighbor, the young translator comments,

> Aunque Owen dejó cartas, algunas entradas de diarios y un puñado de buenos poemas, se sabe poco de su estancia en Nueva York. Se sabe, por ejemplo, que vivió en un viejo edificio de Harlem frente al parque Morningside y que, en esos mismos años, del otro lado del parque, Lorca estaba escribiendo *Poeta en Nueva York*.[6]
>
> [Although Owen left letters, some diary entries, and a handful of good poems, little is known of his period in New York. It is known, I told Salvatore, that Owen lived in an old Harlem building opposite Morningside Park and that during those very years, on the other side of the park, Lorca was writing *Poet in New York*.][7]

This remark offers a first glimpse into the way that Luiselli presents local places in her multivocal novel. Here, the invocation of Morningside Park does not highlight the significance of the park as a physical or historical landmark—rather, it acquires meaning from the overlaps and contacts that happen there, as a place where paths intersect and experiences are layered atop one another. Luiselli's novel encourages the reader to consider narrative settings as intersections of disparate experiences of local place. Seen from this perspective, Morningside Park is a site of affective processes: it is where Federico García Lorca wrote *Poeta en Nueva York* (*Poet in New York*) to capture his sense of alienation while witnessing the stock market crash, where Gilberto Owen lived in a sparsely furnished room and wrote endless letters to his correspondents in Mexico about the time-space vertigo of city life—and much later, where Luiselli herself passed by as a doctoral student at Columbia University. As I will discuss, the novel's traversals of New York further give preference to the patterning of lived experience over fixed geographic coordinates and earth-and-asphalt renderings of locality;[8] indeed the permeable settings of *Los ingrávidos* serve as meeting points between characters rather than determinant anchors.

This approach to local place evokes many of the theoretical contributions of human geographer Doreen Massey, who has emphasized an extroverted, open understanding of *place as process* rather than as a bounded entity of contained interactions: "What gives a place its specificity is not some long internalized history but the fact that it is constructed out of a particular constellation of social relations, meeting and weaving together at a particular locus. . . . Each 'place' can be seen as a particular, unique point of their intersection. It is, indeed, a meeting place."[9] In line with Massey's commentary on place, what we understand as *local* is constituted by the intersections of paths, by the people who populate a place and act within it. Here, the emphasis is on the proximity of lived physical spaces, another manifestation of Luiselli's focus on experience. The narrator endows her spatial routes with meaning based on their intersections with those of other people, particularly Owen. These contacts with other lives—or the possibility of such contacts—drive forward her search to understand Owen, while also blurring the boundaries and revealing the impossibility of representing a singular life or locality without leaving room for the intrusion of other places and perspectives. The novelist reconstructs the landscape of Owen's Harlem Renaissance–era New York and immerses herself in a web of possible literary encounters, eventually going so far as to forge the translations of his poems in the name of another author.[10] These literary figures, among them Federico García Lorca and Nella Larsen, emerge as characters in their own right when Owen assumes the primary narrative voice and traverses—in another time—the same physical spaces as the young translator.[11] The two come into contact through chance encounters that occur in passing, plausibly deniable and evocative of the work's title: each is but one of many faces in the crowd, and their contacts are made visible only through the retellings of place from different perspectives.[12] As such, Luiselli's ruminations on the construction and collapse of material and literary worlds highlight the permeability of the locale, the other times and spaces that trickle into a place through the shared routines of daily life and the voices of past inhabitants.

CLEARING NARRATIVE SPACE

Luiselli's fascination with writing as an architectural process has precedent in several of her earlier works, including the essay "Relingos: The Cartography of Empty Spaces" in her collection *Sidewalks*.[13] Pondering Mexico City's many *relingos* (patches of unused or leftover space), Luiselli describes the act of writing as "an inverse process of restoration" rather than as one of filling in the gaps of an established structure. Like a stonemason, "a writer starts from the fissures and the holes"—a task more akin to the work of an architect. Thus, a writer becomes a person who "distributes silences and empty spaces." Luiselli writes, "writing: making relingos."[14] This dedication to writing as a matter of broadening fissures, of opening a story to let in new voices, further preoccupies the narrator's early musings in *Los ingrávidos,* as she composes her novel from Mexico City: "I need to generate a structure full of holes so that I can always find a place for myself on the page, inhabit it; I have to remember never to put more in than is necessary, never overlay, never furnish or adorn. Open doors, windows. Raise walls and demolish them."[15] Notably, this commitment to opening space contrasts with the physical settings of the narrator in Mexico City, who seems to be trapped in her own home. Throughout *Los ingrávidos,* her writing is further disrupted by her husband's intrusions into the text. Indeed, he reads the pages she has written and asks probing questions about her time in New York, often expressing discomfort at what her narrative of the past might reveal about their present. However, at the exposition, these intrusions are often coded in terms of domestic and maternal obligation, with abundant barriers to writing all around her, including diapers, toy cars, and Transformers.[16] A little later, she again highlights this intrusion in the context of the mental space needed for writing, pushing the physicality of narrative space: "Las novelas son de largo aliento. . . . Yo tengo una bebé y un niño mediano. No me dejan respirar. Todo lo que escribo es—tiene que ser—de corto aliento. Poco aire" (Novels need a sustained breath. . . . I have a baby and a boy. They don't let me breathe. Everything I write is—has to be—in short bursts. I'm short of breath).[17] Although she never leaves the house, much of this narrator's time is spent looking out the window, standing at the threshold of the front door to whistle to the tamale seller in the evenings and waving through the window to her neighbors. Despite her confinement, the outside world leaks into the house through the water dripping through the cracks in the walls and the radio of the construction workers next door, which tells of an earthquake and electoral fraud in Asia, a mass grave discovered in Tamaulipas.

In contrast, the young translator's New York City apartment is seemingly liberated from the fixedness traditionally associated with place. "It all began in another city and another life,"[18] writes the novelist in Mexico City, as she lays the foundation for another situated narrative voice. She emphasizes the barrenness of her apartment, which contains only five permanent pieces of furniture and a rotating cast of houseplants and library books. Against this empty canvas, the narrator writes in order to weave her body syntactically into the world she inhabits: "Cuando alguien ha vivido solo durante mucho tiempo, el único modo de constatar que sigue existiendo es articular las actividades y las cosas en una sintaxis compartible: esta cara, estos huesos que caminan, esta boca, esta mano que escribe" (When a person has lived alone for a long time, the only way to confirm that they still exist is to express activities and things in an easily shared syntax: this face, these bones that walk, this mouth, this hand that writes).[19] The focus on writing and walking as means of patterning space with personal experience is echoed repeatedly throughout the novel and provides a basis for understanding the translator's approach to inhabiting the city. Indeed, the young translator imbues public spaces with a depth of meaning conventionally assigned to more private places, including streets and subway stations.[20] The translator's focus on shared public spaces recalls Michel de Certeau's attention to the way that different actors endow the same place with multiple forms of meaning. Certeau explores the act of walking and being part of the city, a public place that he describes as multiple, social, and experiential, though ultimately "lacking a place" and always in search of itself.[21] Certeau goes on to argue that the relationships and intersections in the city weave together to form an urban fabric, which he argues is "a universe of rented spaces haunted by a nowhere or by dreamed-of places."[22] Just as a street could be transformed in the young translator's mind by the recitations of a particular poet, the narrator evokes Certeau in crafting an entire universe out of connections and subjective spatial routes that are built from thoughts and experiences in geographic locations. The young translator often occupies spaces that are not her own, turning them into zones not codified by the affect traditionally associated with place.

One striking example is when the young woman allows others to enter into her New York City apartment, bedfellows from across town in a similar predicament of loneliness. In doing so, she converts what would otherwise have been a closed space, the space of her home, into one of transit, a realm designated for the late-night comings and goings. The young woman narrates an entire ecosystem of interchangeable apartments with corresponding keys, through which people would circulate, spending the night in shared beds and rooms on borrowed furniture.[23] While it is unclear what exactly goes on in these rotating apartments—the narrator gestures at sexual contact but is vague in her wording—she portrays her apartment and those of others as a singular place with a revolving door, unsettling the boundary between public, shared zones and ostensibly personal or private spaces: for example, we can look to Yi-Fu Tuan's assertion that "from the security and stability of place we are aware of the openness, freedom, and threat of space, and vice versa."[24] Following Tuan's argument, the narrator's flexible approach to inhabiting unfamiliar spaces is a direct affront to the notion of place as secure, closed, and stable. It is rewritten and transformed, rather, into realms that are open, free, unstable, and in motion because of the bodies that enter with varying degrees of anonymity. However, the sharing of apartments also speaks to an overwhelming need for human presence as a form of anchoring—one that trumps both privacy and arguably personal safety, while also troubling the classic distinction between fixed place and open space. At times, this association creates a kind of spatial and discursive liberty for the young translator, who mentions that she sleeps better in other people's beds and takes great joy in returning to the street the next morning to buy a coffee and read a newspaper in the morning sunlight.[25]

In some ways, the presence of other beings in the home turns a place associated with rootedness into a zone of transit. However, that same presence becomes, at times, stifling: in one fragment, for example, the young translator flees to Philadelphia when a friend and a former lover take up residence in her apartment for the weekend.[26] Rather than through location, the places of the novel are oriented through the lens of experience and proximity to the affective spaces of other people, as the young translator maps the city through fleeting stays in others' apartments. This repurposing of others' spaces is echoed in her gleeful acquisition (in some cases, theft) of objects—a chair stolen from the editorial office, and a writing desk found on a sidewalk. While searching through the Hispanic studies archives at Columbia University, she learns that Gilberto Owen lived just a few blocks away from her apartment. Upon visiting the address, the young translator finds a dead orange tree on the rooftop of Owen's former apartment building. Recalling that Owen had mentioned having a similar tree in one of his letters, she takes the lifeless plant home and continues to water it, hanging on to it after she disposes of all her other furnishings.[27] This act marks an important rupture in the boundaries of representation in the novel—fictional and real, dead and alive, material and immaterial—creating an otherwise impossible contact zone. While the reader and the translator herself are aware of the absurdity of the idea that the tree could have belonged to Owen, they gleefully surrender their disbelief in order to open up further possibilities of contact between the translator and her quarry. Indeed, whether the plant belongs to Owen or not, the young translator's use of borrowed and stolen objects may allude to a commentary on writing and translation, which inevitably involve borrowing and repurposing the words and ideas of others, even if only to move them from one language to another.

The task of bringing protagonists into contact with one another dominates Luiselli's novel, as her careful construction of serendipitous contact zones recalls Álex Rigola's use of a treadmill in his adaptation of Robert Bolaño's *2666* to align the mysterious writer Archimboldi with protagonists from his past, including those who pursued him. Beyond her opening of private spaces, the young woman engages liminal spaces as zones of narrative contact that operate as meeting points between protagonists. The metro offers a perfect liminal space for these encounters, as a contained yet mobile space of infinite possible encounters. Luiselli writes,

> Conocí a Moby en el metro. Y aunque ésa sea la verdad, no es verosímil, porque la gente normal, como Moby y yo, no se conoce nunca en el metro. Podría escribir, en vez: conocí a Moby en la banca de un parque. . . . Lo previsible es que la banca se imagina verde y de madera. Entonces debo escribir, por artificio: Moby estaba leyendo un periódico en una de las bancas de cemento blancas, un poco despostilladas, del parque Morningside. Eran las diez de la mañana y el parque estaba casi vacío, como la palabra "parque" y la palabra "banca."[28]
>
> [I write: I met Moby on the subway. And though that is the truth, it's not really credible, because normal people, like Moby and I, never meet on the subway. Instead, I could write: I met Moby on a park bench. A park bench is any park, any bench. . . . Typically, the bench would be green and made of wood. So, not to be predictable, I should write: Moby was reading a newspaper on one of the white, slightly battered concrete benches in Morningside Park. . . . It was 10 a.m. and the park was almost empty, like the word *park* and the word *bench*.][29]

The meaning of the park bench, Luiselli implies, is the people who sit on it, the conversations they have, the daily life they witness as they watch the world go by. Here, the narrator's imprinting of experience onto public spaces recalls Tuan's canonical work on the role of experience in differentiating place from space. Tuan argues that as one gets to know a place better and imbue it with meaning, differentiated from the mobility of space, place becomes an interlude or a "pause."[30] Tuan's discussion of pauses in movement highlights the power of overlapping experiences to render a local specificity out of formerly undifferentiated space. Similarly, the *local* dimension of the metro—and perhaps the feature that lends it a certain flair for creative liberty—is not the location of the tunnels and trains, but the social order of their routes, the people who get on or off at certain stops, the chance encounters that occur when shuttling passengers from place to place beneath the city.

It is useful to recall here Pierre Bourdieu's assertion that a life should be studied as "a ride on the metro," paying attention to not only the ride itself but the tunnels, the stations, the workings of the train.[31] Riding the metro is a practice that puts us into contact with other subjectivities, other ways of seeing and being seen, that inevitably become part of the accumulated affective social relations of a local place, even a liminal transit passage such as a subway train. The communal and liminal features of many public spaces also echo Gayatri Chakravorty Spivak's work on translation. Spivak notes that translation, a matter of working with a language that "belongs to many others," provides a means of circumnavigating the confines of identity in writing. Translation, she says, is a "simple miming of the responsibility to the trace of the other in the self."[32] In bringing a text across, the translator must negotiate meanings within a liminal zone between self and other. In a similar vein, Sarah K. Booker notes in her examination of the role of the translator in *Faces in the Crowd* that the narrator is primed for melding into her subject, given her namelessness.[33] Indeed, neither her younger self in New York nor her older self who is a new mother in Mexico City is a named protagonist, giving her a marked anonymity in contrast to the often referenced poet, Gilberto Owen. Booker has interpreted this namelessness as an homage to the invisibility of the translator, whose identity often gets buried below that of an author, rarely exalted.[34] In her study of the role of the translator in *Los ingrávidos*, Booker also notes that the metro itself acts as a compelling analogy for the process of translation: "The New York subway . . . serves as a means of spatial and temporal transportation and urban connection, but is located underground, or out of sight. In its displacement, the train itself—like the translator—disappears."[35]

In her fixation on the metro, Luiselli echoes many of Owen's own musings on the social mores of 1930s New York, particularly in his letters to Areceli Otero:

> No soy egoísta, no ronco y no atropello a las gentes sino a la entrada del subway. . . . Es todo Nueva York. Es lo más monstruoso, lo más duro, lo más bestial. Gentes que los domingos van sin falta a sus iglesias, (católicas, judías, budistas,

todos); gentes que en el Home no son sino más bien corteses y educados, se vuelven fieras en las estaciones del subway.[36]

> [I'm no egoist, I don't snore or trample over people except at the subway entrance. . . . And that's just New York. It's the most monstrous, most rough, most beastly. People who go to church on Sunday without fail (Catholics, Jews, Buddhists, all of them); people who at home could not be more polite and courteous, become rabid in the subway stations.]

As Owen's comment highlights, the metro offers a place to look beyond the metro, toward a multiplicity of experiences that lead out of the stations and along the diverse spatial routes of a city's inhabitants. Similarly, commenting on the need for a "global sense of local, a global sense of place,"[37] Massey writes of the necessity of factoring the openness of a given locale, the many comings and goings of its inhabitants and its constant reconstitution, into the way we consider place. Urban travel—and accordingly, the patterning of space through mobility—reveals infinite and undeniably rich social relations that make up the fabric of social life. However, they also point beyond a bounded understanding of the local, as they move people and objects across and outside the boundaries of a given place, highlighting the openness of both the places of the subway and Luiselli's narration. The tracks of Line 1 of the subway, spanning the length of Manhattan, extend, for instance, also beyond the length of this story.[38] In this way, Luiselli further opens her narrative settings, inviting distant influences to enter her story while she pointedly notes the limits of her narration. In the parks and subway stations of Harlem, the young translator writes herself into shared spaces with the poet, propelling readers to accept a permeable rendering of the local in time and space. In line with the cover image of the English version—the interior of a New York subway car—the young translator believes that she has seen Owen several times while traveling underground, an experience that moves her. The syncing of two trains becomes the stage for a momentary encounter, one that is rendered unstable and fleeting by the speed with which the two trains run alongside each other—and also by the fact that the young translator questions what she sees. The novel does not portray such encounters as supernatural events, but rather as unexpected, dizzying sightings that leave the narrator unsure as to what has happened. She states,

> Iba mirando por la ventana . . . cuando se acercó por atrás otro tren y por unos instantes anduvo a la misma velocidad que el tren donde iba yo. Lo vi sentado, en la misma posición que yo había adoptado, con la cabeza reclinada sobre la ventana del vagón. Y después nada. . . . Cuando otra vez hubo oscuridad detrás de la ventana vi contra el vidrio mi propia imagen difusa. Pero no era mi rostro; era mi

> rostro supuesto al de él—como si su reflejo se hubiera quedado plasmado en el vidrio y ahora yo me reflejara dentro de ese doble atrapado en la venta de mi vagón.[39]
>
> [I was looking out the window—nothing except the heavy darkness of the tunnels—when another train approached from behind and for a few moments traveled at the same speed as the one I was on. I saw him sitting in the same position as me, his head resting against the carriage window. And then nothing. . . . When there was once again darkness outside the window, I saw my own blurred image on the glass. But it wasn't my face; it was my face superimposed on his—as if his reflection had been stamped onto the glass and now I was reflected inside that double trapped on my carriage window.][40]

In this way, Owen and the narrator fleetingly occupy the same space, while their superimposed countenances add a dimension of ambiguity to the meeting: was she truly seeing Gilberto Owen, or seeing him within herself?[41] The moment at which the two trains run alongside each other offers a means of understanding a transitional period in which both Owen and the young translator speak within the text, as if vying for control of the narration. This tense contact between voices gains significance when Luiselli interjects with a metatextual commentary that recalls the *archein* of destruction and reconstruction discussed in chapter 3 and is structured around a metaphor of fabric and files, her narrator's reality steadily imbricated with fiction. To unwire the "mesh" of this modified reality and divorce fiction from reality definitively, stories must first be torn apart and leveled to the ground to then be forged anew and saved in separate files.[42]

The narrator's desire to raze the plot foreshadows another significant moment of opening within the text. When the translator decides to leave New York for Philadelphia after her editor discovers the forged translation, she comments, "Me iba porque era incapaz de sostener y habitar los mundos que yo mismo fabricaba" (I was going because I was incapable of sustaining and inhabiting the worlds I myself had fabricated),[43] an admission that echoes beautifully the overlap between the labor of sustaining the integrity of a plot and that of inhabiting place. To "unwrite" herself from the story, the young translator confesses the forgery of Owen's translations, quits her job at the publishing house, and sells all of her belongings, save for the orange tree. She flees to Philadelphia and once again tries to find Owen's grave, in order to leave the dead tree there. She is not successful, however, and instead leaves the plant with her sister Laura and her partner, Erea, who keep it by their front door and continue to water it.[44]

This clearing of space also preoccupies the novelist in Mexico City, who comments all the while on her struggle to write without giving in to the prying questions of her husband or the domestic strain of caring for her children. Eventually, the tension in the house becomes insurmountable, and the husband appears to leave. In the first mention of this news, one has the impression that his departure is due to the deterioration of their marriage. Soon, however—and with characteristic metatextual distancing—this same event is rewritten as a creative decision: the narrator writes, "El final no importa. Mi marido se mudó a otra ciudad. Digamos, Filadelfia. . . . Digamos que encontró a otras mujeres" (The rest isn't important. My husband moved to another city. Let's say, Philadelphia. . . . Let's say he met other women. . . . Or maybe he just got fed up, locked himself in an apartment in Philadelphia, and allowed himself to slowly die).[45] The dialogue comes to a head as the narrator's husband reads about his own departure to Philadelphia in the pages of his wife's novel and asks why she sends him away. She responds, "Para que pase algo" (So that something happens).[46] This is a narrative moment in which—to steal a metaphor from Luiselli, or perhaps from Owen himself—the two subway trains of the narration run alongside each other for a moment before pulling apart, foreshadowing the many crossings and eventual narrative collapse that characterize the second half of the novel. We understand that the city could be any city. The geographic locale of Philadelphia is not integral; rather, it is its notion as another city, as an elsewhere that the husband leaves to. It is only later that readers find out that Gilberto Owen moves to the same city, eventually dying there.

CROSSINGS AND COLLAPSE

As the author in Mexico City does at the beginning of the novel, Owen passes the chief narrative perspective over to his younger self with a declaration of place. For him, "todo sucedió en otra ciudad y en otra vida. Era el verano de 1928. Trabajaba como escribiente en el consulado mexicano de Nueva York, redactando oficios sobre el precio de cacahuate mexicano en el mercado yanqui, que estaba a punto de reventar" (it all began in another city and another life. It was the summer of 1928. I was working as a clerk in the Mexican consulate of New York, writing official reports on the price of peanuts on the US market, which was about to crash).[47] Pondering the quarter century that has passed since, he echoes the authorial concession that the first narrator offers at the beginning of *Los ingrávidos*: "No podría escribir esa historia como si todavía estuviera ahí y fuera ese joven flaco y lleno de entusiasmo, traduciendo a Dickinson y a Williams, enfundado en una bata gris" (I couldn't write this story as if I still lived there and were that thin young man, full of enthusiasm, translating Dickinson and Williams, wrapped in a gray bathrobe).[48] Although Owen appears several times earlier in the text, this formal introduction of his narrative voice also operates as a kind of translation: the control of the plot is brought across to another perspective, another way of patterning the lived space of the novel. The reader finds that even the course of the text itself can be reworked from another perspective, as Owen outlines the experiences behind his vertiginous narrations of

Manhattan, commenting drily, "En el fondo, yo mismo no creía nada de lo que escribía, pero me gustaba la idea de ser un poeta despechado en Nueva York" (At heart, even I didn't believe anything I wrote, but I liked the idea of being a despairing poet in New York).[49] The reader follows along as Owen fills in the empty spaces in his biography that the young translator sought desperately to fill, as the Mexican poet-cum-consulate-clerk sits next to his potted orange tree and writes himself into place, drafting the long letters that the young translator reads decades later: "Contaba mi vida en la gran urbe una y otra vez como para hacerla mía. . . . 'Querido X, vivo en Morningside Av. No. 63,' una y otra vez" (I told them about my life in the metropolis, again and again, as if to make it my own. . . . Dear X, I live at 63 Morningside Ave., again and again).[50] Owen's retellings of the events of the first half of the novel act as subjective practices of space that further the game between hunted poet and the narrator—at times, these retellings involve direct mimicry of the phrases and motifs established earlier in the chapter, as is the case with the orange tree. Other meeting places (to borrow again from Massey) often emerge as thematic crossings in the experiences of place. Both narrators express profound discomfort with the wealthy cosmopolitan *criollismo*[51] that dominates the Latin American literary scene in New York—Owen attends a poetry reading at the lavish apartment of his ex-wife, recalling the young translator's reluctant attendance at a Latin American art celebration where the "trustafarian" guests show up in costume. Further echoes of the translator's narration appear when Owen has seemingly parallel experiences in public and shared spaces, as when he takes his children to Morningside Park and meets a young woman named Dolores who goes by "Do," who appeared in the translator's visit to his old apartment building.[52]

Just as the young translator catches glimpses of Owen on the metro, in turn, Owen seems to see the translator, although of course he does not recognize her as such. He remarks on "a woman [he] kept seeing on another train."[53] The woman, described as having brown skin and sad eyes, wearing a red coat, matches the earlier descriptions of the young translator. Although Luiselli offers only a vague description that gestures at the young woman, it is a sufficient coincidence that readers eagerly wonder whether the first narrator has successfully written herself into Owen's world: in one sighting on the subway, Owen sees the woman reading a book entitled *Obras*,[54] which we understand is the collected volume of his poetry that the young translator borrows from the Columbia University archive.[55] Without recognizing his own published work, Owen is surprised to see that the woman is reading a text in Spanish.[56] Echoing the spatial practices of the young translator, Owen describes instances in which her interventions seem to intrude into his reality through repositioned objects. In another scene, Owen sees the woman in the red coat passing by carrying a chair—the reader eagerly assumes that this is the young translator carrying the chair she stole from the editorial office.[57] In others, Luiselli takes great narrative liberty, often tying knots in space and time: in one fragment, Owen mentions the death of an orange tree that he used to write letters next to: "Un día se me murió el naranjo. Me había ido de viaje a las cataratas de Niágara, y no lo regué antes de salir. Cuando volví estaba completamente seco—como si hubieran pasado años y no apenas dos semanas" (I'd gone on a trip to Niagara Falls, and didn't water it before leaving. When I returned, it was completely withered, as if years had passed, instead of scarcely two weeks).[58] Dismayed by the sudden death of the plant, Owen takes it up to the roof terrace of his apartment and abandons it. Later, as he watches the sunrise, Owen observes that the orange tree has vanished from the roof of his building:[59] perhaps, the reader wonders eagerly, because the translator has removed it? Later, on a drunken walk home through the streets of Philadelphia, the older, shambolic Owen stops to relieve himself on a porch. He knocks over a potted plant and, "nomás por no dejar huella" (for no other reason than not leaving traces),[60] decides to take it home to his apartment, where he makes a discovery:

> Supe casi de inmediato que no era cualquier maceta. Pude constatar, repasando sus relieves, que era mi maceta, la de las llamas verdes, junto a la cual había escrito todas las cosas buenas que escribí en mi juventud. Y si no era mi vieja maceta, era igual, y con eso bastaba.[61]
>
> [I knew almost immediately that it wasn't just any old plant pot. Running my fingers over the surface, I was able to confirm that it was my pot, the one with green flames, beside which I had penned all the good things I'd written in my younger days. And if it wasn't my old plant pot, it was exactly the same, and that was good enough.][62]

The serendipitous reappearance of the orange pot is one of many motifs that resound across the constellation of chance encounters and mimicries that Luiselli spins across the pages of *Los ingrávidos*. In mingling her narrative settings, Luiselli risks losing the vivid materiality that complements the novel's lofty metatextual reflections, but for the newspapers that clutter Owen's suffocating Philadelphia apartment and the cockroaches that populate the cracked foundation of the house in Mexico City. Indeed, by weaving a playful serendipity into her local constructions, Luiselli keeps the reader engaged in the game of hide-and-seek between the narrators.

As Owen and the narrator achieve physical and temporal proximity and their formerly disparate spheres collide, the material universe of the novel undergoes a similar conversion. Perhaps, as she writes herself into Owen's life, the narrator finds that her pen has started to tear through the paper, creating cracks and fissures in the material universe of the novel as the protagonists' formerly disparate spheres collide. Part of this collapse is the result of an earthquake that shakes the house in a literal fracturing of the structures that uphold Luiselli's disparate settings.[63] The earthquake is only the final stage of the steady foundering of the house, a building that seems to be in a constant state of disrepair throughout the novel: the narrator describes the cracks in the walls and the faulty plumbing, often attributing these to the "ghosts" who move through the house. In fact, it is unclear whether the rubble the narrator speaks of is literal or figurative; across the novel, the gradual disintegration of the house directly mirrors the collapse of narrative boundaries. This collapse is perhaps the result of many rereadings and rewritings of the novel's events and spaces, of a plot that has been translated back and forth so often between perspectives that the structure of the original text is fractured beyond repair. Yet the earthquake also offers a much-needed sense of relief, of opening the story again to let outside voices filter in. The accordion pleats referenced in the introduction to this chapter collapse, as the novel exhales a gust of times and spaces, and the delicate architecture of the story turns inward, bringing the many configurations of characters and settings, in all of their literary and imagined manifestations, together.

After the earthquake, the literary and physical worlds of the novel become near indistinguishable, as the two settings intermingle in the clutter of Owen's apartment and the debris knocked onto the floor of the first narrator's house in Mexico City. Owen watches a note fall from the branches of his orange tree that recounts a portion of a letter he wrote to Mexican literary critic José Rojas Garcidueñas. The note, we assume, is one of the sticky notes that the translator writes as she feverishly gathers information about Owen's life, a piece of paper that has somehow been translated across space and time into the poet's own reality. Accordingly, the author comments that he does not remember writing the note,[64] although it is uncertain whether he means the letter or the note itself. Just as the narrator's notes seem to bleed into Owen's reality, the earthquake seems to have knocked loose reminders of his foothold in her own lived space. While looking for her husband in the living room, the narrator finds a note she wrote while researching Gilberto Owen: "De niño, Owen poesía 'los seis sentidos mágicos.' Vaticinaba temblores" (As a child, Owen had "the six magic senses." He predicted earthquakes).[65] Again, it is unclear whether these comments are metaphorical or based in reality, though readers have growing faith in all things imagined by their untrustworthy narrator as the text comes to a close.[66] Similarly, Owen's own personal space comes to host new voices: despite his progressive blindness, he somehow sees Federico Garcia Lorca and Ezra Pound in his kitchen—in the English translation of the novel, Owen notes bitterly, "They're taking up all my space."[67] As the family in Mexico City search for the father, who is missing because of the rubble that blocks the second floor of the house, Owen searches for a plot to call his own, repeatedly invoking indirect references to the novel-within-a-novel of *Los ingrávidos*, as he ponders, "La novela estaría narrada en primera persona, por ~~un árbol~~ una mujer de rostro moreno y ojeras hondas que tal vez ya se haya muerto. La primera línea se la voy a robar a Emily Dickinson: Escuché el zumbido de una mosca al morirme" (The novel will be narrated in the first person, by ~~a tree~~ a woman with a brown face and dark shadows under her eyes, who has perhaps died. The first line will be these words by Emily Dickinson: "I heard a fly buzz when I died").[68] Here, Owen mingles and mimics the motifs of the first stream of narration, echoing the mosquito buzz at the beginning of the novel. He repeatedly outlines a sketch of a novel populated by ghosts, searching desperately for a stable piece of narration, a vector for the creation of this novel. Eventually, exhausted from their respective searches, Owen tries to get some sleep while lying on top of his kitchen table, while in Mexico City the author and her children shelter underneath their own table, taking cover from possible aftershocks of the earthquake. Here, Luiselli's tense oscillation between locales once again recalls the subway, as one reality runs underneath another. Owen begins to hear the cry of a baby and the sound of a young boy singing a nursery rhyme. Finally, the novel closes with a relieving gust, as Owen awakes to the gleeful cry of a young boy who has, we assume, been searching for his father in the rubble of the house in Mexico City: "¡Encontrado!" (Found!).[69]

CONCLUSION

Throughout *Los ingrávidos,* Luiselli represents her locales as stories under construction. In reading her work, we learn that creating a text to represent the present necessarily mimics the process of representing place in contemporary life: opening windows, letting other voices in, demolishing the walls, beginning anew. As Luiselli's narrator negotiates how to build and inhabit a story, she opens the empty spaces of her text to outside intervention, creating a multifaceted, intertextual web of representations. Here, Luiselli highlights the irresolvable plurality of perspectives that intersect in contemporary life and inform the act of writing. Beyond the direct references that she discloses within her work, many features of *Los ingrávidos* recall the affective tropes of other recent novels. The intertangled lives of artists and their audiences preoccupy, among many others, Adriana Lisboa's *Rakushisha* (*Hut of Fallen Persimmons*),[70] a novel that begins with a chance encounter in a Rio de Janeiro metro station between two strangers who travel to Kyoto to visit the home of seventeenth-century poet Matsuo Bashō. There is a relentless desire here to write oneself into the spaces of the great thinkers, to understand what it means to occupy the same niche in space, if not the same time, as other people. Although many of her contemporaries artfully weave together disparate lives on the stage of contemporary life, Luiselli distinguishes herself for her tendency to disclose the process of construction behind her texts, whether in metatextual musings on the nature of taking up space in the literary canon, in her character's digressions and "rewritings," or in the splitting of narrative voices. In his review of Luiselli's *Lost Children Archive,* author Edmundo Paz Soldán offers a commentary on her desire to reveal the scaffolding of her own narrative constructions, as if tapping on the glass of the window to awaken the reader:

> A estas alturas todo esto es parte del arsenal posmoderno; lo que cambia es la valencia, el objetivo con que se usa ese arsenal, pues si otros autores usaron estos trucos para criticar la posibilidad misma de representar el presente a través de la novela realista, lo que quiere Luiselli es buscar otra forma de documentar ese presente.[71]
>
> [At this point, this may be part and parcel of the postmodern arsenal; what changes is the motive, the objective with which Luiselli employs such an arsenal, so if other authors use these tricks to critique the very possibility of representing the present in the form of a realist novel, what Luiselli wants is to find another form of documenting the present.]

As Paz Soldán argues, Luiselli's fixation is not on the impossibility of representing the present but rather on a celebration of the text as an open, polyvocal, iterative means of narrating the world. Luiselli reveals the author not as a distant figure who speaks from afar to transmit watertight representations of a contemporary present but as someone who lives within a world of collaborations and chance encounters that later emerge in writing. In an essay on Owen published in *Letras Libres*, Luiselli writes, "No es descubrimiento ni paranoia mía: vivimos en un tiempo obsesionado con la voz del autor. Un escritor dedica todo su empeño a esa búsqueda de la voz propia—sea lo que esto sea—, como si un día fuera de veras a encontrarla en alguna parte" (This is neither a discovery nor a paranoia that belongs exclusively to me: we live in a time obsessed with the voice of the author. A writer dedicates an entire endeavor to the search of their own voice—whatever that may mean—as if one day they would miraculously discover it somewhere).[72] The novel's illustration of interwoven creative processes clashes with the assumed discrete nature of literary identities—we tend to perceive an author's work as wholly his or her own, rather than thinking about the collaborative processes, borrowed or stolen ideas, and chance encounters that emerge on the printed page. By revealing these intersecting dialogues that lie beneath her novels, Luiselli suggests that the simultaneities and multiplicities of contemporary life may best be understood through the contacts between lives, through a playful narrative serendipity that sustains a mutable local woven from active stories.

In this sense, Latin American literature at the turn of the millennium offers readers a set of fractured and multiple modes of perceiving the overlapping and symbiotic relationship of our spatial and narrative identities. Whether through nonlinear narrative voices that invent multiple realities as they negotiate a sense of place, as I have ruminated on at length in this chapter, or the many reflections on ruin as a spatial trope for multilayered identity, literature has the unique ability to expose how individuals practice and play with locality. It is fitting to end this book with a commentary on play, a theme so central to *Los ingrávidos*. Creativity, inventiveness, and play are crucial to understanding literary interventions into practices of locality in our increasingly globalized era. The writing of identities into the nooks and crannies of narrative is a process that comes alive in *Latin American Literature at the Millennium*, placing the power back in the hands of this book's many protagonists. While much of the theory from the Global North on the impacts of globalization might aim to flatten or diminish difference, what the protagonists of this work show us across these four chapters is that difference, as expressed through identity, language, the crafting of homes, and the parsing of the rubble of time and space, is in fact alive and well. Though social theory may help to guide our discussions on locality and globality in the contemporary era, literature offers depth and nuance to the complex interplay between the two.

CONCLUSION

Ser de un interval

Across the chapters of *Latin American Literature at the Millennium,* I have examined the narrative construction of the local as a vector for mediating distant and global processes. Global life is marked by contact with an *elsewhere,* by cultural encounters that expose vulnerability to phenomenological developments. Contemporary Latin American literature sheds light on the heterotopias that characterize our era and thereby enriches our understanding of the historical, political, and social developments of recent years in the region. At the same time, there is a great deal of play at work in these novels. Whether it be through the deliberate coding of language explored in chapter 1 or through Valeria Luiselli's inversion of the place-space dichotomy examined in chapter 4, the Latin American authors discussed in this book draw our attention to a heterogeneous and dynamic global experience that is rich with local traces. The six authors examined employ a range of creative tactics to engage locality and identity across space and time, in the quotidian routines of day-to-day life as well as in the phenomenological processes of globalization that loom in the distance and take root locally. These works provide harrowing lessons of local resistance, struggle, and occupation in the face of the multifaceted set of processes that define globalization: the unequal access to temporal and spatial resources for young women in the borderland factories of the North American Free Trade Agreement, or the eerie mixture of belonging and estrangement that plays out as a migrant struggles to speak his parents' heritage language. Through its focus on local lives in movement, this study highlights the push and pull of fluctuating identities at the turn of the millennium in Latin America.

The last few decades have borne a wealth of scholarship at the intersection of literature and globalization in Latin America, including studies by Francine Masiello and Josefina Ludmer.[1] This book more specifically joins a recent set of analyses that examine temporal and spatial life in contemporary Latin American texts from the turn of the twentieth and the beginning of the twenty-first centuries, including those by Gustavo Guerrero, Erica Durante, and Héctor Hoyos.[2] These explorations have shed light on the diminishment of the nation as a frame of reference for identity and setting, the fragmentation of historic narrative, the machinations of global capitalist trade networks, and the task presented to contemporary literature of representing the world in its entirety. *Latin American*

Literature at the Millennium intervenes most prominently in its examination of practices of locality. Indeed, there has yet to be a dedicated study on the ways in which Latin American literary authors address the concursion of local lives and phenomenological undercurrents of global economic processes. At the same time, the novels examined in this book form part of a historical canon of Latin American authors who have responded to the inundation of popular culture from the Global North through experimentation with style and language, led first by the Macondo movement of the 1990s and writers including Alberto Fuguet, Sergio Gómez, and Edmundo Paz Soldán. Scholars on the post-Boom, including Donald Shaw,[3] have argued that the region's recent writing has certain aesthetic features that respond to global processes, that it is cleaner, less symbolic and metaphorical. There has also been ample scholarly attention to the mutualistic relationship between digital and analog streams of literary production, which has been documented by scholars including Hilda Chacón, Thea Pitman and Claire Taylor, Carolina Gainza, and Scott Weintraub.[4] However, this book is less about the aesthetics of globalization as a factor affecting contemporary literature, and more about how protagonists negotiate their local identities, languages, and memories into the tangible spaces of the narrative present. This can be seen in *Estive em Lisoba,* where Lisbon becomes a mnemonic landscape for protagonists who are caught between familiarity and global estrangement, or in the handling of language in *Mar paraguayo,* as the protagonist asserts her sense of self and creates territories of alternative identity and sites for individual memory.

Indeed, explorations of memory lie at the heart of this study, whether in its connection to language as a mnemonic site or in the ways that individual experiences and connections to physical spaces serve as mediating tactics in the face of global modernity. We can see these connections not only in how Lisbon is narrated in chapter 1 but also in chapter 3's exploration of João Gilberto Noll's Harmada and Bernardo Carvalho's *país das maravilhas.* Both novels are narrated from the position of the in-between and are abundant with explorations of memory through spaces and imaginaries in conflict. In the case of *Harmada,* readers experience a crumbling city to which the protagonist returns, himself slowly descending into ruins. In fact, nothing seems permanent in either work, neither the cities they portray nor the identities of their precarious and peripheral protagonists. In the case of *Teatro,* Carvalho uses the border to ruminate on questions of the in-between, of language, voice, and power, reflecting on the often incongruous experience of migration, one that can be ambivalent and disorienting. Both works operate in the liminal zone that intersects belonging and estrangement as a metaphor for the ills of globalization, with characters that battle isolation and socioeconomic strife in countries that go unnamed. In the face of these challenges for self-making and identity assertion, protagonists navigate return to their territories of memory that often provide short-lived stability or connection. This frequently plays out in their speech and language practices, even when performative. Language as a site of memory and identity in the face of unstable worlds is a theme that draws the many novels of this study together.

Equally central to this book is spatial multiplicity. As for Roberto Bolaño's *2666,* this plays out in a multiterritorial narrative that makes leaps between Europe and North America, with the borderland between Mexico and the United States an eerie epicenter for exploring the socioeconomic incongruencies of globalization. In the case of *Los ingrávidos,* the novel is not about a specific locale, but rather many urban settings that are bound together through explorations on inhabiting and narrating places, in a world populated by other people. In transit zones and shared spaces, Luiselli explores missed connections and attempts to bring protagonists in contact with one another across times and spaces that are vast and disparate. As *Los ingrávidos* comes to a close, the metatextual fictional and lived narrative worlds collapse together, perhaps the ultimate point of contact as the fragile architecture of the novel closes in upon itself and readers and writers meet in the denouement of an earthquake. Luiselli and Bolaño gesture at the notion that the simultaneities and multiplicities of contemporary life may best be understood through contact between lives, weaving hyperlocal details of everyday existence, with global stories that touch, dialogue, and play with other times and other spaces. It is worth mentioning that Luiselli and Bolaño join a chorus of contemporary regional authors who experiment with shorter narrative forms to interrogate the relationship between the local and the global, the phenomenological and the minute. These include *La vida interior de las plantas de interior* by Argentine Patricio Pron, *Instrucciones para ser feliz* by Chilean María José Navia, and *A chave de casa* by Brazilian Tatiana Salem Levy.[5]

With that said, the novels studied here expose the notion that all reality begins at the level of the local, and it is through locality that the global most vividly expresses itself. As narration operates as a mode of fixing representation, contemporary Latin American authors are tasked with representing (without reducing) conflicting historical imaginaries and inequitable experiences. Extended metatextual reflections on the nature of authorship and the question of representation in stories highlight the multiplicity of perspectives and impossibility of presenting a complete portrait of the present. Indeed, the journey of *Latin American Literature at the Millennium* approaches locality not as a fixed concept but as one that is plastic and malleable. From the cosmopolitan academics landing in the borderlands of Mexico in search of an obscure writer, to second-generation migrants clinging to their mother tongue as a site of culture, to an economic migrant who journeys back to the heart of colonial empire, to the many layers of place and placelessness felt by a young woman chasing an obscure poet, this book attempts to capture the multiple, iterative, and dynamic encounter of local lives with global spaces. This is an encounter that is difficult to pin down, as it is constantly in motion, just as protagonists shift and transform across locales and temporalities, reminding us of the agility of spatial experiences in the contemporary era.

Much like the ruins of the decaying city of *Harmada*, the local representations of Latin American literature must be understood in terms of their own makings and unmakings, as they are painstakingly rebuilt from the rubble only to collapse in favor of a new stream of self-narration. These multiple, simultaneous iterations of the local are always *in a state of becoming*, at once multiple and partial as they relentlessly cycle through stages of deconstruction and resurrection. The writer-narrator of Luiselli's *Los ingrávidos* deletes her paragraphs, cutting and pasting segments of an old plot into a new Word document and changing the names of her characters. In *2666*, the forensic reports of the victims are edited and newspaper reports publish details later found to be incorrect. At the moment of enunciation, where the global subject speaks from a local interval—here recalling the words of Carlos Mario Yory—Luiz Ruffato's lusophone protagonist confronts what Néstor García Canclini referred to as "words which have lost their meanings,"[6] as his Brazilian *mineiro* speech distinguishes him as a foreigner in Portugal, serving as a textual reminder of the migrant subjects' position of in-betweenness,[7] which reveals complex experiences of simultaneous assimilation and marginalization. These ephemeral and contingent spoken intervals make a case for a local that communicates the workings of globalization at the ground level, highlighting the plasticity of the places from which contemporary subjects speak in contemporary narrative, and the problem of building coherent representations on unstable ground.

APPENDIX

TESTING REGIONALISM, MIGRANT NARRATIVES, AND THE CONSTRUCTION OF BRAZIL

An Interview with Luiz Ruffato

Luiz Ruffato is one of the most prominent writers in contemporary Brazilian literature. Born in 1961 in Cataguases, Minas Gerais, he recently gained significant exposure through his opening speech at the Frankfurt International Book Fair in October 2013, the focus of which was on Brazilian literature. Rather than praising his home country, Ruffato spoke at length about the complex socioeconomic challenges facing Brazil, including poverty, lack of access to education, illiteracy, and income inequality. The speech generated a great deal of polemical dialogue in Brazil on the cusp of two major international events: the 2014 World Cup and the 2016 Summer Olympic Games in Rio de Janeiro. Raised in a lower-middle-class family of Italian immigrants (his father was a popcorn vender and his mother a washerwoman), Ruffato has faced many of the hardships he notes in his speech. This experience shapes Ruffato's writings, in which he consistently explores poverty, immigration, and socioeconomic marginalization. A selection of his extensive body of work includes the critically acclaimed *Eles eram muitos cavalos*, his five-volume collection *Inferno provisório*, and his most recent novel, *Flores artificiais*.[1] He has published numerous short stories, collections of poetry, and essays, and he serves as a prominent public figure in Brazil.

During our meeting in August 2013, I spoke with Ruffato about a range of topics, from regionalism to migrant literature, his decision to participate in the Amores Expressos collection, and specifically *Estive em Lisboa e lembrei de você*.[2] Our dialogue included discussions on migration, contemporary literature, language use, and the construction and appropriation of space within the fluid terrain of contemporary Brazil.[3]

RAYNOR: Firstly, could you introduce yourself and discuss with us how you came to be a writer?

RUFFATO: It's a long road. I have a trajectory within Brazilian literature that is very unusual. Here in Brazil, as you may have noticed, there is a huge social gap and all writers, almost without exception, come from a middle-class or upper middle-class background. I come from a place that is not middle-class, or even lower middle-class, it's lower-lower middle-class. My mother was a laundress and my father was popcorn seller. Imagine! This profession has not existed in the United States for centuries, right? My mother was illiterate, as was my father. I worked for a long time as my father's helper, as a popcorn seller and also in a tavern. Later, I worked as a mechanic and then as a laborer in the textile industry. Why am I telling you this? I am telling you this because I was not meant to be a writer. I was meant to be anything but a writer. However, when I was in journalism school, I started reading literature, and more specifically Brazilian literature, with great interest. I was startled because I discovered that the universe that I came from was not portrayed in Brazilian literature. This is because middle-class people create literature in Brazil and are only interested in their universe or the universe of gangsters, but not the universe of workers. So, my decision was a conscious one: I want to write about this universe, because there is nothing written in the current literature that represents this universe. It was a political decision that was very clear to me. If I were to write, I had to write about this universe. So more or less this is my path to becoming a writer.

RAYNOR: Could you speak to the genre of the novel, in general terms?

RUFFATO: In my opinion, the novel arose from the need to create a worldview on behalf of the bourgeoisie, and therefore of capitalism. Capitalism has undergone some evident changes over time. And to deal with these changes, the novels and its representations have also changed. Thus, it is clear that the twenty-first-century novel is not the same novel of the nineteenth or twentieth centuries. This is because nineteenth-century capitalism is different from twentieth- or twenty-first-century capitalism. So where does *Estive em Lisboa e lembrei de você* fit into my work at large and what I wanted to achieve? This is a question that I have been asking since the beginning: how do I write about the lower-middle class without relying on the bourgeois form of the novel? The bourgeois novel is always related to identity, it seeks to describe an identity in order to describe a biography. And because my protagonists don't necessarily have a biography, as much of Brazil's poor population, I needed to approach this formal question. So, in 2001, I published *Eles eram muitos cavalos,* which was an attempt to understand part of this formal aspect. Then, throughout the 2000s, I published five volumes of *Inferno provisório,* which is also an attempt to construct a collective novel, in the sense that it does not have protagonists, meaning that people as a collective are the primary protagonist. And out of all of this arose *Estive em Lisboa.* And what is *Estive em Lisboa*? It was my intention to discuss the broad migrations occurring in Brazil during the second half of the twentieth century. This is what I tried to accomplish with *Inferno provisório,* which described the violence inherent in the transformation of the entirety of Brazil over fifty years. For me this illuminates the violence of Brazil today. In the midst of all of this, beyond the internal migrations, there was the 1980s, the so-called lost decade, during which a significant migration abroad occurred. I knew I would have to deal with this matter at some point. This was on my horizon and then I received the proposal to participate in the *Amores Expressos* project, and I chose Lisbon precisely because I wanted to place this particular issue into question. For me the novel is inserted into the discussion about the broad migrations in Brazil during the fifty years between 1950 and 2000.

RAYNOR: *Estive em Lisboa* is written in the form of a testimony. How did Serginho's testimony come to be? Was it a chance meeting in Lisbon or did you already know him?

RUFFATO: This, for me, is the greatest risk the novel takes. I needed to create a false situation, in order to persuade the reader into a false reading of the novel. Serginho does not exist, nor has he ever existed.

RAYNOR: No? I was convinced!

RUFFATO: Great, that was the idea. If I had not put that statement at the beginning of the novel, the story would have existed nonetheless. Now why did I put it there? Precisely to create a sense of ambiguity in relation to the narrative that was being written. It is one thing to write a book under the pretense that Serginho exists and to discuss things happening in his life, etc. It's another matter to read the story knowing that it is fiction. What I did was create an extended joke with the reader and propose to him that what he was reading was not fiction. It was the truth. And as the truth, one undertakes a different type of reading than one might if it were known to be a fiction, though in reality it is fiction. Serginho never existed. That interview never happened. Interestingly, the only thing that was real were the people's names.

RAYNOR: Oh, the names of the protagonists?

RUFFATO: No, the names of the people in the note preceding the text. When I said, "I thank my friend, the engineer X." Or when I thank the journalist Paulo Nogueira; all of these people exist. The café in Lisbon also exists, and the address does as well. When the book came out in Lisbon, some journalists went to the café to talk to Dona Rosa, who is the owner of the restaurant, *Solar dos Galegos,* and she told them, "Of course I remember perfectly! He sat in that very table." And she gave interviews. And this was great because, I thought, well OK then. So it exists.

RAYNOR: The myth is there.

RUFFATO: The myth is there. Later, I returned one day to have a glass of wine with Dona Rosa, and I said: "Dona Rosa, do you remember me?" And she said, "Of course I remember you! I thought it was so cute, you sitting there and talking with him [Serginho]." It's very funny! And once, I remember when I was in São Paulo on a Saturday night, and the phone rang at my house, I answered. On the other end was a person I know in Cataguases, not a friend but a well-known person in the community. So he tells me, "I am here with a guy who wants to talk with you. Talk with him." So I talk with his drunken friend who says, "Is this Luiz Ruffato? The one who wrote that book about Lisbon?" I confirm and he says, "Well, my boy, did you know that Serginho is back in Cataguases?" And I said, "Seriously?" And he said, "It's true. He's back and when you get back here, we are going to take you to have a beer with him."

RAYNOR: How incredible! I wanted to talk to you a little bit more about migration. In your body of work, this theme comes up frequently, particularly Italian immigration to Brazil. Where does this novel fit within this broader theme?

RUFFATO: When considering the last fifty years in Brazil, it was very important for me to think about how people interfere in history and how history interferes in people's lives, because these things are abstract, not concrete. For me, the history of Brazil in the last fifty years is the story of the displaced person. It is a spatial story, a story of space, of the conquering of space and also history changing paradigms across time. You don't just move physically, you also move in time. Time and space are inseparable in physics, so you have to imagine the following. When you have a large transformation from rural space to post-urban space, in a mere fifty years, you also have a change in the quality of time. Time is no longer successive, but rather simultaneous. So it is important to think of how people were or were not prepared for these radical changes in space and time. For me it's important to work with the idea of uprooting. My idea was to focus on a community that had long been migrating, in this case Italians. Italian grandparents had migrated to the interior of Minas Gerais at the end of the nineteenth century. Then in the 1950s, their children were part of the rural exodus, right? So you already have the problem of leaving the rural lands. You go from wide-open spaces in the country, to small and enclosed spaces in the city. Even here in João Pessoa you have small spaces, and you are forced to leave the mythical time of the country, to go to a place where time dominates space and swallows you up. I am interested in these shifts of paradigm. I focused on a community of Italian immigrants in order to understand this microcosm over the last fifty years. There's a song by Caetano Veloso, which sums up my concern. He says, "Here in this country, where what is constructed is already in ruins."

RAYNOR: Right, the important concept of ruin.

RUFFATO: What I have tried to do is precisely to mimic this ruin—the ruin of the disintegration of the family, the ruin of domestic violence—mimic this in the very form of the novel, which is itself a ruin. Even in *Estive em Lisboa* this idea is present. It is less so than in other works, but it is present. There is a moral collapse at the beginning and the end of the narrative. The novel undergoes a series of interferences, including linguistic interferences in the second part that leave it in a state of ruin. The narrative disintegrates over time.

RAYNOR: Language is something you frequently experiment with in your work at large, and it continues to play a role in *Estive em Lisboa*, as you highlight Serginho's language use in an intentional and deliberate way. Can you speak a little bit about this decision? How do you negotiate the question of regionalisms in a novel such as this, especially when we consider the stigma that regionalism has in the history of Brazilian literature?

RUFFATO: This is a great question, but the question preceding this one bothers me a great deal. Who defines what is regional and not regional? Hegemonies decide. For example, if I write about Rio de Janeiro it is not regional because the hegemonic culture is located there, as well as in São Paulo. But if I write about Minas Gerais, it is considered regional because it is not hegemonic. Brazil in relationship to the United States is regional because we are not hegemonic in comparison. So there is always this discussion of center and periphery. So, the first question of a regional novel is defining what is regional. Regional literature does not belong to a hegemonic culture, to begin with. So, this is already a debatable matter. What defines a regionalism? Is a novel regional because of its language? If it's the language, we return to the idea of cultural hegemony. There is an attempt to make Rio de Janeiro the dialectal hegemon of Brazilian Portuguese, something we see frequently in films. Here in João Pessoa, the female news broadcaster is not from Paraíba, neither ethnically nor linguistically. She is a white woman from the South, who speaks with a *carioca* [Rio] dialect. The television soap operas also use the standard accent from Rio, and there is undoubtedly an attempt to impose a cultural hegemony from Rio. Everything that is not from Rio or São Paulo is considered to be regional. This has created a number of problems in Brazil, including for Southern writers from Rio Grande do Sul, who do not use the pronoun "tu" because they would be considered regionalists. So, you end up abandoning your own identity in order to not be considered a regionalist. This is a tragedy! What I have attempted to do is to ignore completely this question of whether or not I am a regionalist. Why? Because I refuse to accept this cultural hegemony, and the role of the writer should always be to question cultural hegemonies. And if I simply assume the hegemonic culture, I can no longer question it. The second thing is that I intentionally wrote this novel in "mineirês" [the dialect spoken in Minas Gerais], rather than Portuguese. However, this is an invention, it is an artificial language in the novel. Here I attempted to reproduce the oral character of spoken "mineirês" within a context that is no longer valued. It was intentional because I wanted to highlight the contrasts of a migrant from Minas Gerais in Lisbon. So I contrasted the language spoken in Brazil with the Portuguese language that is spoken in Portugal, and beyond this, I contrasted this Brazilian Portuguese, because this is not a language spoken in the rest of Brazil. It has a rhythm and a syntax that are completely different than the language you would hear in Paraíba for example. So the idea was to use regionalisms to question what is regional. It would be ridiculous to me for someone to say that the novel is regional, when it takes place in Lisbon. Is it a question of language and not a question of space? It was intentional; that is, this radicalization of one aspect in order to discuss the idea of regionalisms, if they actually exist. For me, this is purely a political question.

RAYNOR: Could you elaborate a bit on your decision to participate in the *Amores Expressos* project?

RUFFATO: The original project was based on a Brazilian film production company, RT Features (Rodrigo Teixera Features), which was resurfacing at a particular moment. The production company wanted to create a series of films. The idea was to send writers overseas to different cities across the world, to write love stories in these cities. Why in other cities in the world? It was easier to create film production agreements in the United States, France, etc. than to do it alone. In the beginning the idea was purely commercial and not intended for literature, but for film. The second step was that *Companhia das Letras* was interested in making a deal to publish the best books of the collection, not all, but the ones they found interesting. The project went from having a purely commercial interest to having a literary one. So what was my intention in all of this? Firstly, I have to pay my bills and they paid very well. Secondly, they said I could choose the city I wanted to travel to. Because if they had told me I needed to live in for example, New Delhi, I would not have accepted. That is because I would be faking my literary interest. Given my interest in working on Brazilian immigration abroad, I had three or four options. One was Japan, when considering the *decasséguis* [Japanese migrants working abroad, here in Brazil]. But Japan didn't exist within the imaginary of my city, Cataguases. In other words, I didn't know anyone who left Cataguases to go to Japan. The other great option was the United States, but there was already someone going to New York. So then I considered Europe, including Italy. But there were not many people going to Italy and I didn't want to get involved in the world that involved primarily transvestites and prostitutes, similar to Spain. The place that was strongest in the migration of the Brazilian working class was Portugal, and I had no doubts about Lisbon. So then I accepted the project, and I knew from that moment that I was not going to write a love story.

RAYNOR: But there is a love story in the novel, right?

RUFFATO: I think so. When I turned the book in to the editor he said, "Wait, only half of this takes place in Lisbon! The book is already short, and half occurs in Cataguases and half in Lisbon. And there is no love story!" And I said, "It does take place in Lisbon, you never said the whole thing had to take place in Lisbon. And it does have a love story." To which he said, "What love story?" And I told him, "You have to look for it!" So, the basic idea in accepting the project was money—I have no problem writing under contract—and because I was interested in the question of Brazilian migration abroad.

RAYNOR: What type of role do you think the *Amores Expressos* project has within Brazilian literature more broadly?

RUFFATO: All of the writers undertook the projects in their own ways. I don't think the project itself is important for Brazilian literature. I think the results of some of the books may or not be important for the body of work of specific writers, but the project itself cannot be evaluated from this point of view, especially because it is so broad, and has a diverse set of authors and projects. I would not look at it as a totality. Some books are still being released and I think it will be easier to see the project in its totality later on. Though, honestly I don't think it will make much of a difference. I don't think you will be able to look at it as a literary project within Brazilian literature.

RAYNOR: Returning to the structure of the novel, it is divided between Cataguases and Lisbon, making the idea of space essential. What role does space play across the novel?

RUFFATO: I enjoy reflecting on the concept of space in my work, not only in this novel. I like to think about how we appropriate space in Brazil. From an outsider's perspective, Brazil is situated in a dichotomy. On the one hand, it is depicted as extremely lyrical and romantic, and also the opposite. But the truth lies in between; it is neither one thing nor the other. If you consider a place like São Paulo in the 1950s, it had about a million people and today it has nine million within the city's limits and almost twenty million in Greater São Paulo. So how do we deal with space in urban areas? We deal with it poorly, because in Brazil we have a very strange concept: that which does not belong to a single person belongs to no one. This is a strange idea, because in the US it is the opposite. In the US, that which belongs to no one belongs to everyone. If you think about this concept, you come to understand Brazil in general and why we have such an issue with public littering, loitering, etc. This is because the only space that matters is my space, not our space. This also explains violence in Brazil. I protect my own home but the moment I go out into the streets, I can drive my car over everyone out there. So the public space is one of confrontation, and the private space is one of domestic violence. The public space is one of confrontation in all ways imaginable; political confrontation, politicians can steal public goods because the public doesn't belong to anyone. Historically, we arrived in Brazil relatively recently, we have an amalgamation of immigrants, and we've always been beaten down. Because we've always been beaten down, we beat down others around us. In Brazil, savage capitalism is not a metaphor, it's the truth. We are savage! This is why Brazil is frequently seen as a romantic place from abroad, because it is savage!

RAYNOR: Right, I see. Importantly, *Estive em Lisboa* is framed in such a way that Serginho quits smoking in the first half and then takes it up again at the end of the second half. What motivated this decision?

RUFFATO: I needed a method of marking time and the turn the tale makes in Serginho's spatial route. I needed markers that were psychological, which was when he quit smoking and when he started again. But these had to be markers of survival and necessity. Quitting in the first half is a metaphor for leaving something that brings him a lot of pleasure, Brazil. For all of its bad points, it's his country. Then quitting smoking becomes quitting something that gives him pleasure. Even if it's a toxic pleasure. Brazil is a toxic pleasure! It is pleasurable, the best place in the world to live, but it kills you. And the second half was exactly the opposite, he is detoxing but he isn't happy because he has no pleasure. So the decision to start smoking again at the end of the novel is indicative of his decision to return to Brazil. It's not explicit, but we see him returning to something that gives him pleasure. Smoking is something that is registered in your memory as pleasurable, but as something that is going to kill you.

RAYNOR: The second half of the text is very rich in memory sequences. What role does memory play within the novel and in migration more generally?

RUFFATO: That is also an important issue because when Italian immigrants came to Brazil they were not only poor, they were miserable. Taking this status and thinking about Brazilian migration in general, what is the great tragedy of migration? It is not losing your food, which is important. It is not losing your language, which is also very important. All of these points are related to culture in general and have to do with breaking away from your history. In Western civilization, where is the connection to memory? It is in the cemetery. Eastern civilization has other traditions, but we have our cemeteries. And when you migrate you cannot take your cemeteries with you. When you migrate, you break with your past and you have to start anew. And so for me, that was a thing that made me uncomfortable. It has to do with the appropriation of space. Why do we sense that public spaces don't belong to anyone? Because we are constantly inaugurating history, regardless of where you go in Brazil, you are unlikely to find people who have four generations of people in a cemetery. It's very hard to find this. What does this mean? It means that we do not appropriate ourselves to our own space; this space is not mine. So for me it was very important to comprehend that memory and a lack of memory determine the construction of society.

RAYNOR: Immigration is frequently depicted in Brazilian literature, both historically and in contemporary literature. Why do you think literature is a particularly effective medium to tell migrant tales? What does it facilitate that other arts do not?

RUFFATO: One thing special about literature is that it supersedes the other arts not because it is better or worse, but because of the way the human mind thinks. We envision our lives in words. We don't think in images, but in words, making literature different than cinema for telling stories. So literature ends up being a repository for the most important thing in Western culture, which is memory, right? It serves as a type of repository for the questioning and self-reflection of our own language, offering up a series of possibilities that other arts do as well, but only precariously. What is interesting is that it is also the most elitist art, because it requires knowledge that is not required of cinema, visual arts, and music.

RAYNOR: Do you agree that it will become more difficult to speak about national literatures in the future? Such as Brazilian literature, Argentine literature and Chilean literature. . . . If you have a text that has no Brazilian protagonists but takes place in Russia, is this Brazilian literature because of the writer's nationality?

RUFFATO: I want to start with this last statement, because I think it determines the first. What determines whether literature is Chilean and not Argentine or Brazilian is the register of the author. As much as I might want to write American literature, I will never be able to. First, because I do not write in English and second, because my worldview is completely contaminated by the environment in which I live. I could even start writing in English tomorrow, but it is not my maternal language, and thus I will never have the same expressiveness in this language. But we are talking about a worldview. Language determines one's worldview. So much so that we say there are no pure translations and that translation is always a betrayal. If true translation were possible, you could mirror the text onto another. However, you cannot translate the worldview; you can translate the expressions, but not the worldview. So what determines the nationality of a piece of writing is the language it was written in because it brings with it a specific worldview. You can say: "I am Russian, my story takes place in Russia, but I am writing in Portuguese and am a Brazilian author, so the literature is Brazilian and not Russian."

RAYNOR: These are difficult questions, right? If you have Brazilian parents and you spent your entire life in Spain and you write about Brazil, is it Brazilian literature or Spanish?

RUFFATO: If you are writing in Spanish and you spent your entire life in Spain, you can write about Brazil, but the literature you write will be Spanish.

RAYNOR: If you spent half your life in Brazil?

RUFFATO: Of course, these are generalizations and everything has its limits. But I think in general, what determines this is the place from which you are writing, which determines your register. Let's take Junot Diaz, for example. He is not a Dominican writer. People refer to him as a "Dominican writer." He was born in the Dominican Republic, that's why. But he writes in English. And he writes from the point of view of an American. He does not write as a Dominican would, he writes as an American, and thus he writes American literature, not Dominican. The best example you could give me would be Puerto Rican literature. Because Puerto Rico obviously has its own culture but it belongs to the United States. But if you ask a Puerto Rican what he is, he will say he is a Puerto Rican. He will have a Puerto Rican worldview and not an American one. It is becoming more and more possible for literature to test the boundaries of national space, but this does not change its essence. Its essence will always be located in the place the author grew up. Literature may become more and more migratory, but the essence is always there.

RAYNOR: Thank you for your time; it's been a pleasure.

RUFFATO: The pleasure was all mine.

ACKNOWLEDGMENTS

No piece of writing is ever composed in a vacuum, and this book is no exception. Many individuals and institutions have accompanied me along the pathways of writing *Latin American Literature at the Millennium*, both during my years at McGill University and prior to them.

I would like to begin by thanking my colleagues in the Department of Languages, Literatures and Cultures, in particular Amanda Holmes, José Jouve Martín, and Jesús Pérez-Magallón, whose support, keen editorial eyes, and advice have been invaluable to the writing of this book. I also wish to express my gratitude to my department chair, Eugenio Bolongaro, who has been fundamental in supporting my early-career research plans. This book would not have been possible without generous grant funding at the provincial and national levels, through the Fonds de recherche du Québec—Société et culture and the Social Sciences and Humanities Research Council of Canada, respectively. I was also fortunate to receive crucial research support from McGill's Internal Social Science and Humanities Development Fund as well as an ARIA Summer Research Grant. During my time at McGill, two research assistants were essential to *Latin American Literature at the Millennium*, Rhian Lewis and Liz Wagner. I would like to thank them both for their time, energy, and relentless belief in this project.

Before McGill, a number of mentors and colleagues were helpful in shaping the ideas that would eventually materialize in this book. In Georgetown University's Department of Spanish and Portuguese, Gwen Kirpatrick, Vivaldo Santos, and Patrícia Vieira were key to the early development of several chapters. In the Department of English, Andrew Rubin's graduate seminar on literary transnationalism was fundamental in thinking through my theoretical apparatus. At Yale University, Aníbal González served not only as an external reader of the doctoral thesis that informed some of the early stages of this book but also as an intellectual companion and professional mentor. Research culminating in this book benefited greatly from a Fulbright Research Grant to Brazil, and thus I would like to extend my appreciation to the Brazilian Fulbright Commission and my academic adviser at the Universidade de Brasília, Regina Dalcastagnè, and her Grupo de Estudos em Literatura Brasileira Contemporânea. I would also like to thank Luiz Ruffato for taking the time to conduct an illuminating interview with me in Brazil, which readers will find in the appendix.

Copanelists, attendees, and members of the extended academic community were crucial in formulating many of the concepts of this book. I presented some of its central arguments at the Institute for World Literature and the Latin American Studies Association Conference in 2015, the International Comparative

Literature Association Conference in 2016, and the Lusophone Studies Association Conferences of 2017 and 2019. Most recently, I was invited to give a lecture on many of the themes of *Latin American Literature at the Millennium* at the Canadian Association of Latin American and Caribbean Studies Conference in Ottawa in 2021. The classroom has also served as a laboratory for testing and exploring central hypotheses, and I would thus like to thank the McGill students from my graduate and undergraduate seminars on the Spanish American novel, contemporary Brazilian literature and film, and Latin American migration narratives for engaging with ideas that would come to inform my thinking and writing processes. I would also like to thank Teatre Lliure in Barcelona for permission to include high-quality stage production images, which help to bring some of the discussions of this book to life.

Finally, I thank friends and family, without whom this journey would never have commenced. This includes friendly support from the academic community, including Mércèdes Baillargeon, Anna Berman, Vanessa Ceia, Regina Dalcastagnè, Robin Desmeules, Patrícia Ferreir, Carl Fischer, Erika Helgen, Denise Kripper, Leila Lehnen, Rafael Esteves Martins, Javier Mocarquer, Maria Morrison, Charles Nagle, María José Navia, Lisa Overholtzer, Thea Pitman, Michael Sinatra, Sandra Sousa, Leonardo Tonus, Ariel Zach, and Katherine Zien. Outside the walls of the academy, dear friends including Amber Beckley, Roxana Donoso, Alice Driver, Virginia Woodside Falvey, Jody Forness, Eric Fortune, Priya Gursahaney, Angela Havenstein, Karishma Jain, Ariel Fox Johnson, Sasha Maseelall, Delphine Mauger, Amanda Nederostek, Daniel O'Maley, Ada Potada, Sara Rouvalis Roberts, Jennifer Sawdey, Patricia Soler, Mónica Vallin, and Elizabeth Van Buren have formed a network of solidarity and support, without which this book simply would not exist. A special note of dedication can be extended to my parents, Dr. Andrew C. Raynor and Janice Raynor, whose faith in my work has known no bounds. I would also like to thank my siblings, Andrew D. Raynor and Alicia Raynor, and their children and spouses, who have surrounded me with familial support of the richest kind. And finally, my biggest debt of gratitude goes to a little human named Xavier who accompanied me in the writing process in ways he will never fully understand—in utero, as a small infant, and now as a budding toddler. His presence fills the pages of this book, penetrating the deepest crevices of my intellectual and affective landscapes. Dream big, little one. Your being in the world inspires and delights.

NOTES

INTRODUCTION

Epigraph: Michel Foucault, "Of Other Spaces: Utopias and Heterotopias," in *The Visual Culture Reader*, 2nd edition, ed. Nicholas Mirzoeff (New York: Routledge, 2002), 231.

1. Ericka Beckman, *Capital Fictions: The Literature of Latin America's Export Age* (Minneapolis: University of Minnesota Press, 2012).

2. One need only turn to texts such as Christopher Columbus's diaries of the fifteenth century or Mário de Andrade's *Macunaíma* (1928) to find evidence of this. Indeed, despite their historical distance, both illustrate how Latin American texts have referenced other times and other places in imaginative and compelling ways. In the case of Columbus, this can be seen in his constant strategic conversation between the imagined New World and empire; in the case of Andrade, readers are drawn into a fictional universe that was heavily researched to craft a Brazilian imaginary aimed at imitating an indigenous subject, Macunaíma. In doing so, Andrade mixed fiction with fact and used historical accounts and invented language, thereby globalizing the imagined local.

3. At the level of language, references to global popular culture have long drawn our attention, led by the McOndo movement of the 1990s and writers such as Alberto Fuguet, Sergio Gómez, and Edmundo Paz Soldán. Clearly, the processes evoked in the words *Macintosh*, *McDonald's*, or *condominium* that form McOndo have had an economic *and* a cultural footprint in Latin America.

Anthony Giddens has commented on the particularity of the modern era, stating,

> In conditions of late modernity, we live "in the world" in a different sense from previous eras of history. Everyone still continues to live a local life, and the constraints of the body ensure that all individuals, at every moment, are contextually situated in time and space. Yet the transformations of place, and the intrusion of distance into local activities, combined with the centrality of mediated experience, radically change what "the world" actually is. This is so both on the level of the "phenomenal world" of the individual and the general universe of social activity within which collective social life is enacted. Although everyone lives a local life, phenomenal worlds for the most part are truly global.

Anthony Giddens, *Modernity and Self-Identity: Self and Society in the Late Modern Age* (Stanford, CA: Stanford University Press, 1991), 187.

4. In an era of increased worldwide integration, contemporary Latin American literature habitually upsets chronological linearity, straddling the local time of multiple geographies or deepening and extending time on a global plane. Of course, time has always played out differently in literature, contracting and expanding based on the parameters of narrative, rather than external chronology. Indeed, Boom writers including Mario Vargas Llosa and Gabriel García Márquez are notorious for their experimentation with time in novels such as *Conversación en la catedral* (1969) and *Cien años de soledad* (1967), respectively. In both works, the barriers of time are made plastic, as protagonists grapple with the cyclicality of quotidian violence, social ills, and corruption. The prominence of geographically diverse micronarratives in contemporary fiction speaks to the transformation of the local into "microenvironments located on global circuits," to draw from Saskia Sassen's "Globalization or Denationalization?"

Review of International Political Economy 10, no. 1 (2003): 13. Such narrative structuring allows readers to observe how time operates locally and globally, constructing and presenting nodes of local specificity and routinely slowing time down.

Numerous scholars have explored the aesthetic impact of globalization on contemporary Latin American texts, resulting in important scholarship including the special issue of *Revista de Estudios Hispánicos* (2012), guest edited by Aníbal González Pérez, whose own contribution to postnationalism has been significant.

5. Gustavo Guerrero, *Paisajes en movimiento—Literatura y cambio cultural entro dos siglos* (Buenos Aires: Eterna Cadencia, 2018); Erica Durante, *Los meridianos de la globalización* (Louvain: UCL, 2016); Héctor Hoyos, *Beyond Bolaño: The Global Latin American Novel* (New York: Columbia University Press, 2015).

6. Santiago Castro-Gómez and Eduardo Mendieta, "Introducción: La translocalización discursiva de 'Latinoamérica' en tiempos de la globalización," in *Teorías sin disciplina: Latinoamericanismo, poscolonialidad y globalización en debate*, ed. Santiago Casto-Gómez and Eduardo Mendiota (México: Miguel Ángel Porrúa, 1998), 12. In Spanish; translation provided by Rhian Lewis. Unless otherwise noted, translations are my own. Santiago Castro-Gómez declares that transnational economic entities define themselves through their local engagement with the global and their interactions with other distant actors. See Santiago Castro-Gómez, "Geografías poscoloniales y translocalizaciones narrativas de 'lo latinoamericano': La crítica al colonialismo en tiempos de la globalización," in *Enfoques sobre Posmodernidad en América Latina*, comp. Roberto Follari and Rigoberto Lanz (Caracas: Editorial Sentido, 1998), 161.

7. Renato Ortiz, *Mundialización y cultura* (Bogotá: Convenio Andrés Bello, 2004), 39.

8. Néstor García Canclini, *Imagined Globalization* (Durham, NC: Duke University, 2014), 18. Néstor García Canclini writes, "The hypothesis is that the statistics released by migration censuses and those agencies that track planetary circulation of investment and consumption make more sense when they are fleshed out with narratives of heterogeneity" (18).

9. Carlos Mario Yory, "Del espacio ocupado al lugar habitado: Una aproximación al concepto de topofilia," *Barrio Taller: Serie Ciudad y Hábitat* 12 (2007): 60.

10. García Canclini, *Imagined Globalization*, 7.

11. George Yúdice, "We Are Not the World," *Social Text*, no. 31/32 (1992): 204. George Yúdice's work dialogues with Samuel Doria Medina's emphasis on the export-heavy status of Latin America within a world economy, one whose terms are often dictated by those at the center for the purposes of benefiting from the development of those at the periphery. See Yúdice, "We Are Not the World," 202–216.

12. Castro-Gómez and Mendieta, "Introducción," 6.

13. *Local*, then, following Arjun Appadurai, is taken to be a relational and contextual concept rather than a spatial dimension.

14. Ángel Esteban and Jesús Montoya Juárez, "¿Desterritorializados o multiterritorializados?: La narrativa hispanoamericana en el siglo XXI," in *Literatura más allá de la nación: De lo centrífugo n la narrativa hispanoamericana del siglo XXI*, ed. Noguerol Jiménez et al. (Madrid: Iberoamericana Vervuert, 2011), 9.

15. Congreso Internacional "Última narrativa latinoamericana: Nuevas corrientes y tendencias," University of Salamanca, 2009.

16. Ángel Esteban et al., eds., *Narrativas latinoamericanas para el siglo XXI: Nuevos enfoques y territorios* (Hildesheim, Germany: Georg Olms Verlag, 2010).

17. Francisca Noguerol Jiménez et al., eds., *Literatura más allá de la nación: De lo centrípeto y lo centrífugo en la narrativa hispanoamericana del siglo XXI* (Madrid: Iberoamericana Vervuert, 2011).

18. Montoya Juárez and Esteban, *Entre lo local y lo global.*

19. Jesús Montoya Juárez and Ángel Esteban, "A modo de introducción: ¿Narrativa latinoamericana más allá del aeropuerto?," in Montoya Juárez and Esteban, *Entre lo local y lo global,* 8. Of particular importance in this volume is contributor Francisca Noguerol's study of the cartographies of contemporary Latin American narrative, in which she notes the use of multisited narratives and geographic plurality to capture universality, and a tendency toward "narrative narcissism," which, as she notes, is more of a literary device than a mere stylistic choice, lending itself to monologue-focused novels often written in a fragmented format, substituting monologue for dialogue. Noguerol cites the distinction Ivan Thays makes between the circular structure of earlier "total" novels and the multilinear narrative structure of today's texts, which draw chaotic narrative threads into an unharmonious yet radiant structure marred by coincidences and cross-contacts: "Actualmente, la totalidad radica en el desorden que nos hace entender que todas las líneas, aún las más absurdas o arbitrarias, pertenecen a la misma línea oscilante y derivativa" (Currently, the totality lies in the disorder that makes us understand that all lines, even the most absurd or arbitrary, belong to the same oscillating and derivative line). Ivan Thays, "Andrea no duerme," in *Palabra de América,* ed. Roberto Bolaño et al. (Barcelona: Seix Barral, 2004), 193. See Francisca Noguerol, "Narrar sin fronteras," in Montoya Juárez and Esteban, *Entre lo local y lo global.*

20. This categorization builds on Deleuze and Guattari's terminology of deterritorialized and reterritorialized subjects, arguing for the absence of a geographical grounding and a fluidity between two spaces, reflected in the prefix *trans-*.

21. As evidenced by the exile writing resulting from the dictatorships and the transterritorialized networks that formed at the close of the twentieth century, the Latin American literary imaginary has long surpassed the parameters of nation. One literary response to the question of ethics and individual justice in relation to the state is Ariel Dorfman's poignant theatrical piece *La muerte y la doncella* (1990), which examines one former victim's obsessive scheme to take the law into her own hands when placed into contact with her former torturer.

Pedro García-Caro studied the erosion of national borders in *After the Nation: Postnational Satire in the Works of Carlos Fuentes and Thomas Pynchon* (Evanston, IL: Northwestern University Press, 2014), proposing that literary narratives destabilize the hegemonic processes of modernity and nationalism while contemplating postnational constellations. Of particular interest in García-Caro's study is his focus on challenging the temporal and spatial design of nation, while questioning the notion of national borders as they are internalized through narrative.

Regina Dalcastagnè notes that recent Brazilian authors are reluctant to construct a portrait of national life and opt instead to focus on the "here and now" of personal experience. Regina Dalcastagnè, "Entrevista: Regina Dalcastagnè: Radiografia da literatura brasileira," interview by Luiz Rebinski Junior, *Cândido: Jornal da Biblioteca Pública do Paraná,* accessed March 1, 2015, https://www.bpp.pr.gov.br/Candido/Pagina/Entrevista-Regina-Dalcastagne.

22. Idelber Avelar, *The Untimely Present: Postdictatorial Latin American Fiction and the Task of Mourning* (Durham, NC: Duke University Press, 1999).

23. Patrick Dove, *Literature and Interregnum: Globalization, War, and the Crisis of Sovereignty in Latin America* (Albany: State University of New York Press, 2016).

24. Timothy Robbins and José González, eds., *New Trends in Contemporary Latin American Narrative: Post-national Literatures and the Canon* (New York: Palgrave Macmillan, 2014).

25. In *Literature and Interregnum,* Dove writes, "Neoliberal globalization presides over the dismantling of an old referential framework in which the national state served as mediator between the global and the local. It coincides with technological evolutions that have resulted in both the automation of tasks formerly performed by manual labor together with the real-time integration of production and demand on a planetary scale" (219).

26. While Mexico did not experience a dictatorship, it did undergo a troubling of the one-party rule that had commenced in 1929, as the first cracks in the political stronghold of the Partido Revolucionario Institucional began to form in the late 1980s. This was largely in response to the governmental cuts to social programs in order to repay federal debts.

27. Indeed, the descendants of some immigrant groups who had migrated to Brazil in search of economic opportunity began to contemplate returning to their parents' countries of origin. See Óscar Nakasato, "Reflections on Japanese-Brazilian Immigration through Narrative: An Interview with Oscar Nakasato," by Cecily Raynor, *Journal of Lusophone Studies* 2, no. 1 (2017): 198–205, https://doi.org/10.21471/jls.v2i1.161.

28. The impact of this debt crisis shook the political foundations of several Latin American governments. For example, in Mexico, oil prices plummeted as the country endured severe economic recession followed by hyperinflation and a currency crisis.

29. The idea of the Washington Consensus was first articulated by John Williamson in his chapter "What Washington Means by Policy Reform," which appeared in his edited volume, *Latin American Adjustment: How Much Has Happened?* (Washington, DC: Institute for National Economics, 1990). Williamson describes ten policy areas in which a fairly broad consensus exists as to what Latin America needs to do to excel economically. These included fiscal discipline, public expenditure priorities, tax reform, foreign direct investment, privatization, deregulation, and property rights. The principles behind the Washington Consensus are macroeconomic prudence, outwardly projected economies, and domestic liberalization. The major case studies of this edited volume included Argentina, Bolivia, Brazil, Chile, Mexico, Peru and Venezuela.

30. The relinquishing of state control over economic affairs had national consequences, as discussed by Néstor García Canclini: "Latin America is losing its national projects. The loss of control over the economies in different countries is evident" ("Introduction: Hybrid Cultures in Globalized Times," in *Hybrid Cultures: Strategies for Entering and Leaving Modernity* [Minneapolis: University of Minnesota Press, 1989], xxxviii). Juan E. De Castro's *The Spaces of Latin American Literature: Tradition, Globalization, and Cultural Production* (New York: Palgrave Macmillan, 2008) studies the historical evolution of Latin American writers, artists, and intellectuals in their relationship with Western culture from the colonial period to the present day. These changes have had inevitable effects on cultural production, as Francine Masiello explores in her critical reflection, *The Art of Transition: Latin American Culture and Neoliberal Crisis* (Durham, NC: Duke University Press, 2001). Masiello tackles this timeframe in the Southern Cone, contributing to our understanding of global capitalism as it relates to culture. She looks at the conflictual efforts of intellectuals, artists, and writers to critically engage and redefine the transition during the postdictatorship period in Argentina and Chile, a timeframe marked by aggressive neoliberal market-driven forces.

31. The term *pink tide* refers to a shift in Latin American governments toward left-leaning regimes and a rejection of neoliberal economic models. Political leaders associated with this period of political history include Hugo Chávez (Venezuela), Luiz Inácio Lula da Silva (Brazil), Cristina Fernández de Kirchner (Argentina) and Evo Morales (Bolivia). A period lasting around a decade, the "pink tide" was said to subside in 2015 following the death of its most radical and visible leader, Hugo Chávez, in 2013. In Venezuela, President Chávez took center stage, challenging Latin America's economic dependence on the United States and pushing for state control of national commodities. Chávez's death led to a notable absence of strong leadership for the most radical segments of the pink tide. The tide is commonly considered to have turned by 2015, with 2016 initiating the emergence of a "new right" in Latin America. This was first articulated by journalists Claire de Oliveira Neto and Joshua Howat Berger in their article "Latin America's 'Pink Tide' Ebbs to New Low in Brazil," *New York Times*, September 1, 2016.

32. García Canclini, *Imagined Globalization*, 152.

33. García Canclini, 26.

34. Gilda Simon, "Les mouvements de population aujourd'hui," in *Immigration et intégration: L'état des savoirs*, ed. Philippe Dewitte (Paris: La Découverte, 1999), 43.

35. Thomas L. Friedman, *The World Is Flat: A Brief History of the Twenty-First Century* (New York: Farrar, Straus and Giroux, 2005); Sheila L. Croucher, *Globalization and Belonging: The Politics of Identity in a Changing World* (Lanham, MD: Rowman and Littlefield, 2004).

36. David Harvey, *Spaces of Neoliberalization: Towards a Theory of Uneven Geographical Development* (Stuttgart: Franz Steiner Verlag, 2005), 59.

37. Anthony Giddens, *The Consequences of Modernity* (Stanford, CA: Stanford University Press, 1990), 140. Giddens posits that local places are constituted, at least in part, by distant global processes, noting that "the 'visible form' of the locale conceals the distanciated relations which determine its nature" (19).

38. Giddens, *Modernity and Self-Identity*, 189. Benedict Anderson, in his study on the imagining of communities in print capitalism, develops the idea of "homogenous, empty time," in which members of the nation move through history as a temporally unified community. Benedict R. O'G. Anderson, *Imagined Communities: Reflections on the Origin and Spread of Nationalism* (London: Verso, 1991), 26. Proceeding from Anderson's work, one line of inquiry that informs this book is how people who have never met one another recognize themselves within an inequitable, heterogeneous network of local actors that make up the global.

39. Giddens, *Modernity and Self-Identity*, 187.

40. Durante, *Los meridianos de la globalización.*

41. However, it should be noted that Quintana Roo's observance of the Hora del Sureste time zone (UTC −5:00) does not follow daylight saving time.

42. Andrés Neuman, *El viajero del siglo* (Madrid: Alfaguara, 2009).

43. César Aira, *Una novela china* (Buenos Aires: Javier Vergara, 1987); César Aira, *Váramo* (Barcelona: Editorial Anagrama, 2002).

44. Roberto Bolaño, *2666* (Barcelona: Editorial Anagrama, 2011), 243.

45. Roberto Bolaño, *2666*, trans. Natasha Wimmer (New York: Farrar, Straus and Giroux, 2004), 189.

46. Sara Ahmed, "Home and Away: Narratives of Migration and Estrangement," *International Journal of Cultural Studies* 2, no. 3 (1999): 343, https://doi.org/10.1177/136787799900200303.

47. Luiz Ruffato, *Estive em Lisboa e lembrei de você* (São Paulo: Editora Companhia das Letras, 2009).

48. Within humanities and social sciences, "Otherness" is commonly understood to stand in opposition to and in tension with Western culture, economy, and power dynamics. For a more detailed exploration on the topic, see Edward W. Said, *Orientalism* (London: Routledge and Kegan Paul, 1978).

49. Wilson Bueno, *Mar paraguayo* (São Paulo: Editora Illuminuras, 1992).

50. For second-generation protagonists, language can become a point of contention, slowly unraveling across generations to expose hybridity, defiance, or loss. For further commentary on the relation between migration, language, and hybrid identity-building, see Gustavo Pérez Firmat, *Life on the Hyphen: The Cuban-American Way* (Austin: University of Texas Press, 2012). My later discussion of Carvalho's *Teatro* in chapter 3 further illuminates this, as a young man returns to his country of origin while struggling to maintain and revive a language spoken by his parents.

51. Antonio Cornejo Polar, *Writing in the Air: Heterogeneity and the Persistence of Oral Tradition in Andean Literatures* (Durham, NC: Duke University Press, 2013).

52. Alastair Pennycook, *Language as a Local Practice* (London: Routledge, 2010).

53. Àlex Rigola and Pablo Ley, *2666* [playbill—Catalán version] (Teatre Lliure, 2007).

54. Bernardo Carvalho, *Teatro: Romance* (São Paulo: Companhia das Letras, 1998); João Gilberto Noll, *Harmada* (São Paulo: Companhia das Letras, 1993).

55. Valeria Luiselli, *Los ingrávidos* (Mexico City: Editorial Sexto Piso, 2011).

56. Doreen B. Massey, *Space, Place, and Gender* (Minneapolis: University of Minnesota Press, 1994); Yi-Fu Tuan, *Space and Place: The Perspective of Experience* (Minneapolis: University of Minnesota Press, 1977).

57. Places are spaces imbued with meaning, just as territories are constructed around collective signification, not only through their material topography. As early as the mid-1970s, Henri Lefebvre theorized space as socially performed, which he models into modes of production, commencing with natural space and culminating in social space. Lefebvre's model centers on the notion that social values and production of meaning are inscribed in space, and that spaces are ultimately reflective of larger systems of power. Lefebvre writes, "(Social) space is a (social) product. The space thus produced also serves as a tool of thought and of action; that in addition to being a means of production it is also a means of control, and hence of domination, of power." Henri Lefebvre, *The Production of Space*, trans. Donald Nicholson-Smith (1974; Oxford: Blackwell, 1991), 26. The shared spaces in the novels examined presently highlight configurations that are common to contemporary Latin American literature broadly. For example, see the work of Nelson de Oliveira, whose *Subsolo infinito* (2000) is a fever dream set in a maze of metro tunnels with few fixed points of reference.

Less traditional liminal spaces provide new readings of contingent human encounters in María José Navia's "Cera." The story follows a bereaved beautician as she enumerates the clients who pass through the chair to be waxed: a champion swimmer, an anthropologist who silently takes notes while the beautician shapes her eyebrows. Here, the malleability of the wax, its hardening and remelting, invokes an aesthetic rumination on the question of fixing representations and opening possibilities. Similarly, in "Afuera," Navia invokes the ghostly rendering of New York that preoccupies Valeria Luiselli in chapter 4 of this book, but in this case Navia refers to the markers of transiting space that her protagonists leave behind them: "Nueva York era una ciudad de fantasmas, de casas embrujadas, de mensajes dejados en un papel sobre la mesa o una nota en el refrigerador anotada con prisa" (New York was a city of ghosts, haunted houses, messages left on paper on the table or a note in the refrigerator written in haste). See María José Navia, "Afuera," in *Lugar* (Santiago de Chile: Ediciones De la Lumbre, 2017), 37–38.

CHAPTER 1 MIGRATION CHRONOTOPES

Epigraphs: Juan Gelman, "El Expulsado," in *Poesía reunida* (Barcelona: Seix Barral, 2012), 45; Marc Augé, *Non-places: An Introduction to Supermodernity*, trans. John Howe (London: Verso, 2008), 118–119.

1. Néstor García Canclini, "Migrants: Workers of Metaphor," in *Art and Visibility in Migratory Culture*, ed. Mieke Bal and Miguel Á. Hernández-Navarro (Leiden: Brill/Rodopi, 2011), 24.

2. Milton Hatoum, *Relato de un cierto Oriente* (São Paulo: Editora Companhia das Letras, 1989); Adriana Lisboa, *Azul-corvo* (Rio de Janeiro: Alfaguara, 2010); Adriana Lisboa, *Rakushisha* (Rio de Janeiro: Rocco, 2007); Adriana Lisboa, *Hanói* (Rio de Janeiro: Alfaguara, 2010); Daniel Galera, *Cordilheira* (São Paulo: Editora Companhia das Letras, 2008); Bernardo Carvalho, *O filho da mãe* (São Paulo: Editora Companhia das Letras, 2009); Chico Buarque, *Budapest: Romance* (São Paulo: Editora Companhia das Letras, 2003).

3. Jeffrey Lesser, *Immigration, Ethnicity, and National Identity in Brazil, 1808 to the Present* (Cambridge: Cambridge University Press, 2013), 197.

4. José Leonardo Tonus, "O imigrante na literatura brasileira: instrumentalização de uma figura literaria," in *Fora do retrato: Estudos de literatura brasileira contemporânea*, ed. Regina Dalcastagnè and Anderson Luis Nunes da Mata (Vinhedo, Brazil: Editora Horizonte, 2012), 94.

5. The term *chronotope* originates with Mikhail Bakhtin, who defines it as such: "We will give the name chronotope (literally, 'time space') to the intrinsic connectedness of temporal and spatial relationships that are artistically expressed in literature. . . . In the literary artistic chronotope, spatial and temporal indicators are fused into one carefully thought-out, concrete whole. Time, as it were, thickens, takes on flesh, becomes artistically visible; likewise, space becomes charged and responsive to the movements of time, plot and history. This intersection of axes and fusion of indicators characterizes the artistic chronotope." Mikhail Bakhtin, "Forms of Time and of the Chronotope in the Novel," in *The Dialogic Imagination: Four Essays*, ed. Michael Holquist (Austin: University of Texas Press, 1981), 84.

6. Luiz Ruffato, *Estive em Lisboa e lembrei de você* (São Paulo: Editora Companhia das Letras, 2009); Wilson Bueno, *Mar paraguayo* (São Paulo: Editora Iluminuras, 1992).

7. Néstor García Canclini, *Hybrid Cultures: Strategies for Entering and Leaving Modernity* (Minneapolis: University of Minnesota Press, 1989); Sara Ahmed, "Home and Away: Narratives of Migration and Estrangement," *International Journal of Cultural Studies* 2, no. 3 (1999): 329–347, https://doi.org/10.1177/136787799900200303.

8. Alastair Pennycook, *Language as a Local Practice* (London: Routledge, 2010); Antonio Cornejo Polar, *Writing in the Air: Heterogeneity and the Persistence of Oral Tradition in Andean Literatures* (Durham, NC: Duke University Press, 2013).

9. Néstor García Canclini, *Imagined Globalization* (Durham, NC: Duke University Press, 2014), 26.

10. Arjun Appadurai, *Modernity at Large: Cultural Dimensions of Globalization* (Minneapolis: University of Minnesota Press, 1996); Tim Oakes and Louisa Schein, "Translocal China: An Introduction," in *Translocal China: Linkages, Identities and the Reimagining of Space*, ed. Tim Oakes and Louisa Schein (London: Routledge, 2006), 1–35.

11. In contrast with Ruffato's prior work, *Inferno provisório*, a set of five panoramic volumes with a shared third-person narrator, the novella is notably brief, occupying fewer than one hundred pages. *Inferno provisório* is composed of (in sequential order) *Mamma, son tanto Felice* (2005), *O mundo inimigo* (2005), *Vista parcial da noite* (2006), *O mundo das impossibilidades* (2008), and *Domingos sem deus* (2011).

12. In the initial project, sixteen Brazilian authors were to embark on a one-month journey to a city overseas, funded by the publisher. Upon their return, they would have the opportunity to publish their work through Companhia das Letras. In the end, not all of the novels were published through the publishing house, nor have all of the initial projects been completed, with several books still to be released. At the same time, not all of the authors adhered to the guidelines of writing a love story. The critical reception has been mixed in the Brazilian literary community, with some books, such as Bernardo Carvalho's *O filho da mãe* (2009) and the Ruffato work examined here, receiving generous critical reception, other works not. Some authors have been eliminated from the project and others have been added. Additionally, a handful of films have been considered and are being launched based on the project. The year 2015 saw the release of a filmic adaptation of *Estive em Lisboa e lembrei de você* directed by Portuguese filmmaker José Barahona.

13. Xutos & Pontapés, "Lisboa, a Magnífica!," track 2 on *Direito ao Deserto* (Lisbon: Universal Music Portugal, 1993).

14. Brasil onde vivi, Brasil onde penei,
Brasil dos meus assombros de menino:
Há quanto tempo já que te deixei,
Cais do lado de lá do meu destino!

Que milhas de angústia no mar da saudade!
Que salgado pranto no convés da ausência!
Chegar. Perder-te mais. Outra orfandade,
Agora sem o amparo da inocência.

Dois pólos de atracção no pensamento!
Duas ânsias opostas nos sentidos!
Um purgatório em que o sofrimento
Nunca avista um dos céus apetecidos.

Ah, desterro do rosto em cada face,
Tristeza dum regaço repartido!
Antes o desespero naufragasse
Ente o chão encontrado e o chão perdido.

Miguel Torga, "Brasil" (1970), in *Diário—Vols. IX a XII* (Alfragide, Portugal: Poblicações Dom Quixote, 2011), 219.

15. Torga, "Brasil," lines 9–12.

16. Luiz Ruffato, *Inferno provisório*, 5 vols. (Rio de Janeiro: Record, 2005–2011); Luiz Ruffato, *Eles eram muitos cavalos* (São Paulo: Boitempo Editorial, 2005). In the latter, Ruffato captures a single day in 2001 in São Paulo through a kaleidoscope of sixty-eight micronarratives written alternately in first- or third-person perspective, or in indirect address through letters or public discourse. The ability to capture the plurality of a cacophony of narrative perspectives is a reoccurring trend throughout Ruffato's work.

17. "O que se segue é o depoimento, mínimamente editado, de Sérgio de Souza Sampaio, nascido em Cataguases (MG) em 7 de agosto de 1969, gravado em quatro sessões, nas tardes de sábado dos 9, 16, 23, e 30 de julho de 2005 . . . [em] Lisboa" (What follows is the testimony, minimally edited, of Sérgio de Souza Sampaio, born in Cataguases (Minas Gerais), on August 7th, 1969, recorded in four sessions on the Saturday afternoons of the 9th, 16th, 23rd and 30th of July 2005 . . . [in] Lisbon).

18. Ruffato, *Estive em Lisboa*, 17.

19. Cecily Raynor, "O global e o particular: Uma leitura espacial de *Eles eram muitos cavalos* de Luiz Ruffato," *Brasil/Brazil: A Journal of Brazilian Literature* 29, no. 54 (2016): 9–24, https://seer.ufrgs.br/index.php/brasilbrazil/article/view/70546. The full interview is presented in the appendix section of this book.

20. Ruffato discusses this in an interview that is available at "Estive em Lisboa e lembrei de você," Companhia das Letras, accessed August 13, 2020, https://www.companhiadasletras.com.br/detalhe.php?codigo=12862.

21. This same tendency is seen in the fragment on page 17: "Respondi que *de-vista*, me ofreceu um, acetei, agradeci" (I responded that we had seen each other around but never spoke, he offered me one, I accepted and thanked him).

22. Ruffato, *Estive em Lisboa*, 67.

23. Ron Scollon and Suzie Wong Scollon, *Discourses in Place: Language in the Material World* (London: Routledge, 2003), ix.

24. García Canclini, "Migrants," 33.

25. Alcides Villaça, "Ruffato cria trama ágil com percepções vivas de Lisboa," *Folha de São Paulo*, October 17, 2009, http://feeds.folha.uol.com.br/fsp/ilustrad/fq1710200914.htm.

26. Ruffato, *Estive em Lisboa*, 32. These are local neighborhoods and regions near the Pomba River in Minas Gerais.

27. Cecily Raynor, "Linguagem, espaço e nação: Um mapeamento das identidades multi-geográficas do protagonista imigrante," *Estudos de Literatura Brasileira Contemporânea*, no. 45 (January–June 2015): 164, http://dx.doi.org/10.1590/2316-4018459.

28. Ruffato, *Estive em Lisboa*, 36.

29. Ruffato, 40.

30. Ruffato, 50.

31. Ruffato, 51.

32. Pennycook, *Language*, 2.

33. Ruffato, *Estive em Lisboa*, 61.

34. Ruffato, 46.

35. Pennycook, *Language*.

36. Ruffato, *Estive em Lisboa*, 83.

37. Ruffato, 16.

38. Ruffato, 44.

39. Óscar Nakasato, *Nihonjin* (São Paulo: Benvirá, 2011).

40. Ruffato connects culture and identity with gastronomic traditions with the Brazilian, Sheila, voicing her desire to eat "arroz-com-feijão" (rice and beans) before the two meet up, a novelty Serginho imagines to be inaccessible in the land of "**arroz com pato, arroz de marisco, arroz de gambas, arroz de polvo, arroz de tamboril**" (**rice with duck, rice with seafood, rice with shrimp, rice with octopus, rice with monkfish**). Ruffato, *Estive em Lisboa*, 63.

41. Ruffato, 62–63.

42. Ruffato, 67.

43. Ruffato, 67.

44. Doreen B. Massey, *Space, Place, and Gender* (Minneapolis: University of Minnesota Press, 1994), 12.

45. Ruffato, *Estive em Lisboa*, 67.

46. Ruffato, 68.

47. Ruffato, 68.

48. Ruffato, 69. The protagonist's use of the expression "por-cima-da-carne-seca," meaning in a position of privilege or "on top," reinforces the informal and local nature of her narrative. More than this, it could be argued that the expression situates her class position as well, given that *carne-seca* is traditionally associated with lower, lower-middle, and nouveau riche classes in Brazil.

49. Torga, "Brasil," 219.

50. Ruffato, *Estive em Lisboa*, 46–47.

51. Ruffato, 78.

52. Marco Antonio Rodrigues, "Mobilidade precária em *Terra estrangeira* e em *Estive em Lisboa e lembrei de você*," *Estudos de Literatura Brasileira Contemporânea* 39 (2012): 190, http://dx.doi.org/10.1590/S2316-40182012000100010.

53. García Canclini, "Migrants," 29.

54. Katherine Brickell and Ayona Datta, eds., *Translocal Geographies: Spaces, Places, Connections* (Farnham, England: Ashgate, 2011).

55. Ahmed, "Home and Away," 336–337.

56. Ahmed, 344.

57. Among many examples, this can be seen in the German-Brazilian dialect Riograndenser Hunsrückisch, spoken by a community in Rio Grande do Sul. See Jeffrey Lesser, *Immigration, Ethnicity, and National Identity in Brazil, 1808 to the Present* (Cambridge: Cambridge University Press, 2013), 39.

58. José Martiniano de Alencar, *Iracema* (São Paulo: Edita Melhoramento, 1865). A range of nineteenth-century texts feature mixed language use, including *En la Sangre* (1887) by Eugenio Cambaceres, which follows the story of an Italian migrant to Buenos Aires and features passages in Italian and *cocoliche*. *Cocoliche* is a Spanish-Italian hybrid language that was prevalent in Buenos Aires between 1880 and 1930. In Brazil, Joaquim de Sousa Andrade's extended poem "O Guesa" (1871) incorporates many languages, including English, given that the author published the piece during his extended stay in the United States.

59. Salim Miguel, "Ponto de Balsa," in *O sabor da forma* (Rio de Janeiro: Record, 2007); Luis Krausz, *Desterro: Memórias em ruínas* (São Paulo: Tordesilhas, 2011); Luiz Ruffato, *Mamma, son tanto felice* (Rio de Janeiro: Record, 2005).

60. Bueno, *Mar paraguayo*, 15.

61. On a handful of occasions, the text also includes lexica in French, "Après midi" (Bueno, *Mar paraguayo*, 48), and English, "en los States" and "technicolor" (51). It is also of note that Erin Moure's recent translation of *Mar paraguayo* yields a text in another blend of languages: this time, English and French.

62. Jens Andermann, "Abismos del tercer espacio: *Mar paraguayo*, portuñol salvaje y el fin de la utopía letrada," *Revista Hispánica Moderna* 64, no. 1 (2011): 17, https://www.jstor.org/stable/41306058.

63. Graciela Montaldo, "El mundo de la cultura," *Revista Hispánica Moderna* 64, no. 1 (2011): 3, https://www.jstor.org/stable/41306057.

64. Néstor Perlongher, "Sopa paraguaya," in *Mar paraguayo*, by Wilson Bueno (São Paulo: Iluminuras, 1992), 8.

65. Bueno, *Mar paraguayo*, 49. Directly afterward, the indirect object pronoun *me* is placed after the first verb and before the infinitive, also in line with Portuguese syntax, rather than "no me voy a poner" (I will not become), as would be grammatical in the Spanish.

66. Bueno, *Mar paraguayo*, 51. *São* and *son* are the plural third-person conjugations of *ser* (to be). This tendency toward amalgamation is also seen in "avuêlos" (42), a fusion of the Spanish *abuelos* and the Portuguese *avós* (grandparents).

67. Bueno, 33.

68. Bueno, 58.

69. Osvaldo Farrés, "Quizás, quizás, quizás," 1947, track B1 on *Ayer, Hoy, y Siempre* (United States: Ofarres, 1979).

70. A further muddling of meaning is created here through almost serendipitous allusions to the landscape of Brazil and Latin America, as *chororó* is also a colloquial name for several species of antbird native to Brazil and Guarará is a town and municipality in Minas Gerais.

71. Perhaps the most widely known example of this practice in nonfiction is the work of Gloria Anzaldúa.

72. Christopher Larkosh, "Flows of Trans-language: Translating Transgender in the Paraguayan Sea," *Transgender Studies Quarterly* 3, no. 3–4 (2016): 559, https://doi.org/10.1215/23289252-3545071. Larkosh's final note to the reader of his translation reads as follows: "Begin here, by all means; but continue on your own, through Spanish and Portuguese, perhaps into Guarani or any other in the myriad combination of other languages, uprooting all impulse for one language alone. Ultimately, this translation and implicit transition will complete itself in each and every committed and attentive reader who enters here" (559).

73. Mikhail Bakhtin, "Discourse in the Novel" (1934), in *The Dialogic Imagination: Four Essays*, ed. Michael Holquist (Austin: University of Texas Press, 2017), 291–292.

74. In postcolonial theory, hybridity has taken manifold forms but continues to be related to the deconstruction and discrediting of a singular authority and dominant discourse, whether cultural or political or linguistic. See Mikhail Bakhtin, *Speech Genres and Other Late Essays*, trans. Vern W. McGee, ed. Caryl Emerson and Michael Holquist (Austin: University of Texas Press, 1986). This can be observed in bilingual environments in which the minor language is literally placed below the major on signs or other public markers of space, as seen frequently in border territories such as between San Diego, California, and Tijuana, Mexico.

75. Pennycook, *Language*, 2.

76. Echoing this theme, and reflecting on the death of Wilson Bueno in 2010, Christopher Larkosh writes that he decided to publish the excerpt of his translation of *Mar paraguayo* as an addendum to his article "not simply for reasons of space but to mark out where I was, and also where he was, at the moment of his death." Larkosh, "Flows of Trans-language," 559.

77. Cornejo Polar, *Writing in the Air*, 165, 170.

78. Andermann, "Abismos del tercer espacio," 13.

79. Andreas Huyssen, *Present Pasts: Urban Palimpsests and the Politics of Memory* (Stanford, CA: Stanford University Press, 2003), 198. In its reflections on the restoration of marginalized identities, the text dialogues with broader trends in contemporary artistic production, as noted in Huyssen's mapping of postmodernism: "Art, writing, film making and criticism of women and minority artists with their recuperation of buried and mutilated traditions, their emphasis on exploring forms of gender- and race-based subjectivity in aesthetic productions and experiences, and their refusal to be limited to standard canonizations . . . [add] a whole new dimension to the critique of high modernism and to the emergence of alternative forms of culture" (24).

80. Bueno, *Mar paraguayo*, 56.

81. Bueno, 16.

82. Bueno, 26.

83. Angélica Madeira, "Línguas na fronteira, línguas na diáspora," *Humanidades* 59 (2012): 55.

84. Rodolfo A. Franconi, "O olhar oblíquo: Uma categoria cultural; conceituação e exemplos," *Revista de Crítica Literaria Latinoamericana* 32, no. 63 (2006): 112, https://doi.org/10.2307/25070326.

85. Bueno, *Mar paraguayo*, 13.

86. Larkosh, "Flows of Trans-language," 560.

87. Bueno, *Mar paraguayo*, 32–33.

88. Bueno, 32.

89. Bueno, 15

90. Bueno, 73.

91. Bueno, 76.

92. Patricio Pron, *El espíritu de mis padres sigue subiendo en la lluvia* (Barcelona: Random House Mondadori, 2012); Tatiana Salem Levy, *A chave da casa* (Rio de Janeiro: Best Bolso, 2013).

93. Huyssen, *Present Pasts*, 18.

94. Regina Dalcastagnè, "O tempo no romance brasileiro contemporâneo," in *Narrativas contemporâneas: Recortes críticos sobre literatura brasileira*, ed. Gina Maria Gomes (Porto Alegre, Brazil: Libretos, 2012), 130.

95. Migration-themed narratives and testimonies are particularly valuable in light of social sciences' conventional focus on statistical data when analyzing migration, as noted by Russell King, John Connell, and Paul White in their preface to their coedited book, *Writing across Worlds: Literature and Migration* (London: Routledge, 1995): "[Social-scientific research] . . . fails to capture the essence of what it is like to be a migrant; and be, or not be, part of a community, a nation, a society—cut off from history and from a sense of place. It fails to portray nostalgia, anomie, exile, rootlessness, restlessness" (ix–x).

CHAPTER 2 SPEED CONTROL

Epigraphs: Gloria Anzaldúa, *Borderlands: The New Mestiza* (San Francisco: Aunt Lute Books, 1987), 25; Michel Foucault, "Of Other Spaces: Utopias and Heterotopias," in *Rethinking Architecture: A Reader in Cultural Theory*, ed. Neil Leach (London: Routledge, 1997), 330.

1. *Traffic*, directed by Steven Soderbergh (USA Films, 2000); Alejandro González Iñárritu, *Amores Perros*, directed by Alejandro González Iñárritu (Studio Home Entertainment, 2000); *Blood Diamond*, directed by Edward Zwick (Warner Bros., 2006); *Syriana*, directed by Stephen Gaghan (Warner Bros., 2005).

2. Roberto Bolaño, *Los detectives salvajes* (Barcelona: Editorial Anagrama, 1998); Roberto Bolaño, *2666* (2004; Barcelona: Editorial Anagrama, 2011).

3. Bolaño's writing style has frequently been seen as a logical consequence of his migratory life between Latin America and Europe. Indeed, he himself famously stated, "My homeland are my son and my library." Roberto Bolaño, *Entre paréntesis: Ensayos, artículos y discursos (1998–2003)*, ed. Ignacio Echeverría (Barcelona: Editorial Anagrama, 2004), 43. Others, however, including Jorge Volpi, have noted a tendency among certain—especially American—critics to overemphasize Bolaño's migrations. To give one of many examples, Patricio Pron's short story "Como una cabeza enloquecida vaciada de su contenido" (in *La vida interior de las plantas de interior* [Barcelona: Random House Mondadori, 2013]) also makes visible the links among a set of protagonists in transnational locations through the use of short, interconnected episodes.

4. This was a decision made by Bolaño's literary executor, Igancio Echevarría, and Jorge Herralde, to whom he verbally communicated his desire to separate the works in the hope of maximizing revenue for his children and estate.

5. *Los detectives salvajes* is a three-part novel, the second of which is composed of fragmented testimonies spanning a nonlinear twenty years and many global locations, ending in Santa Teresa—a significant intertextual link to *2666*. Coincidence is explored at length in *Los detectives salvajes*. One example can be seen in the foundation of the visceral realists, the group of Mexican poets around which much of the novel revolves. The work's fictional Mexican philologist, Ernesto García Grajales, states regarding their formation, "No fue una coincidencia. Más bien fue un homenaje. Una señal. Una respuesta. Quién sabe. De todas formas, yo prefiero no perderme en esos laberintos. Me ciño a la materia tratada y que el lector y el estudioso saquen sus conclusiones. Yo creo que el librito va a quedar bien" (It was not a coincidence. Rather it was a tribute. A signal. An answer. Who knows. Anyway, I prefer not to get lost in those labyrinths. I will stick to the subject matter and the reader and the scholar will draw their conclusions. I think the little book will turn out well) (551). Similarly, *2666*'s mysterious title, a number never mentioned in its 1,100 pages, appears first in *Amuleto* (1999), the story of Uruguayan Auxilio Lacoutre, who gets confined to the bathroom at the Universidad Nacional Autónoma de México during the 1968 student massacre. Among Auxilio's dreams and visions, she recalls wandering around Mexico City with Arturo Belano, Bolaño's alter ego, appearing also in *Los detectives salvajes*. During her walk she sees a "forgotten" cemetery, so haunting she assigns it the futuristic date of 2666. This intertextual reference connects the novel to the death-laden landscape of the massacre and the space of the cemetery, while emphasizing the author's long interest in the border town and the real-life crimes of Ciudad Juárez. Bolaño's literary executor, Ignacio Echevarría, comments, "The writing of *2666* occupied Bolaño in his last years. But the conception and the design of the novel are very old, and, in retrospect, there is room for acknowledging the same heartbeat in this and that novel by Bolaño, more particularly in-between those he published after *Los detectives salvajes*, which does not end in the Sonora by chance" (Bolaño, *Los detectives salvajes*, 1123).

6. The novel begins in the form of a coincidence connecting four European academics in "La parte de los críticos." An unquenchable thirst for knowledge about a shadowy German writer, Benno von Archimboldi, later discovered to be Hans Reiter, ignites friendship and intimate bonds between an Italian, Piero Morini; a Frenchman, Jean-Claude Pelletier; a Spaniard, Manuel Espinoza; and an Englishwoman, Liz Norton, who crisscross European cities via literary conferences to present their work on the author. In the end their search leads three of the four to Santa Teresa after hearing that Archimboldi's enigmatic path had ended in the border town. While their hunts prove futile, Pelletier claims a unique proximity to the author: "Archimboldi está aquí . . . y nosotros estamos aquí, y esto es lo más cerca que jamás estaremos de él" (Bolaño, *2666*, 207) (Archimboldi is here . . . and we're here, and this is the closest we will ever be to him) (Roberto Bolaño, *2666*, trans. Natasha Wimmer [New York: Farrar, Straus and Grioux, 2004], 159). Subsequent citations will refer to these two editions, indicated by "ES" and "EN," respectively. In Santa Teresa, the critics spend most of their time with fellow Archimboldi scholar, Chilean professor Oscar Amalfitano, who is at the center of the second part of the novel. Significantly, each of the novel's five parts brings with it characters from previous sections and works, none of whom are aware of their presence within the larger web, as seen in the introduction of Lalo Cura in part 3, who also appears in *Los detectives salvajes*. These bonds create a broad grid of interconnectivity spanning more than seven decades and multiple geographies. The second part of the novel centers on daily life in Santa Teresa through the lens of Chilean expatriate Oscar Amalfitano, who resides in the middle-class suburbs of the city with his daughter, Rosa. Through memory sequences and dreams, a large part takes place in Barcelona, the city to which Amalfitano migrated during his self-exile from the Chilean military coup. Amalfitano considers exile "un movimento natural, algo que, a su manera, contribuye a abolir el destino o lo que comúnmente se considera el destino" (a natural movement, something that, in its own way, contributes to destiny or what is commonly known as destiny) (157 ES / 117 EN). Thus, it is no wonder that when he becomes concerned for his daughter's safety given the violent crimes against young women occurring around them, he ships her across the border with Oscar Fate, linking the second section of the text with the third, "La parte de fate," the tale of American journalist Quincy Williams, a.k.a. Oscar Fate. Mourning over his mother's recent death, Fate is sent from New York to Santa Teresa to cover a boxing match. His dealings with the locals lead him to uncover the city's dark underbelly while becoming acquainted with Rosa Amalfitano. The final page of this section anonymously introduces the primary suspect in the killings, German expatriate Klaus Haas, further linking the third and the fourth section, in which Haas plays a central role. After the fourth section recounting the crimes, the work's final part, "La parte de Archimboldi," leads readers full-circle to the life of the enigmatic author whom the four academics frantically chased, ending finally with the author's decision to travel to Mexico in the hope of helping his imprisoned nephew, the aforementioned Klaus Haas.

7. Rigola and Ley were the first playwrights to capture the five sections of the novel in a five-part performance, with four intervals, and an approximate running time of five hours. The adaptation has received broad critical acclaim, including the Barcelona Critics Prize for Best Drama Performance, Best Dramaturgy, and Best Set of 2008, as well as the Terenci Moix Prize of Scenic Arts in 2008, the Qwerty 2008 Prize for Best Adaptation from a novel to another format, and the Max 2009 Awards for the Best Theater Show and Best Scenography. Since then, Rigola's stage adaptation of *2666* has been translated into a handful of languages and was most recently performed in Berlin in 2014. Although there have been rumors of an upcoming film adaptation, currently two theatrical adaptations exist: the Rigola play and a piece by Robert Falls and Seth Bockley at the Goodman Theater in Chicago (2016). For the purposes of my discussion of speed and spatial representations in contemporary Latin American literature, I have chosen to discuss Rigola's adaptation because of the director's use of film to uniquely engage the novel's textual representations of movement and mobility.

8. Àlex Rigola, interview by Pablo Ley, 27 February 2006, Barcelona, Spain, in *2666* [playbill—English version] (Theatre Lliure, 2007), 11.

9. Rigola, interview by Ley, 8.

10. Rita Laura Segato, "Territory, Sovereignty, and Crimes of the Second State: The Writing on the Body of Murdered Women," trans. Sarah Koopman, in *Terrorizing Women: Feminicide in the Américas*, ed. Rosa-Linda Fregoso and Cynthia L. Bejarano (Durham, NC: Duke University Press, 2010), 70–92; Rita Laura Segato, "Las nuevas formas de la guerra y el cuerpo de las mujeres," *Sociedade e Estado* 29, no. 2 (2014): 341–371, http://dx.doi.org/10.1590/S0102-69922014000200003; Martin Albrow, *The Global Age* (Stanford, CA: Stanford University Press, 1996); Doreen B. Massey, *Space, Place, and Gender*, (Minneapolis: University of Minnesota Press, 1994); Milton Santos, *Toward an Other Globalization: From the Single Thought to Universal Conscience*, trans. and ed. Lucas Melgaço and Tim Clarke (Cham, Switzerland: Springer International, 2017).

11. Grant Farred, "The Impossible Closing: Death, Neoliberalism, and the Postcolonial in Bolaño's *2666*," *Modern Fiction Studies* 56, no. 4 (2010): 689–708; Sharae Deckard, "Peripheral Realism, Millennial Capitalism, and Roberto Bolaño's *2666*," *Modern Language Quarterly* 73 no. 3 (2012): 351–372, https://doi.org./10.1215/00267929-1631433.

12. Hermann Herlinghaus, "Placebo Intellectuals in The Wake of Cosmopolitanism: A 'Pharmacological' Approach to Roberto Bolaño's Novel *2666*," *The Global South* 5, no. 1, (2011): 106. https://www.muse.jhu.edu/article/449220.

13. Santos, *Toward an Other Globalization*, 43, 44. This assertion is more thoroughly discussed in the introduction to this work, but in short, Santos argues that human activity used to be much slower, and that differences in velocity between territories were not seen as mutually exclusive until recently, when competition between velocities became a primary impetus of global trade networks.

14. Santos, *Toward an Other Globalization*, 37.

15. Jesús Martín-Barbero, "Prólogo," in *Por otra Globalización: Del pensamiento único a la conciencia universal*, by Milton Santos (Bogotá: Convenio Andrés Bello, 2004), 11.

16. It should be noted that factories of this sort had been in existence on a global scale for decades before the passage of the North American Free Trade Agreement.

17. Santos, *Toward an Other Globalization*, 44.

18. Segato, "Territory, Sovereignty, and Crimes," 78.

19. Patrick Dove, *Literature and Interregnum: Globalization, War, and the Crisis of Sovereignty in Latin America* (Albany: State University of New York Press, 2016), 218.

20. Roberto Bolaño, *Estrella distante* (Barcelona: Editorial Anagrama, 1996); Roberto Bolaño, *Amuleto* (Barcelona: Editorial Anagrama, 1999); Roberto Bolaño, *Nocturno de Chile* (Barcelona: Editorial Anagrama, 1999).

21. Sergio González Rodríguez, *Huesos en el desierto* (Barcelona: Editorial Anagrama, 2002).

22. Marcela Valdés, "Alone among the Ghosts: Roberto Bolaño's *2666*," *Nation*, November 19, 2008, https://www.thenation.com/article/archive/alone-among-ghosts-roberto-bolanos-2666/; Patrick Dove, *Literature and Interregnum*, 217.

23. Bolaño, *2666*, 239 ES / 348 EN. For further elaboration on this, see Dove's discussion of Bolaño's process of researching and writing *2666* in *Literature and Interregnum*.

24. Dove, *Literature and Interregnum*, 221.

25. Segato, "Territory, Sovereignty, and Crimes," 84.

26. Farred, "Impossible Closing," 693; Segato, "Territory, Sovereignty, and Crimes," 84.

27. Thomas L. Friedman, *The World Is Flat: A Brief History of the Twenty-First Century* (New York: Farrar, Straus and Giroux, 2005). Sheila L. Croucher argues, like Friedman, that globalization "can be described as a process by which the people of the world are unified into a single society and function together" (Friedman, 10). See Sheila L. Croucher, *Globalization and Belonging: The Politics of Identity in a Changing World* (Lanham, MD: Rowman and Littlefield, 2004).

28. Albrow, *Global Age*, 53.

29. Massey, *Space, Place, and Gender*, 12.

30. Scott Esposito, "*2666* by Roberto Bolaño," *Quarterly Conversation*, 2008, http://quarterlyconversation.com/2666-by-roberto-bolano (site discontinued).

31. Bolaño, *2666*, 15–16 ES.

32. Bolaño, 17 ES / 4 EN. Notably, in Natasha Wimmer's English translation of *2666*, these fragments are separated not only by three full lines but also by a small dot placed in the middle, in order to better distinguish them.

33. Bolaño, 48 ES.

34. Bolaño, 28–29 EN.

35. Roland Robertson, "Glocalization: Time-Space and Homogeneity Heterogeneity," in *Global Modernities*, ed. Mike Featherstone, Scott Lash, and Roland Robertson (London: Sage, 1995), 25–45.

36. Bolaño, *2666*, 716 ES / 573 EN.

37. Albrow, *Global Age*, 52.

38. Bolaño, *2666*, 702 ES / 562 EN.

39. Albrow, *Global Age*, 52.

40. Bolaño, *2666*, 613 ES / 490 EN.

41. Bolaño, 260 ES / 202–203 EN.

42. Bolaño, 172 ES / 129 EN.

43. Bolaño, 221 ES.

44. Bolaño, 157 ES / 117 EN.

45. Laura Barberán Reinares, "Globalized Philomels: State Patriarchy, Transnational Capital and the Femicides on the US-Mexican Border in Roberto Bolaño's *2666*," CUNY Academic Works, 2010, 51–72, https://academicworks.cuny.edu/bx_pubs/6; Ángeles Donoso Macaya, "Estética, política y el posible territorio de la ficción en *2666*," *Revista Hispánica Moderna* 62, no. 2 (2009): 125–142, https://doi.org/10.1353/rhm.0.0023. Significant journalistic accounts of the Juárez femicides include Diana Washington Valdez's book *Cosecha de mujeres: Safari en el desierto mexicano* (Mexico City: Editorial Océano, 2005), as well as the work of Sergio González Rodriguez, as mentioned earlier in the chapter.

46. Saskia Sassen, *The Global City: New York, London, Tokyo* (Princeton, NJ: Princeton University Press, 2001).

47. Bolaño, *2666*, 449 ES / 282 EN.

48. Bolaño, 650 ES.

49. Bolaño, 590 EN.

50. Gilles Deleuze and Félix Guattari, *Anti-Oedipus: Capitalism and Schizophrenia*, trans. Robert Hurley, Mark Seem, and Helen R. Lane (Minneapolis: University of Minnesota Press, 1972), xx.

51. Julia Estela Monárrez Fragoso, "Trama de una injusticia: Feminicidio sexual sistémico en Ciudad Juárez," *Región y Sociedad* 22, no. 47 (2013): 201–206, http://www.scielo.org.mx/pdf/regsoc/v22n47/v22n47a10.pdf; Alicia Gaspar de Alba and Georgina Guzmán, "Introduction: Feminicidio: The 'Black Legend' of the Border," in *Making a Killing: Femicide, Free Trade,* *and La Frontera*, ed. Alicia Gaspar de Alba and Georgina Guzmán (Austin: University of Texas Press, 2010), 1–24.

52. In Mexico, and specifically with respect to the Juárez femicides, this effort has been coordinated by (among many others) Casa Amiga (the organization that published the forensic reports) and Nuestras Hijas de Regreso a Casa AC, a community association composed of family members of missing women. By organizing a summit to discuss the Juárez murders, Alicia Gaspar de Alba has brought substantial scholarly, activist, and journalistic attention in the United States, which eventually led to the formation of the Ni Una Más (Not One More [Femicide]) declaration. Of this gathering, Gaspar de Alba and Georgina Guzmán write, the focus was "not so much on 'who was killing them,' but instead . . . on how we could reassemble the pieces of the puzzle of their deaths to help us understand why they died and why they were killed with such a vicious vengeance against the brown female body." Gaspar de Alba and Guzmán, "Introduction: *Feminicidio*," 8.

Here, it is important to note Gaspar de Alba and Guzmán's positioning of the murders within not only a pervasive culture of misogyny but also the exploitation and commodification of women of color and their labor. Among the many representations of the Juárez murders, there are those that lean toward sensationalizing the murders as a kind of spectacle of third-world tragedy, and those that strive to maintain the agency of "doubly other[ed]" (Segato, "Territory, Sovereignty, and Crimes," 87) women who experience multiple forms of gendered, economic, and racial violence. See Nuala Finnegan, "Sacrificial Screams: Excess in Àlex Rigola's Stage Adaptation of *2666*," in *Cultural Representations of Feminicidio at the US-Mexico Border* (New York: Routledge, 2018), 53–82; and Alicia Schmidt Camacho, "Body Counts on the Mexico-US Border: Feminicidio, Reification, and the Theft of Mexicana Subjectivity," *Chicana/Latina Studies* 4, no. 1 (2004): 22–60, https://www.jstor.org/stable/23014438. These questions may become even more pressing in light of the integration of digital tools of engagement in action against gender violence. One of the most important responses in recent years has been the proliferation of hashtags like #VivasNosQueremos (we want to live) and #NiUnaMás/Menos (not one less [woman]), movements with digital and analog components that spread across Latin America to reach other geographical regions. Participation in these campaigns has been wide ranging, including artists, journalists, and academics who regularly protest, both online (via the popular hashtags) and across the streets of the trans-Hispanic world on days like #8M (March 8) and #24A (April 24). Other examples include the No Estamos Todas collective art project, whose participants create portraits of women who died by femicide, allowing for a community ritual of grief and memorialization.

53. Bolaño, *2666*, 444 ES / 353–354 EN.

54. Bolaño, 476 ES / 450 EN, 518 ES / 359 EN, 533 ES / 454 EN.

55. Bolaño, 470 ES / 375 EN.

56. Bolaño, 469 ES / 374–375 EN.

57. Bolaño, 488 ES / 390 EN, 446 ES / 356 EN, 444 ES / 355 EN.

58. It is also significant that when the bodies are discovered, the forensic reports often characterize the dead women as being out of place. This is the case when a woman is found dead in the waste disposal receptacle of a different industrial park from the one she worked in (489 ES / 391 EN) and in a fragment in which residents of a neighborhood near the site where one of the cadavers is found tell the police that they had never seen her before: "Esta criatura no es de aquí" (She isn't from around here, poor thing) (443 ES / 353 EN). To some degree, this heightens the presence of blame that is attached to women's mobility in the text, as many of the murdered women are implicitly portrayed as recklessly mobile, with stasis perceived to be the safer alternative.

59. Nuala Finnegan, *Cultural Representations of Feminicidio at the US-Mexico Border* (New York: Routledge, 2018), 37.

60. Bolaño, *2666*, 575 ES.
61. Bolaño, 458–459 EN.
62. Elva Orozco Mendoza has explored the notion of thing agency in relation to the "funeralization" of Ciudad Juarez through the proliferation of memorial objects for victims of femicide. See Elva F. Orozco Mendoza, "Feminicide and the Funeralization of the City: On Thing Agency and Protest Politics in Ciudad Juárez." *Theory and Event* 20, no. 2 (2017): 351–380.
63. In *The Femicide Machine*, Sergio González Rodríguez positions the maquila as a sacrificial culture, writing of an endless "flux of sacrifice and self-sacrifice" through which workers are assimilated into the mechanisms of the "productive apparatus." Sergio González Rodríguez, *The Femicide Machine* (Cambridge, MA: MIT Press, 2012), 29–30.
64. Finnegan, *Cultural Representations of Feminicidio*, 62.
65. Finnegan, 72. In her monograph *[Un]framing the "Bad Woman": Sor Juana, Malinche, Coyolxauhqui, and Other Rebels with a Cause* (Austin: University of Texas Press, 2014), Alicia Gaspar de Alba engages the trope of sacrifice as a disruptive mode of conceptualizing the Juárez murders.
66. Segato, "Territory, Sovereignty, and Crimes," 80.
67. Dove, *Literature and Interregnum*, 266–267. See also Segato, "Las nuevas formas de la guerra," 341–371.
68. *Arixiu Bolaño: 1977–2003*, Centre de Cultura Contemporània de Barcelona, Barcelona, March 5–June 30, 2013.
69. Lisa Lacoscio, "Who Was Roberto Bolaño?," *Salon*, June 6, 2013, https://www.salon.com/2013/06/24/myths_and_legends_of_roberto_bolano_exposed_in_new_exhibit_partner/. In a 2011 compilation of Bolaño's memoirs, *Entre paréntesis: Ensayos, artículos y discursos (1998–2003)*, the writer discusses his residence in Blanes, near Barcelona, where he lived between 1985 and 2003. Bolaño comments on his friendship with the small-town video store owner Narcís Serra, with whom he "spent whole afternoons discussing the films of Woody Allen or talking about thrillers that only he and I had seen" (251).
70. Rigola, interview by Ley, 9.
71. For more on this, see Arjun Appadurai, *Modernity at Large: Cultural Dimensions of Globalization* (Minneapolis: University of Minnesota Press, 1996).
72. Jara Martínez Valderas and Javier J. González Martínez, "Àlex Rigola: Dramaturgia y dirección se unen para golpear al público," in *La escenificación española contemporánea: Una mirada más allá de nuestras fronteras*, ed. Margarita del Hoyo Ventura, La excepción y la regla (Granada: Ediciones Tragacanto, 2017), 110.
73. Herbert Blau discusses this, stating, "To be sure, it was the escalation of mediatization that appeared to bring into the theater itself, and to the live bodies there, reflexes and habits of mind that seemed less natural or organic than mechanically reproduced." Herbert Blau, "Virtually Yours: Presence, Liveness, Lessness," in *Critical Theory and Performance*, ed. Janelle G. Reinelt and Joseph R. Roach (Ann Harbor: University of Michigan Press, 1992), 538.
74. Gabriela Cordone discusses the inherent sense of violence in this scene, paying particular attention to the suffocating sensation of a framing bound in violence: "Los actores/personajes no hacen referencia al espacio visual superior: encerrados en el asfixiante cuadro verde y exiguo, las imágenes superiores son más bien un catalizador de la violencia y del desquicio de sus actos" (The actors/characters don't make references to the visual space above them: while trapped in a green, exiguous and asphyxiating frame, the images above them are rather a catalyst for the violence and the mayhem of their acts). Gabriela Cordone, "*2666* en escena: Relato, imagen y mestizaje artístico," *Revista Letral* 11 (2013): 15.
75. Rigola continues to work with lighting in this section: the stage is later cast in red (which gives off a strange yellow-green color when combined with the green of the stage), and the

recording is in blue. Here lighting seems to follow the escalation of the night as violence intensifies and Fate and Rosa finally decide to flee.

76. As Giddens notes, the visible form of the locale often obscures the distanciated relations that shape the experience of everyday life at the local level. Anthony Giddens, *The Consequences of Modernity* (Stanford, CA: Stanford University Press, 1990), 19.

77. As Ana Prieto Nadal notes, "En cada una de las partes, un espacio escénico—sala de conferencias, patio con verja, cubo-ring-televisor, desierto, espacio vacío con pantalla y cinta de correr—configura la imagen, arbitraria, de un paisaje contenedor que engloba todos los demás espacios evocados y referenciados" (In each of the parts, the space of the scenes—conference rooms, patio with railings, cubical television, desert, empty space with a screen and treadmill—configures the image, arbitrarily, as a container landscape that encompasses all other evoked and referenced spaces). Ana Prieto Nadal, "La narrativa de Roberto Bolaño a escena: *2666*," *Revista de Literatura* 78, no. 156 (2016): 545, https://doi.org/10.3989/revliteratura.2016.02.023.

78. Saskia Sassen, *Globalization and its Discontents: Essays on the New Mobility of People and Money* (New York: New Press, 1999); Sassen, *Global City*; Saskia Sassen, "Globalization or Denationalization?," *Review of International Political Economy* 10, no. 1 (2003): 1–22. https://www.jstor.org/stable/4177449.

79. Segato, "Territory, Sovereignty, and Crimes," 88.

CHAPTER 3 AMBIVALENT SPACES

Epigraph: Diana Taylor, "Performing Ruins," in *Telling Ruins in Latin America*, ed. Michael Lazzara and Vicky Unruh (New York: Palgrave Macmillan, 2009), 13.

1. Canonical writers including Machado de Assis, Jorge Luis Borges, and Guimarães Rosa have long argued for a denationalized aesthetic.

2. Bernardo Carvalho, *Teatro: Romance* (São Paulo: Companhia das Letras, 1998); João Gilberto Noll, *Harmada* (São Paulo: Companhia das Letras, 1993).

3. Andreas Huyssen, "Nostalgia for Ruins," *Grey Room* 23 (2006): 8, https://doi.org/10.1162/grey.2006.1.23.6.

4. Marc Augé states, "I noticed the proliferation, in the contemporary world, of spaces in which no lasting social relations are established (transit spaces, spaces people pass through), I suggested calling those spaces non-places to suggest that in those contexts there were a total absence of symbolic ties, and evident social deficits." "Places and Non-places: A Conversation with Marc Augé," *On the Move*, 2006, http://onthemove.autogrill.com/gen/lieux-non-lieux/news/2009-01-26/places-and-non-places-a-conversation-with-marc-auge (site no longer accessible).

5. In her work on the performance of ruins, Taylor discusses such convergences of there and then, of past and present ("Performing Ruins," 17).

6. Among others, Gaston Gordillo and Quetzil Castañeda have carried out anthropological study of these relationships with ruin.

7. Alfredo González-Ruibal, "Ruins of the South," in *Contemporary Archaeology and the City: Creativity, Ruination, and Political Action*, ed. Laura McAtackney and Krysta Ryzewski (Oxford: Oxford University Press, 2017), 150.

8. González-Ruibal, 162.

9. Pablo Neruda, *Alturas de Machu Picchu* (Santiago: Iberoamérica, Archivo de la Palabra, 1947); Carlos Fuentes, *Cambio de piel* (Mexico City: J. Mortiz, 1967); Carlos Drummond de Andrade, *Antologia poética. Organizada pelo autor* (São Paulo: Companhia das Letras, 2012).

10. Juan Rulfo, *Pedro Páramo* (Mexico City: Fondo de Cultura Económica, 1955).

11. Huyssen, "Nostalgia for Ruins," 9. Despite the enduring presence of ancient ruins, it was not until the eighteenth century that the aesthetic of ruin would come to occupy a central position in Western society via art, literature, and architecture. During this period, a motif of collapse and decay perceived as picturesque gained a foothold across Europe, particularly among the aristocracy, which would go so far as to replicate ruins in their garden landscapes.

12. Brian Dillon, "Fragments from a History of Ruin," *Cabinet*, Winter 2005–2006, 55, http://www.cabinetmagazine.org/issues/20/dillon.php.

13. Notably, recent theorists including González-Ruibal have argued that the postindustrial ruins of the Global South predate those of the North, because of the disparity in the chronological boom and bust of the economic growth and collapse of the regions.

14. González-Ruibal, "Ruins of the South," 164.

15. Beatriz Resende, *Contemporâneos: Expressões da literatura brasileira no século XXI* (Rio de Janeiro: Casa da Palavra, 2008), 20.

16. Leila Lehnen, "What Is Contemporary in Brazilian Literature?," *Luso-Brazilian Review* 48, no. 2 (2011): 207, https://doi.org/10.1353/lbr.2011.0050.

17. Clarice Lispector, *Para não esquecer* (São Paulo: Editora Ática, 1978), 9.

18. Here, Lispector understands Brasília as a constructed ruin, a "landscape of insomnia," that "never sleeps." Clarice Lispector, "Five Days in Brasília," in *The Foreign Legion: Stories and Chronicles*, trans. Giovanni Pontiero (New York: New Directions Publishing, 1992), 139. Lispector's reference to sleep evokes the critiques of Brasília that have been taken up since the city's founding: to sleep is to pause, to accumulate long-term memory.

19. The Templo Mayor (main temple) district was dismantled as the Spaniards built their colonial city over the top of Tenochtitlan. Later, subsections of the Templo Mayor were excavated beginning in the early twentieth century.

20. González-Ruibal, "Ruins of the South," 151.

21. González-Ruibal writes, "Left to their own devices or restored to their former grandeur, the delicate ruins of Belem, Pelotas, or Rio Grande continue to tell only half the story, the same story that their owners would have told" (162).

22. Gastón R. Gordillo, *Rubble: The Afterlife of Destruction* (Durham, NC: Duke University Press, 2014), 265.

23. Gordillo states, "The fetishization of ruins is one of the ways in which the rubble created by capitalist and imperial expansion, and thereby the abyss generated by their destruction of space, is deflected and disregarded" (254).

24. González-Ruibal, "Ruins of the South," 161.

25. Henri Lefebvre, *The Production of Space*, trans. Donald Nicholson-Smith (1974; Oxford: Blackwell, 1991), 161.

26. Taylor, "Performing Ruins," 14.

27. Michael Lazzara and Vicky Unruh, "Introduction: Telling Ruins," in Lazzara and Unruh (eds.), *Telling Ruins in Latin America*, 1–12, 4.

28. Idelber Avelar, *Alegorias da Derrota: A Ficção Pós-Ditatorial e o Trabalho do Luto na América Latina* (Belo Horizonte, Brazil: Editora UFMG, 2003).

29. González-Ruibal, "Ruins of the South," 153.

30. Noll, *Harmada*, 5.

31. Noll, 6.

32. Noll, 14.

33. Fermín Rodríguez, "João Gilberto Noll / *Harmada*," review, Inrocks Libros, October 21, 2010, https://inrockslibros.wordpress.com/2010/10/21/joao-gilberto-noll-harmada/.

34. Noll, *Harmada*, 16.

35. Anthony Giddens, *The Consequences of Modernity* (Stanford, CA: Stanford University Press, 1990), 140–141.

36. Noll, *Harmada*, 6, 100.

37. Noll, 91.
38. Noll, 39.
39. David Treece, "'It Could All Be Different': An Introduction to the Fiction of João Gilberto Noll," *Portuguese Studies* 14 (1998): 272, https://www.jstor.org/stable/41105098.
40. Noll, *Harmada*, 44.
41. Noll, 46.
42. Noll, 43.
43. Avelar, *Alegorias da Derrota*, 202.
44. José Castello, quoted in "*Harmada*—João Gilberto Noll," *Teco poeta sonhador* (blog), 2016, https://tecopoetasonhador.blogspot.com/2016/11/harmada-joao-gilberto-noll.html?m=1.
45. Noll, *Harmada*, 68.
46. Noll, 100.
47. Noll, 70.
48. Noll, 81.
49. Idelbar Adelar, "Bildungsroman at a Standstill," in *The Untimely Present: Postdictatorial Latin American Fiction and the Task of Mourning* (Durham, NC: Duke University Press, 1999), 186–209. As noted by Avelar, there are a number of references to *Pedro Páramo* in the novel, including a play that the protagonist and Cris construct together, described as a "peça, um monólogo de um autor mexicano, falava de uma mulher enlutada, por acreditar com ódio e desespero na eternidade. Isto, ela não se cobria de luto no corpo e na alma pela morte de alguém, pela finitude de um ser, não: o seu luto ao contrário expressava sua tristeza pela dura, pela descomunal herança da eternidade" (a play, a monologue from a Mexican author, which spoke of a bereaved woman, who believed with hatred and despair in eternity. She was not consumed by mourning in body and soul for the death of one person, for the finitude of one being, no: on the contrary, her mourning expressed a sadness for the hard and enormous inheritance of eternity) (Noll, *Harmada*, 71).
50. Noll, *Harmada*, 111.
51. Noll, 111.
52. Noll, 100.
53. Noll, 102.
54. Noll, 103.
55. Noll, 77.
56. González-Ruibal, "Ruins of the South," 161.
57. Noll, *Harmada*, 78.
58. Noll, 112.
59. Noll, 117.
60. Noll, 123.
61. Noll, 124.
62. Noll, 124.
63. Noll, 125.
64. Gloria Anzaldúa, *Borderlands: The New Mestiza* (San Francisco: Aunt Lute Books, 1987).
65. Anzaldúa, 3.
66. Anzaldúa, 82.
67. Sara Ahmed, "Home and Away: Narratives of Migration and Estrangement," *International Journal of Cultural Studies* 2, no. 3 (1999): 343, https://doi.org/10.1177/136787799900200303.
68. Marc Augé, *Non-places: Introduction to an Anthropology of Supermodernity*, trans. John Howe (London: Verso, 2008).

69. Carvalho, *Teatro*, 10.
70. Carvalho, 10.
71. Carvalho, 22.
72. Carvalho, 22.
73. Carvalho, 11.
74. Carvalho, 19.
75. Carvalho, 74.
76. Anderson Luís Nunes da Mata, "À Deriva: Espaço e Movimento em Bernardo Carvalho," *Revista de História e Estudos Culturais* 2, no. 2 (2005): 11, https://www.revistafenix.pro.br/PDF3/Artigo%20Anderson%20da%20Mata.pdf.
77. Bernardo Carvalho, *Nove Noites* (São Paulo: Companhia das Letras, 2002); Bernardo Carvalho, *Magnólia* (São Paulo: Companhia das Letras, 2003).
78. In Stefania Chiarelli's words, "um universo ficcional onde não mais é possível que se estabeleça uma só verdade, que se torna 'mais inverossímel do que a mentira'" (a fictional universe where it is no longer possible to establish a single truth, which becomes more unlikely than a lie). Stefania Chiarelli, "As Coisas Fora do Lugar: Modos de Ver em Bernardo Carvalho," *Estudos de Literatura Brasileira Contemporânea* 30 (2007): 77.
79. Carvalho, *Teatro*, 32.
80. Anzaldúa, *Borderlands*, 12–13.
81. Carvalho, *Teatro*, 50.
82. Carvalho, 56.
83. In his writings on power and knowledge, Foucault reminds us, "Each society has its regime of truth, its 'general politics' of truth; that is, the types of discourse which it accepts and makes function as true; the mechanisms and instances which enable one to distinguish true and false statements, the means by which each is sanctioned; the techniques and procedures accorded value in the acquisition of truth; the status of those who are charged with saying what counts as true." Michel Foucault, "Truth and Power," in *Power/Knowledge: Selected Interviews and Other Writings, 1972–1977*, ed. Colin Gordon and trans. Colin Gordon et al. (New York: Pantheon Books, 1980), 131.
84. Paulo César Thomaz, "Poéticas do dilaceramento e da desolação: Bernardo Carvalho e Sergio Chejfec," *Estudos De Literatura Brasileira Contemporânea* 36 (2010): 236, http://dx.doi.org/10.1590/2316-40183615.
85. Carvalho, *Teatro*, 10.
86. Carvalho, 22.
87. Carvalho, 22.
88. "Além da idéia do artifício, da fabricação de uma multiplicidade de versões, comparece também a discussão da linguagem como índice da não integração, da marginalidade e do degredo, não só cultural, mas também psicológico" (Beyond the idea of the artifice, of the manufacturing of a multiplicity of versions, it also compares the discussion of language as an index of non-integration, marginality and exile, not only in a cultural sense, but also in a psychological one) (Chiarelli, "As Coisas Fora do Lugar," 77).
89. Noll, *Harmada*, 40.
90. Noll, 24.
91. Noll, 46.
92. He is not alone, however; in addition to the narrator's own storytelling, his adopted daughter, Cristina, goes so far as to construct a false story stating that her mother had died early on and that the narrator raised her.
93. Caio Yurgel, *Landscape's Revenge: The Ecology of Failure in Robert Walser and Bernardo Carvalho* (Berlin: De Gruyter, 2018), 136.

94. Notably, Anthony Giddens has identified this tension as a central attribute of the period that follows modernity. In *The Consequences of Modernity*, 18–19.

95. Eduardo Grüner, "Recuerdo de un futuro (en ruinas): La Nación como no-espacio en la ideología de la Globalización," *La Jiribilla*, 2005, http://www.lajiribilla.co.cu/2004/n174_09/174_23.html.

CHAPTER 4 ANOTHER CITY AND ANOTHER LIFE

Epigraph: Gilberto Owen to Celestino Gorostiza, September 18, 1928, quoted in Valeria Luiselli, *Los ingrávidos* (Mexico City: Editorial Sexto Piso, 2011), 122; Valeria Luiselli, *Faces in the Crowd*, trans. Christina MacSweeney (Minneapolis: Coffee House, 2014), 119.

1. The materiality of the work is highlighted by its many reflections on writing as an architectural practice and the fact that in the English translation of the novel, *Faces in the Crowd*, the narrator's husband is an architect who envisions physical spaces that she argues eclipse the construction of literary worlds. The plasticity of time is explored at length in the novel. For example, there is a moment when Owen is told, "If you dedicate your life to writing novels, you're dedicating yourself to folding time," to which he responds, "I think it's more a matter of freezing time without stopping the movement of things, a bit like when you're on a train, looking out of the window" (115).

2. Regina Cardoso Nelky, "Fantasmas y Sosias en *Los ingrávidos*, de Valeria Luiselli," in "Escritoras mexicanas del siglo XXI: Miradas líquidas fragmentadas," special issue, *Romance Notes* 54 (2014): 80.

3. Luiselli, *Los ingrávidos*, 50–51; Luiselli, *Faces in the Crowd*, 44. Later, when he occupies the primary narrative voice, Owen retorts, "I was leading an imbecilic life, but I liked it" (69).

4. Luiselli, *Los ingrávidos*, 11; Luiselli, *Faces in the Crowd*, 1.

5. She describes her loneliest days in New York City as an incomplete outline: "Lo único que perdura de aquel período son los ecos de algunas conversaciones, un puñado de ideas recurrentes, poemas que me gustaban y releía una y otra vez hasta aprenderlos de memoria. Todo lo demás es *elaboración posterior*. Mis recuerdos de esa vida no podrían tener mayor contenido. Son andamiajes, estructuras, casas vacías" (All that has survived from that period are the echoes of certain conversations, a handful of recurrent ideas, poems I liked and read over and over until I knew them by heart. Everything else is a *later elaboration*. It's not possible for my memories of that life to have more substance. They are scaffolding, structures, empty houses). (Luiselli, *Los ingrávidos*, 14; Luiselli, *Faces in the Crowd*, 4).

6. Luiselli, *Los ingrávidos*, 51.

7. Luiselli, *Faces in the Crowd*, 44.

8. In Luiselli's interview with Ezio Neyra of *Asymptote*, she states, "I was very interested in telling Owen's story, not the history of New York, but one of the fragments of Owen's story that I was most interested in narrating happened in New York in the twenties. At first, out of some kind of timidity or fear, I even strongly resisted naming the city." "An Interview with Valeria Luiselli," by Ezio Neyra, *Asymptote*, 2015, https://www.asymptotejournal.com/interview/an-interview-with-valeria-luiselli/.

9. Doreen B. Massey, *Space, Place, and Gender* (Minneapolis: University of Minnesota Press, 1994), 154.

10. Indeed, the poet's marginalization is compounded by the limited market for English translations of lesser-known Latin American authors. This leads the narrator down a path of deception as she attests to having found rough translations of Owen's poetry by Joshua Zvorsky (a fictionalized Louis Zukofsky) in the archives. Eventually, the forged translations of Owen's poetry are published in a new edited volume and the work achieves widespread popularity, wrenching Owen from the shadows of obscurity to stand on a more global stage thanks to his supposed link to a more well-known writer.

To further my reflections, I offer some commentary on the interplay between the novel's English translation, *Faces in the Crowd,* and the original Spanish, *Los ingrávidos.* The translation by Christina MacSweeney differs substantially from the original text, particularly in terms of the chronological progression of the work, whose fragments often appear in a different order when compared with the Spanish. Luiselli has spoken publicly about these translations, discussing how she perceives them to be versions of the original Spanish rather than close, idiomatic adaptations. In an interview with National Public Radio, she discusses the issue of language in her work and across its translations: "I like to think of my books in English more as versions of the Spanish ones, and the Spanish ones as versions of the English ones. A lot of things change when I go from one language to the other." Valeria Luiselli, "Smashing Snow Globes: A Writer on Essays, Novels and Translations," interview broadcast on National Public Radio, December 24, 2014, https://www.npr.org/2014/12/21/371261474/smashing-snowglobes-a-writer-on-essays-novels-and-translation. Many of the same lessons on translation embedded in the text emerge in the creative decisions made by MacSweeney, the translator of two of Luiselli's other works, *Sidewalks* (2014) and *The Story of My Teeth* (2015). The fact that the translator of *Los ingrávidos* makes herself visible through falsifying, reworking, or adapting translations of Owen's work is unsurprising, as it conforms to Luiselli's vision of the role of the translator of her own works, one of presence, creative intervention, and acts of visibility. Translation, as in the novel, becomes an act of writing toward a different place, with its own set of practices and cultural norms, a creative mediation. These differences compel the reader to reckon with the ontological products of translation and other acts of rewriting: such practices produce many versions of a text, texts whose events play out differently from fragment to fragment, whose unfolding of accordion pleats happens in other ways. Indeed, the devil is in the details, or to draw from Gayatri Chakravorty Spivak, "The task of the translator is to facilitate [a] love between the original and its shadow, a love that permits fraying." Gayatri Chakravorty Spivak, "The Politics of Translation," in *Outside in the Teaching Machine* (London: Routledge, 1993), 313. It is precisely this fraying that MacSweeney achieves in her translation, small strayings from the original that are at times ornamental and aesthetic, on other occasions linguistic or idiomatic, and in the most common cases, slight structural changes that produce a peculiar reordering of narrative time and space. Generally, the differences between the English and the Spanish versions of *Faces in the Crowd* fall into three broad categories: the reordering of fragments; changes in the details surrounding characters; and the addition or removal of details from narrative fragments. With regard to the latter two categories, these include modifications that have an impact on the rest of the novel, including the husband's profession—he is a writer in the Spanish version and an architect in the English version, as mentioned in an earlier note. Given the significance of architecture in the English version, which Luiselli uses as a way to ponder the construction of narrative, readers of the original might take particular note of this absence in the Spanish version. In minute ways that one might even miss when reading the two versions one after the other, MacSweeney and Luiselli succeed in disorienting and shifting the narrative patterning of the novel, in "relocating" the narrative in ways that surpass changing the language of the text.

11. The fervent intertextuality of the narrative draws our attention, even in the first pages of the work: contemplating how to begin her novel, the narrator writes, "I would have liked to start the way Hemingway's *A Moveable Feast* ends" (Luiselli, *Faces in the Crowd,* 1). Hemingway's *A Moveable Feast* is perhaps a novel without an end, as the chapters may read as standalone entities, and in any chronological order. Interestingly, when Owen appears to readers as narrator rather than subject, he also begins with a literary reference, stating, "I would have liked to start the way Fitzgerald's *The Crack-Up* begins" (58).

12. The title of MacSweeney's translation is an intertextual reference to Ezra Pound's poem "In a Station of the Metro" and specifically to the line reading, "The apparition of these faces in the crowd: Petals on a wet, black bough." This reference is important given that the young narrator-translator encounters Gilberto Owen on the New York subway, as discussed earlier. It is also an instance in which MacSweeney is given creative freedom in her rendering of the English text, as noted by Denise Kripper in "On Translators in Translation: Spanish Novels about Translators Available in English Translation," *Asymptote Journal*, 2018, https://www.asymptotejournal.com/blog/2018/03/28/on-translators-in-translation-spanish-novels-about-translators-available-in-english-translation/.

13. Valeria Lusielli, "Relingos: The Cartography of Empty Spaces," in *Sidewalks*, trans. Christina MacSweeney (Minneapolis: Coffee House, 2014).

14. Luiselli, 78.

15. Luiselli, *Faces in the Crowd*, 10.

16. "En esta casa tan grande no tengo un lugar para escribir. Sobre mi mesa de trabajo hay pañales, cochecitos, transformers, biberones, sonajas, objetos que aún no termino de descifrar" (In this big house I don't have a place to write. On my worktable, there are diapers, toy cars, Transformers, bibs, rattles, things I still can't figure out) (Luiselli, *Los ingrávidos*, 13; Lusielli, *Faces in the Crowd*, 4.

17. Lusielli, *Los ingrávidos*, 14; Lusielli, *Faces in the Crowd*, 4.

18. Luiselli, *Faces in the Crowd*, 1.

19. Luiselli, *Los ingrávidos*, 12; Luiselli, *Faces in the Crowd*, 2. In an interview with Nichole Reber, Luiselli ruminates on the possibility of writing oneself into Mexico City, her place of birth and one whose syntax is coded in a language that is hers but from which she feels a distance: "I decided to write *Sidewalks* in order to appropriate a language and a space that was not entirely my own. It was an aspirational gesture on my part: I wanted to become a writer, a Mexican writer, an inhabitant of a city in which I had been born but had never lived, a speaker of a language that had always been only a small portion of myself. Writing is a way of writing yourself into the world, I guess. . . . I finished *Sidewalks*, the book that would finally insert me into my hometown, I had already begun living somewhere else." Valeria Luiselli, "Writing Yourself into the World: A Conversation with Valeria Luiselli," interview by Nichole Reber, *World Literature Today*, January 1, 2016, 12–13, https://www.worldliteraturetoday.org/2016/january/writing-yourself-world-conversation-valeria-luiselli-nichole-l-reber.

20. She writes, "Los espacios públicos, como las calles y las estaciones del metro, se iban volviendo habitables a medida que las asignara algún valor y se les imprimiera alguna experiencia. Si yo recitaba un pedazo de Paterson cada vez que caminaba por cierta avenida, con el tiempo esa avenida sonaría a William Carlos Williams" (Public spaces, such as streets and subway stations, became inhabitable as I assigned them some value and imprinted an experience on them. If I recited a snatch of *Paterson* every time I walked along a certain avenue, eventually that avenue would sound like William Carlos Williams) (Luiselli, *Los ingrávidos*, 17; Lusielli, *Faces in the Crowd*, 26).

21. Michel de Certeau, *The Practice of Everyday Life* (Berkeley: University of California Press, 1984), 103.

22. Certeau, 103.

23. "No me gustaba dormir sola en mi departamento. Estaba en un séptimo piso. Prefería prestar mi casa a amistades lejanas y buscaba otros cuartos, sillones prestados, camas compartidas para pasar la noche. Le repartí copias de mis llaves a mucha gente. Otras personas me dieron copia de las suyas. No generosidad: reciprocidad" (I didn't like sleeping alone in my apartment. I lived on the seventh floor. I would lend my apartment to people and seek out other rooms, borrowed armchairs, shared beds in which to spend the night. I gave copies of my keys to a lot of people. They gave me copies of theirs. Reciprocity, not generosity) (Luiselli, *Los ingrávidos*, 17; Lusielli, *Faces in the Crowd*, 7).

24. Yi-Fu Tuan, *Space and Place: The Perspective of Experience* (Minneapolis: University of Minnesota Press, 1977), 6.

25. Lusielli, *Faces in the Crowd*, 73.

26. Luiselli, 80–81.

27. Luiselli, 25. Earlier in the novel, the narrator mentions reading a letter written by Owen in which "Owen listed the objects in a room he was renting in Harlem: writing desk, pictures, plant, magazines, a piano" (22).

28. Lusielli, *Los ingrávidos*, 27. Note here that the Spanish version of the novel has a slightly different order to the sentences compared with the later English translation.

29. Luiselli, *Faces in the Crowd*, 17–18.

30. "What begins as undifferentiated space becomes a place as we get to know it better and endow it with value. . . . If we think of space as that which allows movement, then place is a pause; each pause in movement makes it possible for location to be transformed into place" (Tuan, *Space and Place*, 6).

31. Pierre Bourdieu, cited in Helene Lipstadt, "Life as a Ride in the Métro: Piere Bourdieu on Biography and Space," in *Biographies & Space: Placing the Subject in Art and Architecture*, ed. Dana Arnold and Joanna Sofaer Derevenski (London: Routledge, 2007), 36. In one of her sticky notes, the narrator writes, "The New York subway was constructed in 1904, the year of Owen's birth" (Lusielli, *Faces in the Crowd*, 36).

32. Spivak, "Politics of Translation," 179.

33. Sarah K. Booker, "On Mediation and Fragmentation: The Translator in Valeria Luiselli's *Los ingrávidos*," *Revista Canadiense de Estudios Hispánicos* 41, no. 2 (2017): 278.

34. Booker, 275.

35. Booker, 288.

36. Gilberto Owen, *Me muero de sin usted: Cartas de amor a Clementina Otero*, ed. Marinela Barrios Otero and Vicente Quirarte (Mexico City: Siglo XXI Editores, 2004), 167.

37. Massey, *Space, Place, and Gender*, 4.

38.

> La línea uno cruza Manhattan de sur a norte. Empieza en el embarcadero situado en el extremo sur de la isla, atraviesa parte de Chelsea, y llega hasta la Universidad de Columbia por ahí de la calle 116, donde Owen tomaba el tren todos los días hacia el extremo sureño de la ciudad, después de pesarse en una báscula junto a la taquilla. La línea sube hacia Harlem y después no sé qué más. La vía sigue y sigue, más allá de la isla, más allá de esta historia. (Luiselli, *Los ingrávidos*, 70–71)
>
> [The 1 Line runs the length of Manhattan. It starts at the ferry terminal at the southern tip of the island, goes through part of Chelsea and up to Columbia University on 116th Street, where Owen used to take the train every day to the south of the city, after weighing himself on a machine by the ticket office. Line continues up to Harlem and I don't know how much farther. The track goes on and on, beyond the island, beyond this story.] (Luiselli, *Faces in the Crowd*, 66)

39. Luiselli, *Los ingrávidos*, 66.

40. Luiselli, *Faces in the Crowd*, 60.

41. To complicate matters, Owen duplicates the encounter when he assumes control of the narrative later in the book, becoming fixated on the idea that he encountered Ezra Pound on the subway (Luiselli, *Los ingrávidos*, 92; Luiselli, *Faces in the Crowd*, 88–89). When the poet describes the sighting to his peers, they ridicule him on the basis of a spatial impossibility, presuming Pound to be in Europe at that time. This encounter also mimics an event that the translator's editor recounts to her earlier on, in which the poet Ezra Pound encountered author Herni Gaudier-Brezska in the metro.

42. Luiselli, *Los ingrávidos*, 63; Luiselli, *Faces in the Crowd*, 58.

43. Luiselli, *Los ingrávidos*, 86; Luiselli, *Faces in the Crowd*, 81.

44. Lusielli, *Los ingrávidos*, 84; Luiselli, *Faces in the Crowd*, 78.

45. Luiselli, *Los ingrávidos*, 87; Luiselli, *Faces in the Crowd*, 81.

46. Lusielli, *Los ingrávidos*, 89; Luiselli, *Faces in the Crowd*, 85.

47. Lusielli, *Los ingrávidos*, 64; Luiselli, *Faces in the Crowd*, 58.

48. Lusielli, *Los ingrávidos*, 64; Luiselli, *Faces in the Crowd*, 58.

49. Lusielli, *Los ingrávidos*, 74; Luiselli, *Faces in the Crowd*, 69.

50. Lusielli, *Los ingrávidos*, 92–93; Luiselli, *Faces in the Crowd*, 90.

51. Emerging in the nineteenth century, *criollismo* refers to a Latin American regionalist artistic and literary movement centering native traditions, landscapes, sceneries, and styles. David Rozotto, "El criollismo en la América de habla hispana: Revisita y reflexiones sobre el patrimonio de una literatura centenaria," *Lit. Teor. Hist. Crit.* 21, no. 1 (2019): 11–141, http://dx.doi.org/10.15446/lthc.v21n1.74868.

52. "Chubby" Dolores helps the translator escape from the rooftop of the very apartment complex where she fetches the dead tree (Luiselli, *Faces in the Crowd*, 25). In the case of Owen, "sturdy" and "cheerful" Dolores appears in Morningside Park, one of many children in a family he encounters (102). Of interest is also the fact that the narrator's Dolores bears the surname Preciado, an intertextual nod to Juan Preciado, the main character of Juan Rulfo's *Pedro Páramo* (1955). This also connects the work with João Gilberto Noll's *Harmada* from chapter 3. Given the supernatural elements of Rulfo's work, which is filled with ghosts and specters in the ruinous town of Comala, this also connects the text thematically to the earlier work.

53. Luiselli, *Faces in the Crowd*, 89.

54. Luiselli, *Los ingrávidos*, 108.

55. Luiselli, *Los ingrávidos*, 31; Luiselli, *Faces in the Crowd*, 22.

56. Luiselli, *Los ingrávidos*, 111; Luiselli, *Faces in the Crowd*, 108.

57. Luiselli, *Faces in the Crowd*, 114.

58. Luiselli, *Los ingrávidos*, 111; Luiselli, *Faces in the Crowd*, 107.

59. Luiselli, *Faces in the Crowd*, 122.

60. Luiselli, *Los ingrávidos*, 113; Luiselli, *Faces in the Crowd*, 111.

61. Luiselli, *Los ingrávidos*, 114.

62. Luiselli, *Faces in the Crowd*, 111.

63. Luiselli, *Los ingrávidos*, 133; Luiselli, *Faces in the Crowd*, 131.

64. Luiselli, *Los ingrávidos*, 137; Luiselli, *Faces in the Crowd*, 136.

65. Luiselli, *Los ingrávidos*, 137; Luiselli, *Faces in the Crowd*, 137.

66. Further diminishing the narrator's reliability, the young boy does not seem to be aware of the breakdown of the house around him. When the narrator suggests they keep out of the kitchen in case the house begins to shake again, the boy asks, "¿Cómo que si vuele a temblar?" (As if it starting shaking again?) (Luiselli, *Los ingrávidos*, 141). In the English translation, when the narrator suggests that the ghost could help them glue the house back together after the earthquake, the boy brings her back into his reality, stating, "Earthquakes don't exist, Mama" (Luiselli, *Faces in the Crowd*, 138).

67. Luiselli, *Faces in the Crowd*, 143.

68. Luiselli, *Los ingrávidos*, 114; Luiselli, *Faces in the Crowd*, 111.

69. Luiselli, *Los ingrávidos*, 146; Luiselli, *Faces in the Crowd*, 146.

70. Adriana Lisboa, *Rakushisha* (Rio de Janeiro: Rocco, 2007); Adriana Lisboa, *Hut of Fallen Persimmons*, trans. Sarah Green (Austin: Texas Tech University Press, 2011).

71. Edmundo Paz Soldán, "Valeria Luiselli: Retrato de familia con niños extraviados al fondo," review of *Lost Children Archive*, by Valeria Luiselli, *OtroLunes*, December 2019, https://otrolunes.com/53/otra-opinion/valeria-luiselli-retrato-de-familia-con-ninos-extraviados-al-fondo/.

72. Valeria Luiselli, "Gilberto Owen, Narrador," *Letras Libres* 11, no. 121 (2009): 58–59, https://www.letraslibres.com/mexico/gilberto-owen-narrador.

CONCLUSION

1. Francine Masiello, *The Art of Transition: Latin American Culture and Neoliberal Crisis* (Durham, NC: Duke University Press, 2001); Josefina Ludmer, *Aquí América latina: Una especulación* (Buenos Aires: Eterna Cadencia Editora, 2010).

2. Gustavo Guerrero, *Paisajes en movimiento—Literatura y cambio cultural entro dos siglos* (Buenos Aires: Eterna Cadencia, 2018); Erica Durante, *Los meridianos de la globalización* (Louvain: UCL, 2016); Héctor Hoyos, *Beyond Bolaño: The Global Latin American Novel* (New York: Columbia University Press, 2015).

3. Donald L. Shaw, "The Post-Boom in Spanish American Fiction," *Studies in 20th Century Literature* 19, no. 1.3 (1995): 11–27, https://doi.org/10.4148/2334-4415.13591995.

4. Hilda Chacón, *Online Activism in Latin America* (London: Routledge, 2018); Thea Pitman and Claire Taylor, *Latin American Identity in Online Cultural Production* (London: Routledge, 2013); Carolina Gainza, *Narrativas y poéticas digitales en América Latina: Producción literaria en el capitalismo informacional* (México: Secretaría de cultura / Centro de Cultura Digital, 2019); Scott Weintraub, *Latin American Technopoetics: Scientific Explorations in New Media* (New York: Routledge, 2018).

5. Patricio Pron, *La vida interior de las plantas de interior* (Barcelona: Random House Mondadori, 2013); María José Navia, *Instrucciones para ser feliz* (New York: Sudaquia Editores, 2015); Tatiana Salem Levy, *A chave de casa* (Rio de Janeiro: Editora Record, 2007).

6. Néstor García Canclini, "Migrants: Workers of Metaphors," in *Art and Visibility in Migratory Culture: Conflict, Resistance, and Agency*, ed. Mieke Bal and Miguel Á. Hernández-Navarro (Leiden: Brill/Rodopi, 2011), 21–35.

7. See Victoria A. Lawson, "Arguments within Geographies of Movement: The Theoretical Potential of Migrants' Stories," *Progress in Human Geography* 24, no. 2 (2000): 174.

APPENDIX

1. Luiz Ruffato, *Eles eram muitos cavalos* (São Paulo: Boitempo Editorial, 2005); Luiz Ruffato *Inferno provisório*, 5 vols. (Rio de Janeiro: Record, 2005–2011); Luiz Ruffato, *Flores artificiais* (São Paulo: Editora Companhia das Letras, 2014).

2. Luiz Ruffato, *Estive em Lisboa e lembrei de você* (São Paulo: Editora Companhia das Letras, 2009).

3. This interview was made possible through the Brazilian Fulbright Commission, in bilateral collaboration with the U.S. Department of State. This interview was originally published by the American Portuguese Studies Association in *Ellipsis* 13 (2015): 215–229.

BIBLIOGRAPHY

Ahmed, Sara. "Home and Away: Narratives of Migration and Estrangement." *International Journal of Cultural Studies* 2, no. 3 (1999): 329–347. https://doi.org/10.1177/136787799900200303.

Aínsa, Fernando. "Del espacio vivido al espacio del texto: Significación histórica y literaria del estar en el mundo." *Cuyo: Anuario de filosofía argentina y americana* 20 (2003): 19–36.

Aira, César. *Una novela china.* Buenos Aires: Javier Vergara, 1987.

———. *Váramo.* Barcelona: Editorial Anagrama, 2002.

Albrow, Martin. *The Global Age.* Stanford, CA: Stanford University Press, 1996.

Alencar, José Martiniano de. *Iracema.* São Paulo: Edita Melhoramento, 1865.

Andermann, Jens. "Abismos del tercer espacio: *Mar paraguayo*, portuñol salvaje y el fin de la utopía letrada." *Revista Hispánica Moderna* 64, no. 1 (2011): 11–22. https://www.jstor.org/stable/41306058.

Anderson, Benedict R. O.'G. *Imagined Communities: Reflections on the Origin and Spread of Nationalism.* London: Verso, 1991.

Anzaldúa, Gloria. *Borderlands: The New Mestiza.* San Francisco: Aunt Lute Books, 1987.

Appadurai, Arjun. "Disjuncture and Difference in the Global Cultural Economy." *Theory, Culture & Society* 7, no. 2–3 (1990): 295–310.

———. *Modernity at Large: Cultural Dimensions of Globalization.* Minneapolis: University of Minnesota Press, 1996.

———. "The Production of Locality." In *Counterworks: Managing the Diversity of Knowledge*, edited by Richard Fardon, 204–225. London: Routledge, 1995.

Apter, Emily S. "Untranslatables: A World System." *New Literary History* 39, no. 3 (2009): 581–598. https://doi.org/10.1353/nlh.0.0055.

Arac, Jonathan. "Anglo-globalism?" *New Left Review* 16 (July–August 2002): 35–46. https://newleftreview.org/issues/II16/articles/jonathan-arac-anglo-globalism.

Assis, Machado de, and Neto M. Sanches. *O Ideal Do Crítico.* Rio de Janeiro: José Olympio Editora, 2008.

Augé, Marc. *Non-places: An Introduction to Supermodernity.* Translated by John Howe. London: Verso, 2008.

Avelar, Idelber. *Alegorias da derrota: A ficção pós-ditatorial e o trabalho do luto na América Latina.* Belo Horizonte, Brazil: Editora UFMG, 2003.

———. "Bildungsroman at a Standstill." In *The Untimely Present: Postdictatorial Latin American Fiction and the Task of Mourning*, 186–209. Durham, NC: Duke University Press, 1999.

———. *The Untimely Present: Postdictatorial Latin American Fiction and the Task of Mourning.* Durham, NC: Duke University Press, 1999.

Bachelard, Gaston. *The Poetics of Space.* Translated by Maria Jolas. Boston: Beacon, 1994.

Bakhtin, Mikhail. "Discourse in the Novel." 1934. In *The Dialogic Imagination: Four Essays*, edited by Michael Holquist, 259–422. Austin: University of Texas Press, 2017.

———. "Forms of Time and of the Chronotope in the Novel." In *The Dialogic Imagination: Four Essays*, edited by Michael Holquist, 84–258. Austin: University of Texas Press, 1981.

———. *Speech Genres and Other Late Essays.* Translated by Vern W. McGee. Edited by Caryl Emerson and Michael Holquist. Austin: University of Texas Press, 1986.

Barberán Reinares, Laura. "Globalized Philomels: State Patriarchy, Transnational Capital and the Femicides on the US-Mexican Border in Roberto Bolaño's *2666*." CUNY Academic Works, 2010, 51–72. https://academicworks.cuny.edu/bx_pubs/6.

Beckman, Ericka. *Capital Fictions: The Literature of Latin America's Export Age*. Minneapolis: University of Minnesota Press, 2012.

Benedetti, Mario. *Viento Del Exilio*. Mexico City: Editorial Nueva Imagen, 1981.

Bhabha, Homi. *The Location of Culture*. New York: Routledge, 1994.

Blau, Herbert. "Virtually Yours: Presence, Liveness, Lessness." In *Critical Theory and Performance*, edited by Janelle G. Reinelt and Joseph R. Roach, 532–547. Ann Harbor: University of Michigan Press, 2010.

Bolaño, Roberto. *Amuleto*. Barcelona: Editorial Anagrama, 1999.

———. *Entre paréntesis: Ensayos, artículos y discursos (1998–2003)*. Edited by Ignacio Echevarría. Barcelona: Editorial Anagrama, 2004.

———. *Estrella distante*. Barcelona: Editorial Anagrama, 1996.

———. *Los detectives salvajes*. Barcelona: Editorial Anagrama, 1998.

———. *Nocturno de Chile*. Barcelona: Editorial Anagrama, 1999.

———. *2666*. Barcelona: Editorial Anagrama, 2011.

———. *2666*. Translated by Natasha Wimmer. New York: Farrar, Straus and Grioux, 2004.

Booker, Sarah K. "On Mediation and Fragmentation: The Translator in Valeria Luiselli's *Los ingrávidos*." *Revista Canadiense de Estudios Hispánicos* 41, no. 2 (2017): 273–295.

Borges, Jorge L. *El escritor argentino y la tradición*. Washington, DC: Unión Panamericana, Dept. de Asuntos Culturales, 1953.

———. *El jardín de senderos que se bifurcan*. Buenos Aires: SUR, 1942.

———. *Nueva refutación del tiempo*. Buenos Aires: Oportet and Haereses, 1947.

Borges, Jorge L., and P. D. James. *The Borges Lectures*. London: Anglo-Argentine Society, 1999.

Brands, Hal. *Latin America's Cold War*. Cambridge, MA: Harvard University Press, 2010.

Brickell, Katherine, and Ayona Datta, eds. *Translocal Geographies: Spaces, Places, Connections*. Farnham, England: Ashgate, 2011.

Buarque, Chico. *Budapest: Romance*. São Paulo: Editora Companhia das Letras, 2003.

Bueno, Wilson. *Mar paraguayo*. São Paulo: Editora Illuminuras, 1992.

Camacho, Alicia Schmidt. "Body Counts on the Mexico-US Border: Feminicidio, Reification, and the Theft of Mexicana Subjectivity." *Chicana/Latina Studies* 4, no. 1 (2004): 22–60. https://www.jstor.org/stable/23014438.

Cardoso Nelky, Regina. "Fantasmas y Sosias en *Los ingrávidos*, de Valeria Luiselli." In "Escritoras mexicanas del siglo XXI: Miradas líquidas fragmentadas." Special issue, *Romance Notes* 54 (2014): 77–84.

Carvalho, Bernardo. Interview by Natalia Brizuela. Translated by Clélia Donovan. *Bomb*, January 1, 2008. https://bombmagazine.org/articles/bernardo-carvalho/.

———. *Magnólia*. São Paulo: Companhia das Letras, 2003.

———. *Nove noites*. São Paulo: Companhia das Letras, 2002.

———. *O filho da mãe*. São Paulo: Companhia das Letras, 2009.

———. *Teatro: Romance*. São Paulo: Companhia das Letras, 1998.

Casanova, Pascale. *The World Republic of Letters*. Translated by M. B. DeBoise. Cambridge, MA: Harvard University Press, 2004.

Castañeda, Quetzil. *In the Museum of Maya Culture*. Minneapolis: University of Minnesota Press, 1996.

Castro-Gómez, Santiago. "Geografías poscoloniales y translocalizaciones narrativas de 'lo latinoamericano': La crítica al colonialismo en tiempos de la globalización." In *Enfoques sobre Posmodernidad en América Latina*, comp. Roberto Follari and Rigoberto Lanz, 155–182. Caracas: Editorial Sentido, 1998.

Castro-Gómez, Santiago, and Eduardo Mendieta. "Introducción: La translocalización discursiva de 'Latinoamérica' en tiempos de la globalización." In *Teorías sin disciplina: Latinoamericanismo, poscolonialidad y globalización en debate*, edited by Santiago Castro-Gómez and Eduardo Mendieta, 5–30. Mexico City: Miguel Ángel Porrúa, 1998.

Centre de Cultura Contemporània de Barcelona. *Arixiu Bolaño: 1977–2003*. Barcelona, Spain, March 5–June 30, 2013.

Certeau, Michel de. *The Practice of Everyday Life*. Berkeley: University of California Press, 1984.

Chacón, Hilda. *Online Activism in Latin America*. London: Routledge, 2018.

Chiarelli, Stefania. "As coisas fora do lugar: Modos de ver em Bernardo Carvalho." *Estudos de Literatura Brasileira Contemporânea* 30 (2007): 71–78.

Conrad, Joseph. *Youth; Heart of Darkness; The End of the Tether: Three Stories*. London: J. M. Dent, 1946.

Cordone, Gabriela. "2666 en escena: Relato, imagen y mestizaje artístico." *Revista Letral* 11 (2013): 11–23.

Cornejo Polar, Antonio. *Writing in the Air: Heterogeneity and the Persistence of Oral Tradition in Andean Literatures*. Durham, NC: Duke University Press, 2013.

Cortázar, Julio. *El Perseguidor*. Madrid: Alianza Editorial, 1993.

Croucher, Sheila L. *Globalization and Belonging: The Politics of Identity in a Changing World*. Lanham, MD: Rowman and Littlefield, 2004.

Dalcastagnè, Regina. "Entrevista: Regina Dalcastagnè: Radiografia da literatura brasileira." Interview by Luiz Rebinski Junior. *Cândido: Jornal da Biblioteca Pública do Paraná*. Accessed March 1, 2015. https://www.bpp.pr.gov.br/Candido/Pagina/Entrevista-Regina-Dalcastagne.

———. "O tempo no romance brasileiro contemporâneo." In *Narrativas contemporâneas: Recortes críticos sobre literatura brasileira*, edited by Gina Maria Gomes, 129–144. Porto Alegre, Brazil: Libretos, 2012.

De Castro, Juan E. *The Spaces of Latin American Literature: Tradition, Globalization, and Cultural Production*. New York: Palgrave Macmillan, 2008.

Deckard, Sharae. "Peripheral Realism, Millennial Capitalism, and Roberto Bolaño's *2666*." *Modern Language Quarterly* 73, no. 3 (2012): 351–372. https://doi.org./10.1215/00267929-1631433.

Deleuze, Gilles, and Félix Guattari. *Anti-Oedipus: Capitalism and Schizophrenia*. Translated by Robert Hurley, Mark Seem, and Helen R. Lane. Minneapolis: University of Minnesota Press, 1972.

———. *Kafka: Toward a Minor Literature*. Translated by Dana Polman. Minneapolis: University of Minnesota Press, 1986.

Dillon, Brian. "Fragments from a History of Ruin." *Cabinet*, Winter 2005–2006, 55–59. http://www.cabinetmagazine.org/issues/20/dillon.php.

Dimock, Wai-chee. *Through Other Continents: American Literature across Deep Time*. Princeton, NJ: Princeton University Press, 2006.

Donoso Macaya, Ángeles. "Estética, política y el posible territorio de la ficción en *2666*." *Revista hispánica moderna* 62, no. 2 (2009): 125–142. https://doi.org/10.1353/rhm.0.0023.

Dove, Patrick. *Literature and Interregnum: Globalization, War, and the Crisis of Sovereignty in Latin America*. Albany: State University of New York Press, 2016.

Drummond de Andrade, Carlos. *Antologia poética. Organizada pelo autor*. São Paulo: Companhia das Letras, 2012.

Duffy, Enda. *The Speed Handbook: Velocity, Pleasure, Modernism*. Durham, NC: Duke University Press, 2009.

Durante, Erica. *Los meridianos de la globalización*. Louvain: UCL, 2016.

Esposito, Scott. "*2666* by Roberto Bolaño." *Quarterly Conversation*, 2008. http://quarterlyconversation.com/2666-by-roberto-bolano (site discontinued).

Esteban, Ángel, and Jesús Montoya Juárez. "¿Desterritorializados o multiterritorializados? La narrativa hispanoamericana en el siglo XXI." In *Literatura más allá de la nación: De lo centrípeto y lo centrífugo en la narrativa hispanoamericana del siglo XXI*, edited by Francisca Noguerol Jiménez, María Ángeles Pérez López, Ángel Esteban, and Jesús Montoya Juárez, 7–13. Madrid: Iberoamericana Vervuert, 2011.

Esteban, Ángel, Jesús Montoya, Francisca Noguerol, and María Ángeles Pérez López, eds. *Narrativas latinoamericanas para el siglo XXI: Nuevos enfoques y territorios*. Hildesheim, Germany: Georg Olms Verlag, 2010.

Falls, Robert, and Bockley, Seth, dirs. *2666* [theatrical production]. Written by Roberto Bolaño. Goodman Theatre, Chicago, February 6–March 20, 2016.

Farred, Grant. "The Impossible Closing: Death, Neoliberalism, and the Postcolonial in Bolaño's *2666*." *Modern Fiction Studies* 56, no. 4 (2010): 689–708.

Finnegan, Nuala. *Cultural Representations of Feminicidio at the US-Mexico Border*. New York: Routledge, 2018.

———. "Sacrificial Screams: Excess in Àlex Rigola's Stage Adaptation of *2666*." In *Cultural Representations of Feminicidio at the US-Mexico Border*, 53–82. New York: Routledge, 2018.

Foucault, Michel. *The Archeology of Knowledge*. Translated by A. M. Sheridan Smith. London: Routledge, 1989.

———. "Of Other Spaces: Utopias and Heterotopias." In *The Visual Culture Reader*, 2nd ed., edited by Nicholas Mirzoeff, 229–236. London: Routledge, 2002.

———. *The Order of Things: An Archaeology of the Human Sciences*. New York: Pantheon Books, 1971.

———. "Truth and Power." In *Power/Knowledge: Selected Interviews and Other Writings, 1972–1977*, edited by Colin Gordon and translated by Colin Gordin et al., 109–133. New York: Pantheon Books, 1980.

Farrés, Osvaldo. "Quizás, quizás, quizás." 1947. Track B1 on *Ayer, Hoy, y Siempre*. United States: Ofarres, 1979.

Franconi, Rodolfo A. "O olhar oblíquo: Uma categoria cultural; conceituação e exemplos." *Revista de crítica literaria latinoamericana* 32, no. 63 (2006): 105–115. https://doi.org/10.2307/25070326.

Fregoso, Rosa-Linda, and Bejarano, Cynthia, eds. *Terrorizing Women: Feminicide in the Americas*. Durham, NC: Duke University Press, 2009.

Freitag, Ulrike, and Achim von Oppen, eds. *Translocality: The Study of Globalising Processes from a Southern Perspective*. Leiden: Brill, 2010.

Fresán, Roberto. *La velocidad de las cosas*. Barcelona: Random House Mondadori, 2002.

Friedman, Thomas L. *The World Is Flat: A Brief History of the Twenty-First Century*. New York: Farrar, Straus and Giroux, 2005.

Fuentes, Carlos. *Cambio de piel*. Mexico City: J. Mortiz, 1967.

Gaghan, Stephen, dir. *Syriana*. Warner Bros., 2005.

Gainza, Carolina. *Narrativas y poéticas digitales en América Latina: Producción literaria en el capitalismo informacional*. México: Secretaría de cultura / Centro de Cultura Digital, 2019.

Galera, Daniel. *Cordilheira*. São Paulo: Editora Companhia das Letras, 2008.

García Canclini, Néstor. *Hybrid Cultures: Strategies for Entering and Leaving Modernity*. Minneapolis: University of Minnesota Press, 1989.

———. *Imagined Globalization*. Durham, NC: Duke University Press, 2014.

———. "Introduction: Hybrid Cultures in Globalized Times." In *Hybrid Cultures: Strategies for Entering and Leaving Modernity*, xxiii–xlvi. Minneapolis: University of Minnesota Press, 1989.

———. "Migrants: Workers of Metaphors." In *Art and Visibility in Migratory Culture: Conflict, Resistance, and Agency*, edited by Mieke Bal and Miguel Á. Hernández-Navarro, 21–35. Leiden: Brill/Rodopi, 2011.

Garcia-Caro, Pedro. *After the Nation: Postnational Satire in the Works of Carlos Fuentes and Thomas Pynchon*. Evanston, IL: Northwestern University Press, 2014.

Gaspar de Alba, Alicia. "Alice Driver, More or Less Dead: Feminicide, Haunting, and the Ethics of Representation in Mexico." *Canadian Journal of Latin American and Caribbean Studies / Revue canadienne des études latino-américaines et caraïbes* 41, no. 2 (2016): 282–287. https://doi.org/10.1080/08263663.2016.1180784.

———, ed. *Making a Killing: Femicide, Free Trade, and La Frontera*. With Georgina Guzmán. Austin: University of Texas Press, 2010.

———. *[Un]framing the "Bad Woman": Sor Juana, Malinche, Coyolxauhqui, and Other Rebels with a Cause*. Austin: University of Texas Press, 2014.

Gaspar de Alba, Alicia, and Georgina Guzmán. "Introduction: *Feminicidio*: The 'Black Legend' of the Border." *Making a Killing: Femicide, Free Trade, and La Frontera*, edited by Alicia Gaspar de Alba and Georgina Guzmán, 1–24. Austin: University of Texas Press, 2010.

Gelman, Juan. *Com/posiciones*. Barcelona: Ediciones del Mall, 1986.

———. "El Expulsado." In *Poesía reunida*, 471. Barcelona: Seix Barral, 2012.

Giddens, Anthony. *The Consequences of Modernity*. Stanford, CA: Stanford University Press, 1990.

———. *Modernity and Self-Identity: Self and Society in the Late Modern Age*. Stanford, CA: Stanford University Press, 1991.

Gleick, James. *Faster: The Acceleration of Just About Everything*. New York: Pantheon Books, 1999.

González Pérez, Aníbal, ed. *Revista de estudios hispánicos* 46, no. 1 (2012).

González Rodríguez, Sergio. *The Femicide Machine*. Cambridge, MA: MIT Press, 2012.

———. *Huesos en el desierto*. Barcelona: Editorial Anagrama, 2002.

González-Ruibal, Alfredo. "Ruins of the South." In *Contemporary Archaeology and the City: Creativity, Ruination, and Political Action*, edited by Laura McAtackney and Krysta Ryzewski, 149–170. Oxford: Oxford University Press, 2017.

Gordillo, Gastón R. *Rubble: The Afterlife of Destruction*. Durham, NC: Duke University Press, 2014.

Grüner, Eduardo. "Recuerdo de un futuro en (ruinas): La Nación como no-espacio en la ideología de la Globalización." *La Jiribilla*, 2005. http://www.lajiribilla.co.cu/2004/n174_09/174_23.html.

Guerrero, Gustavo. *Paisajes en movimiento—Literatura y cambio cultural entro dos siglos*. Buenos Aires: Eterna Cadencia, 2018.

"*Harmada*—João Gilberto Noll." *Teco poeta sonhador* (blog), 2016. https://tecopoetasonhador.blogspot.com/2016/11/harmada-joao-gilberto-noll.html?m=1.

Harvey, David. *Spaces of Neoliberalization: Towards a Theory of Uneven Geographical Development*. Stuttgart: Franz Steiner Verlag, 2005.

Hatoum, Milton. *Dois irmãos*. São Paulo: Editora Companhia das Letras, 2000.

———. *Relato de un cierto Oriente*. São Paulo: Editora Companhia das Letras, 1989.

Heidegger, Martin. *The Fundamental Concepts of Metaphysics: World, Finitude, Solitude*. Translated by William McNeill and Nicholas Walker. Bloomington: Indiana University Press, 1995.

Herlinghaus, Hermann. "Placebo Intellectuals in the Wake of Cosmopolitanism: A 'Pharmacological' Approach to Roberto Bolaño's Novel *2666*." *Global South* 5, no. 1 (2011): 101–119. https://www.muse.jhu.edu/article/449220.

Holland, Eugene. *Deleuze and Guattari's "Anti-Oedipus": Introduction to Schizoanalysis*. London: Routledge, 1999.

Holston, James. *The Modernist City: An Anthropological Critique of Brasília*. Chicago: University of Chicago Press, 1989.

hooks, bell. "Choosing the Margin as Space of Radical Openness." In *Yearning: Race, Gender and Cultural Politics*, 145–153. Boston: South End, 1990.

Hoyos, Héctor. *Beyond Bolaño: The Global Latin American Novel*. New York: Columbia University Press, 2015.

Huyssen, Andreas. "Nostalgia for Ruins." *Grey Room* 23 (2006): 6–21. https://doi.org/10.1162/grey.2006.1.23.6.

———. *Present Pasts: Urban Palimpsests and the Politics of Memory*. Stanford, CA: Stanford University Press, 2003.

IBGE (Instituto Brasileiro de Geografia e Estatística). *Resistência e Integração: 100 anos de Imigração Japonesa no Brasil*. Rio de Janeiro: IBGE, 2008.

Iñárritu, Alejandro González, dir. *Amores Perros*. Studio Home Entertainment, 2000.

Ivanic, Roz. "I Is for Interpersonal: Discoursal Construction of Writer Identities and the Teaching of Writing." *Linguistics and Education* 6, no. 1 (1994): 3–15. https://doi.org/10.1016/0898-5898(94)90018-3.

Jay, Paul. *Global Matters: The Transnational Turn in Literary Studies*. Ithaca, NY: Cornell University Press, 2010.

Katz, Solomon H., ed. *Encyclopedia of Food and Culture*. New York: Scribner, 2003.

Kaygusuz, Sema. "A National Literature." Edinburgh World Writers' Conference, Edinburgh, Scotland, February 27, 2013. http://www.edinburghworldwritersconference.org/national-literature/kaygusuz-karnezis-a-national-literature/.

Kenzari, Bechir, and Yasser Elsheshtawy. "Crossing Boundaries: Architecture and the 'Influence' of Other Disciplines." *Built Environment* 31, no. 1 (2005): 5–8.

King, Russell, John Connell, and Paul E. White, eds. *Writing across Worlds: Literature and Migration*. London: Routledge, 1995.

Krausz, Luis. *Desterro: Memórias em ruínas*. São Paulo: Tordesilhas, 2011.

Kripper, Denise. "On Translators in Translation: Spanish Novels about Translators Available in English Translation." *Asymptote Journal*, 2018. https://www.asymptotejournal.com/blog/2018/03/28/on-translators-in-translation-spanish-novels-about-translators-available-in-english-translation/.

Lacoscio, Lisa. "Who Was Roberto Bolaño?" *Salon*, June 6, 2013. https://www.salon.com/2013/06/24/myths_and_legends_of_roberto_bolano_exposed_in_new_exhibit_partner/.

Larkosh, Christopher. "Flows of Trans-language: Translating Transgender in the Paraguayan Sea." *Transgender Studies Quarterly* 3, no. 3–4 (2016): 552–568. https://doi.org/10.1215/23289252-3545071.

Lawson, Victoria A. "Arguments within Geographies of Movement: The Theoretical Potential of Migrants' Stories." *Progress in Human Geography* 24, no. 2 (2000): 173–189.

Lazzara, Michael, and Vicky Unruh. "Introduction: Telling Ruins." In *Telling Ruins in Latin America*, edited by Michael Lazzara and Vicky Unruh, 1–12. New York: Palgrave Macmillan, 2009.

———, eds. *Telling Ruins in Latin America*. New York: Palgrave Macmillan, 2009.

Lefebvre, Henri. *The Production of Space*. Translated by Donald Nicholson-Smith. Oxford: Blackwell, 1991. First published 1974.

Lehnen, Leila. "What Is Contemporary in Brazilian Literature?" *Luso-Brazilian Review* 48, no. 2 (2011): 203–211. https://doi.org/10.1353/lbr.2011.0050.

Lepore, Jill. "The Cobweb: Can the Internet Be Archived?" *New Yorker*, January 19, 2015. https://www.newyorker.com/magazine/2015/01/26/cobweb.

Lesser, Jeffrey. *Immigration, Ethnicity, and National Identity in Brazil, 1808 to the Present*. Cambridge: Cambridge University Press, 2013.

Levy, Tatiana Salem. *A chave de casa*. Rio de Janeiro: Editora Record, 2007.

———. "O silência da representação: Uma leitura de *Eles eram muitos cavalos*." *Estudos de Literatura Brasileira Contemporânea* 22 (2003): 173–184.

Lionnet, Françoise, and Shumei Shi. *Minor Transnationalism*. Durham, NC: Duke University Press, 2005.

Lipstadt, Helene. "Life as a Ride in the Métro: Piere Bourdieu on Biography and Space." In *Biographies & Space: Placing the Subject in Art and Architecture*, edited by Dana Arnold and Joanna Sofaer Derevenski, 35–54. London: Routledge, 2007.

Lisboa, Adriana. *Azul-corvo*. Rio de Janeiro: Alfaguara, 2010.

———. *Hanói*. Rio de Janeiro: Alfaguara, 2010.

———. *Hut of Fallen Persimmons*. Translated by Sarah Green. Austin: Texas Tech University Press, 2011.

———. *Rakushisha*. Rio de Janeiro: Rocco, 2007.

Lispector, Clarice. "Five Days in Brasília." In *The Foreign Legion: Stories and Chronicles*, translated by Giovanni Pontiero, 136–140. New York: New Directions Publishing, 1992.

———. *Para não esquecer*. São Paulo: Editora Ática, 1978.

———. *Visão do esplendor: Impressões leves*. Rio de Janeiro: F. Alves, 1975.

Llosa, Mario Vargas. *Conversación en la catedral*. Madrid: Alfaguara, 2013.

Ludmer, Josefina. *Aquí América latina: Una especulación*. Buenos Aires: Eterna Cadencia Editora, 2010.

Luiselli, Valeria. *Faces in the Crowd*. Translated by Christina MacSweeney. Minneapolis: Coffee House, 2014.

———. "Gilberto Owen, Narrador." *Letras Libres* 11, no. 121 (2009): 58–59. https://www.letraslibres.com/mexico/gilberto-owen-narrador.

———. "An Interview with Valeria Luiselli." By Ezio Neyra. *Asymptote*, 2015. https://www.asymptotejournal.com/interview/an-interview-with-valeria-luiselli/.

———. *Los ingrávidos*. Mexico City: Editorial Sexto Piso, 2011.

———. *Sidewalks*. Translated by Christina MacSweeney. Minneapolis: Coffee House, 2014.

———. "Smashing Snow Globes: A Writer on Essays, Novels and Translations." Interview broadcast on National Public Radio, December 24, 2014. https://www.npr.org/2014/12/21/371261474/smashing-snowglobes-a-writer-on-essays-novels-and-translation.

———. *The Story of My Teeth*. Minneapolis: Coffee House, 2015.

———. *Tell Me How It Ends: An Essay in Forty Questions*. Minneapolis: Coffee House, 2017.

———. "Writing Yourself into the World: A Conversation with Valeria Luiselli." Interview by Nichole Reber. *World Literature Today*, January 1, 2016, 11–15. https://www.worldliteraturetoday.org/2016/january/writing-yourself-world-conversation-valeria-luiselli-nichole-l-reber.

Macaya, Ángeles Donoso. "Estética, política y el posible territorio de la ficción en *2666* de Roberto Bolaño." *Revista Hispánica Moderna: Boletín Del Instituto De Las Españas* 62, no. 2 (2009): 125–142.

Madeira, Angélica. "Línguas na fronteira, línguas na diáspora." *Humanidades* 59 (2012): 47–55.

Márquez, Gabriel García. *Cien años de soledad*. Buenos Aires: Editorial Sudamericana, 1971.

Martín-Barbero, Jesús. "Artes de la memoria y regímenes de visibilidad." Keynote address at "Staging Citizenship: Cultural Rights in the Americas," Hemispheric Institute, Universidad Nacional, Bogotá, August 21, 2009.

———. "Comunicación y cultura mundo: Nuevas dinámicas mundiales de lo cultural." *Signo y pensamiento* 29, no. 57 (2010): 20–34. https://doi.org/10.11144/Javeriana.syp29-57.ccmu.

———. "La globalización en clave cultural: Una mirada latinoamericana." *Renglones: Los desafíos de América Latina: Cultura y globalización*, March–April 2003. https://rei.iteso.mx/bitstream/handle/11117/357/53_02_globalizacion.pdf?sequence=2.

———. "Prólogo." In *Por otra Globalización: Del pensamiento único a la conciencia universal*, by Milton Santos, 9–14. Bogotá: Convenio Andrés Bello, 2004.

Martínez Valderas, Jara, and Javier J. González Martínez. "Àlex Rigola: Dramaturgia y dirección se unen para golpear al público." In *La escenificación española contemporánea: Una mirada más allá de nuestras fronteras*, edited by Margarita del Hoyo Ventura, 105–120. La excepción y la regla. Granada: Ediciones Tragacanto, 2017.

Masiello, Francine. *The Art of Transition: Latin American Culture and Neoliberal Crisis*. Durham, NC: Duke University Press, 2001.

Massey, Doreen B. *Space, Place, and Gender*. Minneapolis: University of Minnesota Press, 1994.

Mata, Anderson Luís Nunes da. "À Deriva: Espaço e Movimento em Bernardo Carvalho." *Revista de História e Estudos Culturais* 2, no. 2 (2005): 1–20. https://www.revistafenix.pro.br/PDF3/Artigo%20Anderson%20da%20Mata.pdf.

Mello, Jefferson Agostini. "Duplicidades e contradições em Bernardo Carvalho: O estético e o político; o universal e o particular." *Revista Faac* 2 (2012): 131–144.

Miguel, Salim. "Ponto de Balsa." In *O sabor da forma*, 136–152. Rio de Janeiro: Record, 2007.

Monárrez Fragoso, Julia E. "An Analysis of Feminicide in Ciudad Juárez: 1993–2007." In *Strengthening Understanding of Femicide: Using Research to Galvanize Action and Accountability*, 78–83. Washington, DC: Program for Appropriate Technology in Health, InterCambios, Medical Research Council of South Africa, and World Health Organization, 2009. https://path.azureedge.net/media/documents/GVR_femicide_rpt.pdf.

———. "Trama de una injusticia: Feminicidio sexual sistémico en Ciudad Juárez." *Región y Sociedad* 22, no. 47 (2013): 201–206. http://www.scielo.org.mx/pdf/regsoc/v22n47/v22n47a10.pdf.

Moniz, Naomi Hoki. "Race, Gender, Ethnicity and the Narrative of National Identity in the Films of Tizuka Yamazaki." In *New Worlds, New Lives: Globalization and People of Japanese Descent in the Americas and from Latin America in Japan*, edited by Lane R. Hirabayashi, Akemi Kikumura-Yano, and James A. Hirabayashi, 221–236. Stanford, CA: Stanford University Press, 2002.

Montaldo, Graciela. "El mundo de la cultura." *Revista Hispánica Moderna* 64, no. 1 (2011): 1–9. https://www.jstor.org/stable/41306057.

Montoya Juárez, Jesús, and Ángel Esteban. "A modo de introducción: ¿Narrativa latinoamericana más allá del aeropuerto?" In *Entre lo local y lo global: La narrativa latinoamericana en el cambio del siglo, 1990–2006*, edited by Jesús Montoya Juárez and Ángel Esteban, 7–18. Madrid: Iberoamericana Editorial, 2008.

———, eds. *Entre lo local y lo global: La narrativa latinoamericana en el cambio de siglo, 1990–2006*. Madrid: Iberoamericana Editorial, 2008.

Nakasato, Oscar. *Nihonjin*. São Paulo: Benvirá, 2011.

———. "Reflections on Japanese-Brazilian Immigration through Narrative: An Interview with Oscar Nakasato." By Cecily Raynor. *Journal of Lusophone Studies* 2, no. 1 (2017): 198–205. https://doi.org/10.21471/jls.v2i1.161.

Navia, María José. "Afuera." In *Lugar*, 36–48. Santiago de Chile: Ediciones De la Lumbre, 2017.

———. *Instrucciones para ser feliz*. New York: Sudaquia Editores, 2015.

Neruda, Pablo. *Alturas de Machu Picchu*. Santiago: Iberoamérica, Archivo de la Palabra, 1947.

Neuman, Andrés. *El viajero del siglo*. Madrid: Alfaguara, 2009.

Noguerol, Francisca. "Narrar sin fronteras." In *Entre lo local y lo global: La narrativa latinoamericana en el cambio de siglo, 1990–2006*, edited by Jesús Montoya Juárez and Ángel Esteban, 19–33. Madrid: Iberoamericana Editorial, 2008.

Noguerol Jiménez, Francisca, María Ángeles Pérez López, Ángel Esteban, and Jesús Montoya Juárez, eds. *Literatura más allá de la nación: De lo centrípeto y lo centrífugo en la narrativa hispanoamericana del siglo XXI*. Madrid: Iberoamericana Vervuert, 2011.

Noll, João Gilberto. *Harmada*. São Paulo: Companhia das Letras, 1993.

Oakes, Tim, and Louisa Schein. "Translocal China: An Introduction." In *Translocal China: Linkages, Identities and the Reimagining of Space*, edited by Tim Oakes and Louisa Schein, 1–35. London: Routledge, 2006.

Orozco Mendoza, Elva F. "Feminicide and the Funeralization of the City: On Thing Agency and Protest Politics in Ciudad Juárez." *Theory and Event* 20, no. 2 (2017): 351–380.

Ortiz, Renato. *Mundialización y cultura*. Bogotá: Convenio Andrés Bello, 2004.

Otero, Jaime. "La comunidad panhispánica: Para la proyección global del español." *Política Exterior* 18, no. 101 (2004): 32–39.

Owen, Gilberto. *Me muero de sin usted: Cartas de amor a Clementina Otero*. Edited by Marinela Barrios Otero and Vicente Quirarte. Mexico City: Siglo XXI Editores, 2004.

Paz Soldán, Edmundo. "From Macondo to McOndo: Latin American Fiction Today." *Borders Features*, 2004. https://www.bordersstores.com/features/feature.jsp?filepazsoldan (site discontinued).

———. "Valeria Luiselli: Retrato de familia con niños extraviados al fondo." Review of *Lost Children Archive*, by Valeria Luiselli. *OtroLunes*, December 2019. https://otrolunes.com/53/otra-opinion/valeria-luiselli-retrato-de-familia-con-ninos-extraviados-al-fondo/.

Pennycook, Alastair. *Language as a Local Practice*. London: Routledge, 2010.

Pérez Firmat, Gustavo. *Life on the Hyphen: The Cuban-American Way*. Austin: University of Texas Press, 2012.

Perlongher, Néstor. "Sopa paraguaya." In *Mar paraguayo*, by Wilson Bueno, 7–11. São Paulo: Iluminuras, 1992.

Pitman, Thea, and Claire Taylor. *Latin American Identity in Online Cultural Production*. London: Routledge, 2013.

"Places and Non-places: A Conversation with Marc Augé." *On the Move*, 2006. http://onthemove.autogrill.com/gen/lieux-non-lieux/news/2009-01-26/places-and-non-places-a-conversation-with-marc-auge (site no longer accessible).

Prieto Nadal, Ana. "La narrativa de Roberto Bolaño a escena: *2666*." *Revista de Literatura* 78, no. 156 (2016): 543–567. https://doi.org/10.3989/revliteratura.2016.02.023.

Pron, Patricio. *El espíritu de mis padres sigue subiendo en la lluvia*. Barcelona: Random House Mondadori, 2012.

———. *El libro tachado: Prácticas de la negación y del silencio en la crisis de la literatura*. Madrid: Turner, 2014.

———. *La vida interior de las plantas de interior*. Barcelona: Random House Mondadori, 2013.

Raynor, Cecily. "Linguagem, espaço e nação: Um mapeamento das identidades multigeográficas do protagonista imigrante." *Estudos de Literatura Brasileira Contemporânea*, no. 45 (January–June 2015): 159–182. http://dx.doi.org/10.1590/2316-4018459.

———. "O global e o particular: Uma leitura espacial de *Eles eram muitos cavalos* de Luiz Ruffato." *Brasil/Brazil: A Journal of Brazilian Literature* 29, no. 54 (2016): 9–24. https://seer.ufrgs.br/index.php/brasilbrazil/article/view/70546.

Redhead, Steve. "The Art of the Accident: Paul Virilio and Accelerated Modernity." *Fast Capitalism* 2, no. 1 (2006): 11–18.

Resende, Beatriz. *Contemporâneos: Expressões da literatura brasileira no século XXI*. Rio de Janeiro: Casa da Palavra, 2008.

Rigola, Àlex. Interview. 27 February 2006, Barcelona, Spain. In *2666* [playbill—English version], 8–12. Teatre Lliure, 2007.

Rigola, Àlex, and Pablo Ley. *2666* [playbill—Catalán version]. Teatre Lliure, 2007.

Robbins, Timothy, and José González, eds. *New Trends in Contemporary Latin American Narrative: Post-national Literatures and the Canon*. New York: Palgrave Macmillan, 2014.

Robertson, Roland. "Glocalization: Time-Space and Homogeneity Heterogeneity." In *Global Modernities*, edited by Mike Featherstone, Scott Lash, and Roland Robertson, 25–45. London: Sage, 1995.

Rodrigues, Marco Antonio. "Mobilidade precária em *Terra estrangeira* e em *Estive em Lisboa e lembrei de você*." *Estudos de Literatura Brasileira Contemporânea* 39 (2012): 181–192. http://dx.doi.org/10.1590/S2316-40182012000100010.

Rodríguez, Fermín. "João Gilberto Noll / *Harmada*." Review, Inrocks Libros, October 21, 2010. https://inrockslibros.wordpress.com/2010/10/21/joao-gilberto-noll-harmada/.

Rozotto, David. "El criollismo en la América de habla hispana: Revisita y reflexiones sobre el patrimonio de una literatura centenaria." In *Lit. Teor. Hist. Crit.* 21, no. 1 (2019): 11–141. http://dx.doi.org/10.15446/lthc.v21n1.74868.

Ruffato, Luiz. *Eles eram muitos cavalos*. São Paulo: Boitempo Editorial, 2005.

———. *Estive em Lisboa e lembrei de você*. São Paulo: Editora Companhia das Letras, 2009.

———. *Flores artificiais*. São Paulo: Editora Companhia das Letras, 2014.

———. *Inferno provisório*. 5 vols. Rio de Janeiro: Record, 2005–2011.

———. *Mamma, son tanto felice*. Rio de Janeiro: Record, 2005.

Rulfo, Juan. *Pedro Páramo*. Mexico City: Fondo de Cultura Económica, 1955.

Rushdie, Salman. *Imaginary Homelands: Essays and Criticism, 1981–1991*. London: Penguin, 1992.

Said, Edward W. *Orientalism*. London: Routledge and Kegan Paul, 1978.

Santos, Milton. *Toward an Other Globalization: From the Single Thought to Universal Conscience*. Translated and edited by Lucas Melgaço and Tim Clarke. Cham, Switzerland: Springer International, 2017.

Sassen, Saskia. *The Global City: New York, London, Tokyo*. Princeton, NJ: Princeton University Press, 2001.

———. *Globalization and Its Discontents: Essays on the New Mobility of People and Money*. New York: New Press, 1999.

———. "Globalization or Denationalization?" *Review of International Political Economy* 10, no. 1 (2003): 1–22. https://www.jstor.org/stable/4177449.

Scarry, Elaine. *The Body in Pain: The Making and Unmaking of the World*. Oxford: Oxford University Press, 1985.

Scollon, Ron, and Suzie Wong Scollon. *Discourses in Place: Language in the Material World*. London: Routledge, 2003.

Segato, Rita Laura. "Las nuevas formas de la guerra y el cuerpo de las mujeres." *Sociedade e Estado* 29, no. 2 (2014): 341–371. http://dx.doi.org/10.1590/S0102–69922014000200003.

———. "Territory, Sovereignty, and Crimes of the Second State: The Writing on the Body of Murdered Women." Translated by Sarah Koopman. In *Terrorizing Women: Feminicide in the Américas*, edited by Rosa-Linda Fregoso and Cynthia L. Bejarano, 70–92. Durham, NC: Duke University Press, 2010.

Shaw, Donald L. "The Post-Boom in Spanish American Fiction." *Studies in 20th Century Literature* 19, no. 1.3 (1995): 11–27. https://doi.org/10.4148/2334-4415.13591995.

Simon, Gilda. "Les mouvements de population aujourd'hui." In *Immigration et intégration: L'état des savoirs*, edited by Philippe Dewitte, 43–54. Paris: La Découverte, 1999.

Siskind, Mariano. *Cosmopolitan Desires: Global Modernity and World Literature in Latin America*. Evanston, IL: Northwestern University Press, 2014.

Soderbergh, Steven, dir. *Traffic*. USA Films, 2000.

Spivak, Gayatri Chakravorty. "The Politics of Translation." In *Outside in the Teaching Machine*, 179–200. London: Routledge, 1993.

Sousa Santos, Boaventura de. "Globalizations." *Theory, Culture & Society* 23, no. 2–3 (2006): 393–399. https://doi.org/10.1177/026327640602300268.

———. "The Processes of Globalisation." Translated by Sheena Caldwell. *Revista Crítica de Ciências Sociais and Eurozine*, 2002, 1–48. https://www.eurozine.com/the-processes-of-globalisation/?pdf.

Taylor, Diana. "Performing Ruins." In *Telling Ruins in Latin America*, edited by Michael Lazzara and Vicky Unruh, 13–26. New York: Palgrave Macmillan, 2009.

Thays, Ivan. "Andrea no duerme." In *Palabra de América*, edited by Roberto Bolaño et al., 185–197. Barcelona: Seix Barral, 2004.

Thomaz, Paulo César. "Poéticas do dilaceramento e da desolação: Bernardo Carvalho e Sergio Chejfec." *Estudos De Literatura Brasileira Contemporânea* 36 (2010): 233–239. http://dx.doi.org/10.1590/2316-40183615.

Tomlinson, John. *Globalization and Culture*. Chicago: University of Chicago Press, 1999.

Tonus, José Leonardo. "O imigrante na literatura brasileira: Instrumentalização de uma figura literária." In *Fora do retrato: Estudos de literatura brasileira contemporânea*, edited by Regina Dalcastagnè and Anderson Luis Nunes da Mata, 93–101. Vinhedo, Brazil: Editora Horizonte, 2012.

Torga, Miguel. "Brasil." 1970. In *Diário—Vols. IX a XII*. Alfragide, Portugual: Poblicações Dom Quixote, 2011.

Treece, David. "'It Could All Be Different': An Introduction to the Fiction of João Gilberto Noll." *Portuguese Studies* 14 (1998): 267–276. https://www.jstor.org/stable/41105098.

Tuan, Yi-Fu. *Space and Place: The Perspective of Experience*. Minneapolis: University of Minnesota Press, 1977.

Valdés, Marcela. "Alone among the Ghosts: Roberto Bolaño's *2666*." *The Nation*, November 19, 2008. https://www.thenation.com/article/archive/alone-among-ghosts-roberto-bolanos-2666/.

Valdez, Diana Washington. *Cosecha de mujeres: Safari en el desierto mexicano*. Mexico City: Editorial Océano, 2005.

Varnelis, Kazys. *Networked Publics*. Cambridge, MA: MIT Press, 2008.

Venuti, Lawrence, ed. *The Translation Studies Reader*. London: Routledge, 2012.

Vieira, Yara Frateschi. "Diante Do Espelho: Refração E Iluminação Em Bernardo Carvalho." *Portuguese Studies* 21 (2005): 210–223.

Villaça, Alcides. "Ruffato cria trama ágil com percepções vivas de Lisboa." *Folha de São Paulo*, October 17, 2009. http://feeds.folha.uol.com.br/fsp/ilustrad/fq1710200914.htm.

Weintraub, Scott. *Latin American Technopoetics: Scientific Explorations in New Media*. New York: Routledge, 2018.

Williamson, John. "What Washington Means by Policy Reform." In *Latin American Adjustment: How Much Has Happened?*, edited by John Williamson, 7–20. Washington, DC: Institute for National Economics, 1990.

Xutos & Pontapés. "Lisboa, a Magnífica!" Track 2 on *Direito ao Deserto*. Lisbon: Universal Music Portugal, 1993.

Yory, Carlos Mario. "Del espacio ocupado al lugar habitado: Una aproximación al concepto de topofilia." *Barrio Taller: Serie Ciudad y Hábitat* 12 (2007): 46–64.

Yúdice, George. "We Are Not the World." *Social Text*, no. 31/32 (1992): 202–216.

Yurgel, Caio. *Landscape's Revenge: The Ecology of Failure in Robert Walser and Bernardo Carvalho*. Berlin: De Gruyter, 2018.

Zwick, Edward, dir. *Blood Diamond*. Warner Bros., 2006.

INDEX

Page numbers in *italics* refer to figures.

ABOUT THE AUTHOR

CECILY RAYNOR is an assistant professor of Latin American literature and digital humanities at McGill University, where she teaches contemporary fiction and digital culture. She holds a PhD in Latin American literature and cultural studies from Georgetown University and resides in Montreal, Canada, with her son.